Industrial Slavery
in the Old South

Industrial Slavery
in the Old South

Robert S. Starobin

OXFORD UNIVERSITY PRESS

LONDON   OXFORD   NEW YORK

OXFORD UNIVERSITY PRESS

Oxford London New York
Glasgow Toronto Melbourne Wellington
Cape Town Salisbury Ibadan Nairobi Lusaka Addis Ababa
Bombay Calcutta Madras Karachi Lahore Dacca
Kuala Lumpur Hong Kong Tokyo

For My Mother and Father

Preface

This study examines the nature of slavery in the United States, the character of the political economy of the Old South, and the causes of the American Civil War from a new perspective—the use of slave labor in southern industries from 1790 to 1861. The study offers, first, an account of the extent of slave employment by such industries as manufacturing, mining, lumbering, turpentine extraction, processing of agricultural crops, and the construction and operation of transportation facilities. The daily living and working conditions of industrial bondsmen are described, and particular emphasis is placed on the resistance and accommodation by slaves to work routines and the slavery regime. An analysis of industrial slavery as a labor system and as a means of economic development is presented. Lastly, the study traces the ways in which the movement for slave-based industries influenced political developments leading up to the Civil War.

By the 1840's and 1850's about 5 per cent of the slave population was working in industrial enterprises, where they were either directly owned by companies or hired by their employers. Most of these businesses were profitable, and the employment of bondsmen by industries was generally more economical than using other labor forces available in the Old South. Most of the capital for slave-employing industries came from slaveowning planters and farmers themselves, who were greatly interested in developing the southern economy. Industrial slaves resisted bondage as frequently and as vigorously as did plantation hands; but employers found that their bonds-men could be disciplined by various brutal and subtle means so as to create a sufficiently tractable work force. Many Southerners had come to believe that they could create a more balanced economy in which their plantation agriculture would be complemented by their ability to operate industries with slave labor. However, leading Southerners also believed that industries had to be directed by slaveowning planters, not new slaveless entrepreneurs, so that existing class and race relation-ships would remain unchanged.

Moreover, between the American Revolution and the Civil War, the idea of industrializing the South on the basis of slave labor was widely discussed and became an important political issue on both the state and federal levels. This issue was in turn related to the problem of the protective tariffs, the role of poor whites and skilled artisans in southern society, the expansion of slavery into the territories and the Caribbean, the building of the transcontinental railroad, and the reopening of the African slave trade. Perhaps most important, the use of slave labor in industries was related to the movement for separate southern nationhood, which culminated in bloody civil war.

During the course of this study I have received assistance from many persons. The archival staffs of the two-score li-braries consulted were quite helpful. The Graduate Research Committee of the University of California at Berkeley pro-vided travel funds, while Berkeley's History Department awarded me the Max Farrand Traveling Fellowship for 1965–66, which enabled me to spend a whole year doing research and writing in the South. Harper's Monthly has given permis-sion to reproduce the drawings of slave workers which appear in the text. Professors Richard Sewell and Morton Rothstein—my colleagues at the University of Wisconsin—criticized por-tions of the manuscript. Professors David B. Davis of Yale, Eugene D. Genovese of Rochester, and Victor Garlin of the

University of California also offered helpful suggestions. I am especially grateful to Professor Kenneth M. Stampp of Berkeley, who read the entire work in its dissertation form. Elsa also displayed sympathetic understanding over a long period of time. I alone, of course, am responsible for whatever errors may appear.

R. S. S.

MADISON, WISCONSIN

July 1969

Contents

ONE   Slavery and Industry in the Old South   3

TWO   Working and Living Conditions   35

THREE   Patterns of Resistance and Repression   75

FOUR   Conversion, Hiring, and Integration of Work
  Forces   116

FIVE   The Economics of Industrial Slavery   146

SIX   The Politics of Industrial Slavery   190

Notes   233

Appendix   289

Bibliographical Essay   299

Index   315

List of Tables

1 Earnings of Slave-employing Textile Mills,
    1838–1861   290

2 Earnings of Slave-employing Canals and Turnpikes,
    1805–1861   293

3 Earnings of Slave-employing Railroads,
    1835–1862   294

4 Annual Maintenance Cost per Industrial Slave,
    1820's–1861   296

Industrial Slavery
in the Old South

CHAPTER ONE

Slavery and Industry in the Old South

Slave Labor [is] the labor indicated by nature, and history, and providential appointment for this region . . . .

James Dunwoody Brownson De Bow

The Old South was a region of diversity and complexity, contrast and contradiction. The section ranged geographically from the fertile lands of the Tidewater, Black Belt, and deltas to the rugged Appalachian mountain chain of the interior. Piney woods divided the coast from the rolling hills of the Piedmont; a great valley punctuated the mountain range. Rivers provided a natural waterway system for virtually every area; the Ohio, the Mississippi, and the Tennessee rivers defined a fertile interior plateau. Lush forests and swamps complemented rich deposits of minerals and metals. The growing season averaged between six and nine months, while the climate varied from temperate to tropical.

The South's economy was predominantly agricultural and heavily dependent upon the cultivation of several commercial crops. Tobacco and hemp were grown in the upper states, especially in Virginia, Kentucky, and Missouri, while a considerable amount of wheat was raised in Maryland and Virginia. Rice was produced along the eastern coast, especially in South Carolina and Georgia. Sugar was cultivated mainly in Louisiana, while corn could be grown almost anywhere. The cotton region, where the South's most important staple grew, extended all the way from the Carolinas to Texas.

Cotton was not only the most important commercial crop in the South but also the leading export of the United States down to the 1850's. The demand by northern and British textile interests after the War of 1812 had stimulated the expansion of cotton cultivation into the Piedmont region and into the Black Belt of the Southwest. In the 1820's and 1830's the cotton crop almost quadrupled, while from 1840 to 1860 it more than doubled, reaching the unprecedented total of 4.9 million bales by the opening of the Civil War. This fantastic increase in cotton production was largely responsible for southern prosperity and greatly contributed to national economic growth in these years.[1]

Several lesser crops contributed to the prosperity of certain southern regions. In Louisiana the value of sugar production quadrupled in the quarter-century before 1860; in Kentucky hemp cultivation also increased dramatically, partly to meet the booming demand for rope and cotton bagging. Tobacco growing responded to the cravings of men at home and abroad, while the harvest of rice, wheat, corn, and livestock also soared rapidly. Corn production competed with cotton cultivation in both volume and value,[2] but as an export crop cotton continued to remain "king."

By 1860, the South's free population totaled eight million whites and one-quarter million free blacks. The white population included poor whites, yeoman farmers and herdsmen, and slaveowning farmers and planters. Several hundred thousand poor whites lived in degradation on marginal lands; they represented an untapped source of agricultural or industrial labor. The middle class, comprising two-thirds of the free population, included yeoman farmers, craftsmen, mechanics, professionals, and commercial interests, all of whom represented potential entrepreneurial groups for industry. Most of the yeoman farmers engaged in self-sufficient agriculture, but some of them produced small marketable crops on about two hundred acres of fairly fertile land or tended livestock that roamed the piney woods and the interior valleys and plateaus.[3]

By 1860, there were about four million Negro slaves in the South, and servitude had long since become firmly entrenched in the southern social structure. Slave ownership was so widespread that almost 400,000 white families held bondsmen, and as many as two million white persons therefore had direct property interests in slavery. The typical slaveholder was a farmer who owned one or two slave families and a few hundred acres of good land; however, 12 per cent of the slaveowners—the planter class—owned more than twenty slaves each, monopolized more than half of the slave population, and possessed the best southern lands of all. Most slaves worked on one of these large plantations.[4] The "peculiar institution" was also integral to the southern economy, since plantation bondsmen produced the bulk of the commercial crops. Slaves raised over 90 per cent of the cotton in the Black Belt, an even greater percentage of the tobacco in Virginia, and cultivated almost all of the Kentucky hemp, Louisiana sugar, and Carolina rice. Slaveowning planters thus dominated the staple-export sector of the southern economy, upon which prosperity and economic growth depended.[5]

Slavery was suitable to plantation agriculture and to the southern economy generally. Under intelligent management and on fertile soils, slave labor was cheaper than free labor and profitable to most agriculturists. Slave labor could be maintained at a subsistence standard of living, and the offspring of black women counted as a bonus to masters. Most slaveowners annually averaged on their capital investments returns which were at least equal to or greater than the average returns on alternative forms of investments. Slave ownership was thus competitive in capitalist terms and gave most planters an economic advantage over slaveless farmers.[6]

The planter class was a "power elite" because of its economic function, wealth, status, and tradition of leadership. Since slave-based plantations dominated the southern economy and were vital to international trade, planters held enormous economic power. Social status depended primarily upon wealth in land and slaves, so that the planters easily remained at the peak of the southern social pyramid. The ideology of agrarianism, which held that farming, not commerce or manufacturing, was the good life, further facilitated planter control. Though in theory state constitutional reforms democratized southern politics, planters continued to control southern power in practice.

The class and racial relationships associated with slavery were also unique. Despite great contrasts in power, wealth, and status among the southern white citizenry, class antagonisms were relatively minor. Between poor whites and slaveless yeomen on the one hand and the planters on the other there was often a degree of hostility, but class conflict seldom became serious so long as economic opportunities for ambitious whites seemed open. The presence of blacks and the effectiveness of proslavery propaganda encouraged white unity and tended to divide the South more along racial lines than along class lines. Fears of miscegenation, racial equality, manumission, and slave rebellion allied slaveless whites with slaveowners, while the aspiration to slave ownership remained the popular ideal of the way to wealth. To most white Southerners, slavery was simply both an economic opportunity and a racial necessity. There was thus little threat from white Southerners themselves to the slave system or to the class that dominated it.[7]

Slavery was essentially a labor system designed to meet the opportunities for the development of the New World. Free white laborers were scarce and they were unwilling to work in hot, sickly climates as agricultural workers when cheap land was available. As whites proved intractable, African labor was enslaved. The effectiveness of this slave labor system depended upon the economic aggressiveness and managerial efficiency of masters and overseers. On small farms masters worked closely with their slaves, while on plantations management was often divorced from ownership. Some owners drove their blacks brutally to obtain maximum production over the short run; other masters sought to obtain a steady amount of work from their slaves by combining punishments with rewards. Whatever the circumstances, slaves worked arduously and their lives were unpleasant.[8]

By the early eighteenth century the legal framework of slavery was fully developed; there was considerable refinement of the old slave codes in the nineteenth century until southern statutes generally provided that black people were slaves for life, that children were to inherit their mother's condition, and that Christian baptism would not automatically assure freedom. Blacks were legally defined both as property and as persons, for whom masters had certain responsibilities. State legislation further directed all white men to assist in the capture of fugitive slaves and to serve in nightly patrols of rural and urban slave districts. The slave codes also prohibited marriages between whites and blacks and forbade bondsmen to acquire or to inherit property, to hold secret gatherings, to be parties to contracts or suits, to marry legally, or to engage in certain trades. Slave mobility, communication, religion, and legal rights were thus severely restricted.[9] Those who violated the slave codes were punished by a variety of means ranging from fines to imprisonment, from whipping to death. Despite such requirements, direct power over the slaves rested almost solely with masters and overseers, whose personalities and self-interests largely determined treatment of their Negroes.[10]

A limited urban development also characterized the Old South, and by 1860, eight slave states claimed cities with populations greater than 22,000 persons. These centers which skirted the perimeter of the South were Baltimore, Richmond, Charleston, Savannah, Mobile, New Orleans, St. Louis, and Louisville. In addition, Washington, D.C., had a population of about 60,000.[11] Few interior cities were developing, however, and five states—North Carolina, Florida, Mississippi, Arkansas, and Texas—lacked a town with a population over 10,000, while two other states—Tennessee and Delaware—lacked one with a population larger than 22,000.[12] Clearly lagging behind the urban development of the free states, which could point to the dramatic growth in the 1850's of Chicago, Cleveland, Cincinnati, or Pittsburgh, as well as to their own seaboard metropolises, the South remained essentially a rural region.

Most southern cities were commercial and residential in character. They harbored the port facilities essential to the cotton and sugar trade, and served the commercial, financial, and social needs of the plantations. Factors, bankers, lawyers, and slave dealers dominated the urban economy, while the townhouses of wealthy planters hosted the urban social life. By the 1840's, only Richmond had clearly become an industrial and transportation center, though some interior towns were also developing in this direction.

Small towns dotted the countryside and sprouted at the falls and forks of rivers. Backcountry towns served initially as centers of politics and trade, where commodities were transshipped around river rapids and where seats of government were located. These towns soon became the sites of industry, because falls yielded water power and rivers offered convenient transportation. Exhibiting remarkable population expansion, such interior towns as Petersburg, Augusta, and Columbus typified the emerging urban centers of the Piedmont, while Lexington, Nashville, and Chattanooga characterized transmontane urbanization. At the same time Norfolk, Wilmington, and Georgetown represented coastal village growth.[13]

After an earlier period of expansion, the population of such seaboard cities as Charleston leveled off between 1840 and 1860, though Savannah revived to expand 45 per cent in the last antebellum decade.[14] By contrast, the river cities boomed after 1840, with New Orleans expanding 45 per cent, Louisville, 55 per cent, and St. Louis by 93 per cent. Mobile's population increased from 809 in 1819 to 30,000 in 1850. Memphis grew from 500 in 1826 to 22,000 in 1860. And, besides the nine largest cities, the Old South boasted twenty-one towns with populations over 8000 on the eve of the Civil War.[15]

Slaves formed substantial portions of urban populations, amounting to as much as 50 per cent in Charleston by 1850. Altogether, 70,000 slaves lived in the eight leading cities at this time, and in Mobile, Savannah, and especially in Richmond (as well as in some interior towns such as Montgomery), the slave population was expanding with considerable vitality.[16] Urban slaves, like most other city workers—free or slave, native and immigrant—engaged in commercial occupations or in domestic service. City slaves were typically artisans and craftsmen, stevedores and draymen, barbers and common laborers, and house and hotel servants. Indeed, the "great bulk," [17] probably two-thirds, of all urban bondsmen were either domestic servants or service tradesmen. Industrial slaves therefore formed only a minority of all urban slaves, and they were not representative of typical city blacks.

Urban slavery allegedly afforded certain advantages to the bondsmen. The quality and amount of food was presumably better, housing was perhaps more comfortable, and back alleys and illicit grog shops may have offered some social life. However, much of the liberality of urban slavery existed because the majority of urban slaves were domestic servants, not because slavery was dying in the cities. The townhouses and city hotels naturally offered more social life and better working conditions than did rural plantations; but the privileges

granted urban domestic servants differed little from those
given plantation house servants. And those privileges afforded
urban domestic slaves did not necessarily mean that in the
cities slavery as an institution was being transformed into freedom. Nor can it safely be assumed, simply because many industrial slaves lived in urban areas, that such privileges pertained
to industrial slavery as well. Urban slavery was often characterized by the drudgery, unhealthiness, protest, and unre-
strained repression similar to that which obtained on plantations. Indeed, as one fugitive slave astutely recalled, urban
slavery "as seen here by the casual observer, might be supposed not to be so hard as one would imagine. . . . But Slavery is *Slavery*, wherever it is found." [18]

Analysis of plantation and urban slavery is vital, of course,
but a study of southern industry and the use of slave labor in
it can also provide important insights into American history.
By the beginning of the nineteenth century, certain industries
had already begun to develop in the Old South. As early as
the 1790's, if not before, for example, the processing of agricultural crops, the extraction of ores, turpentine, and lumber,
and the manufacture of tobacco and hemp were becoming
important southern industries. In this early stage, southern
industries emerged from agriculture and were often so closely
linked to it that certain enterprises remained in rural or small-
town settings. Iron manufacturing and even transportation,
for instance, served plantation needs directly, while sugar
milling, rice milling, and cotton ginning operated largely in
the plantation context. Other rural industries, such as mining
and lumbering, were either linked only indirectly to farming
or remained altogether distinct from the plantation economy. [19]
Increasingly, manufacturing, crop processing, and transportation enterprises tended to separate from agriculture and to
assume independent existences. As this divorce evolved, indus-

trialization accelerated in such southern cities as Richmond and in many interior towns. Simultaneously, industrial output began to increase, small units of production consolidated into larger industrial establishments, and mechanization advanced. Transportation networks originally designed to service agricultural interests began to expand and to meet urban-industrial interests as well. The southern iron and textile manufacturing industries also began slowly to develop.

After the development of southern industries over many decades, by the 1840's and 1850's the South accounted for about 20 per cent of the capital invested in the nation's industry. In the 1850's, the slave states' industrial production almost doubled, so that by 1860, the South contained about 15 per cent of national industrial capacity. The value of southern manufactured goods alone increased from $34 million in 1840 to nearly $100 million in 1860. The value of cotton manufactures, to use another index, increased from $1.5 to $4.5 million during this same period. Even in the predominantly agricultural state of Mississippi capital invested in textile manufacturing rose from $50,000 to $345,000 in the 1850's. Moreover, even though the plantation system still dominated industries and cities alike, some southern industries such as iron working, hemp manufacturing, and mining were crucial to southern economic growth. Other industries, like the processing of staple crops, the extraction of turpentine, and lumbering, were vital to national economic development as well.[20]

Beyond these general characteristics southern industry's most interesting aspect was its wide and intensive use of slave labor. In the 1850's, for example (when the black population grew from 3.2 to 4 million persons), between 160,000 and 200,000 bondsmen—or about 5 per cent of the total slave population—worked in industry.[21] Most of these industrial slaves were men, but many were women and children. The typical industrial slave lived in a rural, small-town, or plantation setting, where most industry was located, not in a large city. Thus, of the 70,000 urban slaves only about 25,000 (or about 15 to 20 per cent) were industrial bondsmen.[22]

There were two basic patterns of industrial slave employment—direct ownership and hiring. About four-fifths of all industrial slaves were directly owned by industrial entrepreneurs; the rest (one-fifth) were rented by employers from their masters by the month or year. The typical industrial slave was therefore owned outright, not hired.[23] But many industrial hirelings did experience a divorce of management from ownership similar to that of those plantation bondsmen who were disciplined by overseers or drivers. There was no clear pattern of industries preferring slave hiring to slave purchase, and each means of employment had advantages and limitations. Whatever the form of employment or ownership, however, the use of slave labor in southern industries had clearly been established between the American Revolution and the Civil War.

One of the most significant antebellum southern industrial efforts was a movement to bring the cotton mills to the cotton fields, presaging the textile manufacturing campaign of the post-Civil War period. Competing against firmly entrenched northern and British manufacturers, Southerners did manage to establish textile milling enterprises in the 1790's, after the War of 1812,[24] and then again in the 1840's. Low cotton prices stimulated the founding of new cotton factories in the 1840's, when, for example, North Carolinians alone commenced thirty-two new mills. By 1861, cotton mills dotted the fall-line towns of Georgia, Virginia, and the Carolinas, as well as the hill country of Alabama and Mississippi. There were many woolen mills as well.

The number of southern textile mills seemed to decline in the 1850's, as rising agricultural prices encouraged investment in farming rather than in manufacturing and as northern and foreign producers outbid southern competitors. In this decade North Carolinians opened only eleven new mills, while the number of Georgia mills dropped from thirty-six to thirty-three and the number of mills in eleven deep-South states remained constant. However, this declining trend was uneven, since there was some consolidation of mills, the value of goods produced in Georgia still increased nearly 70 per cent, the value of textile production in the eleven states increased by 43 per cent, and by 1860, these same states produced one-third of the nation's yarn and 7 per cent of the value of cotton goods. In 1840, the amount of capital invested in southern cotton manufacturing was almost six million dollars, or about 12 per cent of the national total. By 1860, the total capital in southern cotton factories had nearly doubled and the fifteen slave states as a whole produced almost 25 per cent of the nation's cotton and woolen textiles. Still, Lowell, Massachusetts, had as many spindles as all of the southern factories combined.[25]

Many southern textile mills employed either slave labor exclusively or combined both bondsmen and free workers in the same mill, contradicting the myth that southern textile manufacturing was the sole domain of native poor whites. The first southern cotton mill (1789) hired slaves from nearby planters,[26] and many textile millers, such as Edward McGehee, whose Woodville, Mississippi, factory owned about one hundred bondsmen in the 1850's, continued to manufacture textiles entirely with slave labor.[27] Though after 1845 some mills converted from slave labor to free, by 1860 southern cotton and woolen mills together employed more than five thousand slaves.[28] The ability of these bondsmen was testified to by a visitor to the Saluda Factory in South Carolina, which employed 158 slaves in 1851: *

* In all quoted material, the original spelling, punctuation, and syntax have been preserved.

We had the gratification recently of visiting this factory, situated on the Saluda River, near Columbia, and of inspecting its operations. It is on the slave-labor, or anti-free soil system; no operators in the establishment but blacks. The superintendent and overseers are white, and . . . principally from the manufacturing districts of the North, and although strongly prejudiced on their first arrival at the establishment against African labor, from observation and more experience they all testify to their equal efficiency, and great superiority in many respects. So as not to act precipitately, the experiment of African labor was first tested in the spinning department; since which, the older spinners have been transferred to the weaving room . . . . A weaver from Lowell has charge of this department, and she reports that, while there is full as much work done by the blacks, they are much more attentive to the condition of their looms. They all appear pleased with the manipulations on which they are employed . . . .[29]

The manufacture of iron was also heavily dependent upon slave labor. Serving plantation and railroad interests, iron manufacturing expanded into widely scattered centers in the Piedmont and the mountains of Virginia, South Carolina, and Alabama, as well as into Kentucky, Tennessee, and Missouri. After a promising early development, southern pig iron production grew unevenly in the 1850's, when Pennsylvania and Ohio ironmongers posed severe competition. Virginia, Georgia, and South Carolina furnaces made less iron in 1860 than a decade earlier, but Kentucky, after a brief decline in the 1840's, increased its production by 27 per cent and led the South in 1860.[30]

Slaves were the chief labor force at most upper-South iron works, some of which were well-known and nationally important. Early in the nineteenth century, the Oxford Iron

Works of Virginia, which contributed to the war effort of 1812–15, owned 220 Negroes. In the 1840's in the Cumberland River region of Tennessee, Senator John Bell, who would later run for President, controlled one iron establishment owning 365 blacks, while twenty other iron works in the area employed more than 1800 slaves. During the 1850's the Tredegar Iron Company of Richmond, Virginia, used more than one hundred bondsmen. By 1861 this firm employed 900 workers, half of them slaves, to transact one million dollars' worth of business annually. Tredegar was the South's leading iron mill by 1860, and it had the third largest iron-working force in the United States and the largest labor force in Richmond. Capitalized at almost half a million dollars, its furnaces and rolling mills produced virtually every conceivable kind of finished iron. Tredegar's facilities were the most important of Virginia's developing industrial capacity,[31] and they would become the "ironmaker to the Confederacy."

Large numbers of slaves also labored in iron works in other southern regions. In South Carolina the Nesbitt Manufacturing Company owned about 140 Negroes, and the Aera and Aetna Iron Works used 90 bondsmen. Exploitation of the central Alabama and central Missouri iron regions fell to the slave-owning Shelby Iron Company and to the slave-hiring Maramec Iron Works, respectively. In Maryland the Northampton Furnace hired many slaves. Blacksmith shops using slave labor were, of course, common on plantations and in towns.[32] Altogether, probably 10,000 slaves were employed at antebellum southern iron works.

The manufacture of tobacco, centering in Virginia and North Carolina and expanding westward into Kentucky and Missouri in the 1850's, was an important southern industry. Richmond's tobacco factories alone processed more than half of the plug and smoking tobacco of the eastern district. In

Tobacco Factory Worker

this region, the capital investment almost trebled and both the number of slaves and the value of product doubled in the 1850's.[33]

Prospering throughout the antebellum period, southern tobacco factories employed slave labor almost exclusively. Richmond's fifty-two tobaccories employed 3400 slaves in the 1850's, Petersburg's twenty establishments worked more than 2400 slaves, and Lynchburg's forty-seven companies used more than 1600. In 1860, Danville had thirteen tobacco factories employing almost 500 slaves; eighteen other plants in the surrounding county used 400 bondsmen. "Down the centre of a long room," wrote one of the many visitors to

Richmond's tobaccories, "were twenty large presses, at each of which some dozen slaves, stripped to the waist (it was very hot), were tugging and heaving at long iron arms which turned screws, accompanying each push and pull by deep-drawn groans." [34]

Though most tobacco factories were small, three-quarters of them employing less than fifty hands, the trend toward larger labor forces had already begun. By 1833, Petersburg's prominent tobacconist Robert Leslie used more than sixty slaves. By the Civil War, many others had exceeded Leslie, so that three Richmond factories each used about sixty slaves, while the Talbott Brothers employed seventy-eight bondsmen, Turpin and Tarborough used ninety-seven, the Hardgroves had 108, and James H. Grant used 110. Of the fifty-five tobacco manufacturers listed in the Richmond *Directory* for 1860, forty-two paid taxes on ten or more slaves, and sixteen had more than ninety-five bondsmen each.[35] The most successful tobacco manufacturer was James Thomas, Jr., whose Richmond establishment engaged 150 slaves and by 1860 produced more than a million pounds of chewing tobacco annually. At this time, the eastern and western tobacco manufacturing districts together employed almost 15,000 bondsmen.[36]

The manufacture of hemp was another major southern industry. By spinning the fibers of the hemp plant, cotton bagging and bale rope—both of which were vital to the maritime strength of the nation—were produced. In 1850, Kentucky alone housed one-third of the nation's hemp factories, which were concentrated in the Bluegrass towns of Lexington and Louisville. The number of southern enterprises decreased from 159 to forty-two in the last antebellum decade, from cutthroat northern and Russian competition, and by 1860, New York and Massachusetts surpassed Kentucky in the production of cordage. But at this time Missouri still led the South in the production of cordage and Kentucky still manufactured 60 per cent of the nation's cotton bagging and bale rope.[37]

Throughout the pre-Civil War period, slave labor was crucial to hemp manufacturing. In 1850, some 159 Kentucky hemp factories employed almost 3000 Negroes; ten years later, Kentucky's establishments alone used 5000 bondsmen, twice as many as Missouri's hemp factories.[38] In the hemp manufacturing center of Louisville in the 1840's, two representative companies, Worsley's and Golding's, employed 165 and 125 bondsmen respectively. The hemp factory slaves of Lexington, where Senator Henry Clay and the famous Hunt-Morgan families were prominent producers,[39] were described as follows:

> At one of the principal bagging and bale rope establishments, there are employed from 60 to 100 negroes, of all ages,—all stout, hearty, healthy, and merry fellows, some of whom contrive to while away the time and drown the noise of the machinery by their own melody. . . . I could make no more of it than Guildenstern could of Hamlet's pipe, but a friend translated it something after this fashion. The leader would commence singing in a low tone—"Ho! Ho! Ho! Master's gone away." To which the rest replied with rapidity, "Ho! Ho!—chicken-pie for supper, Ho! Ho!—Ho! Ho!" The effect of such noisy mumbling was irresistibly comic. When they get tired of this, anyone who had a little fancy—and precious little would answer the purpose, would start something equally as sentimental; to which the rest again responded, at the same time walking backward and forward about their spinning, with great regularity, and in some measure keeping time with their steps . . . .[40]

It is also significant that most secondary manufacturing industries used bondsmen extensively. For example, Savannah's 1848 census listed seventy-four slave "mechanics," while scores of "well-skilled" slave machinists worked Daniel Pratt's famous cotton gin factory in Alabama. Slave cobblers made slave brogans on many plantations, but in one large shoe factory twenty-six bondsmen produced 11,000 pairs of shoes annually. Slaves operated hundreds of southern tanneries; one Mobile bakery even employed sixteen slaves in 1860.[41] Carolina and Kentucky papermakers used bondsmen, while a young slave in Hagerstown, Maryland, described as "shrewd, active, enterprising, and faithful," with his master's "entire confidence," helped prepare a local newspaper. The printing press of the famous Charleston *Courier* was "driven by the labor of negroes, two of whom may be seen whenever it is in operation, with coats, jackets and shirts off, sweating and chugging like horses."[42] Large brick-manufacturing companies complemented the lesser brick production of many sugar plantations. In the 1820's, John McDonogh's New Orleans brick works owned a hundred Negroes, while in 1850 at one Biloxi Bay plant 116 male and 37 female slaves produced ten million bricks annually.[43] Slave labor was so extensively used in all kinds of southern manufacturing efforts that one visitor concluded that "slaves are trained to every kind of manual labor. The blacksmith, cabinet-maker, carpenter, builder, wheelright—all have one or more slaves laboring at their trades. The negro is a third arm to every working man, who can possibly save money to purchase one."[44]

The processing of agricultural crops was one of the most important southern industries, with sugar refining, rice milling, and gristmilling together employing about 30,000 slaves. Though such processing occurred largely in the plantation context, it nonetheless can be treated as an emerging industrial pursuit. For, as the prominent Louisianan Judah P. Benjamin once observed, "a sugar plantation is incomplete without its workshop, that is, its sugar house. The owner is manufacturer as well as agriculturist, and the manufacture is one of great delicacy and difficulty." [45] Moreover, the export trade of the whole country was heavily dependent on the processing of staple crops.

Louisiana and Texas hosted most sugar mills, but coastal Georgia plantations processed some sugar as well. In the 1850's, as large steam-powered refineries absorbed small horse-driven ones, the number of Louisiana sugar mills declined from 1540 to 1310. But Louisiana sugar production still rose to an average of 300,000 hogsheads per year during the same decade, while Texas annually averaged 8000 hogsheads. Such river cities as Louisville and St. Louis also had huge sugar mills, while New Orleans supported at least three large refineries as early as 1830. One of these, the Louisiana Sugar Refining Company, employed about a hundred slaves,[46] while another representative Louisiana sugar refinery had, according to a visitor,

> one sugar house five hundred and seventy feet long, by seventy-five feet wide, thirty-four feet high between the floor and ceiling, and a "double sawmill." The machinery consists of steam saw-mills and pumping engine at the river for supplying the sugar house with water, steam-engine of eighty horse-power, and sugar-mill for grinding cane, engines, vacuum-pans, and a complete apparatus for making and refining twenty-five thousand pounds of sugar every twenty-four hours direct from the cane-juice, and doing this entirely by steam. . . .[47]

The rice milling industry was especially important to the economy of the South Carolina and Georgia tidewater and was dependent upon slave labor almost entirely. Rice was a basic food in this region, and surpluses were shipped to the North and the Caribbean. Most rice plantations had threshing and pounding mills where the bulk of the slaves worked during the autumn and winter. The 550 rice plantations that each milled at least 20,000 pounds of rice in 1850 [48] were com-

Sugar Refining

plemented by Wilmington, North Carolina's three large rice mills and by Georgetown, South Carolina's twelve rice mills. These urban mills together employed more than 400 workers in 1860. Large-scale facilities also existed in Charleston, where, in 1840, two rice mills each owned over seventy slaves, and in 1860, the West Point Rice Mill employed eighty-nine bondsmen and the Lucas Rice Mill 160. At the same time, the rice mill of a leading Savannah merchant, Robert Habersham, used more than twenty-five slaves, while William Lake's rice mill owned fifty-five.[49]

Slave labor was also essential to gristmilling, a leading industry in most southern regions, where thousands of small water- or horse-powered mills ground corn and flour to serve local needs. Westward Mills of Brunswick County, Virginia, operated by only four slaves, was typical of the rural gristmilling establishments. In addition, commercial milling for the export trade flourished in Richmond and Baltimore. Richmond's Gallego Mills—largest in the world—and the Haxall

Company, both of which employed many slave millers and coopers (Haxall owned at least sixty-four), were representative of large urban flour mills. Baltimore alone processed 240,000 barrels of flour in 1857 valued at $2.5 million. The value of cereals milled in eleven slave states at this time was about $38 million.[50]

Both cotton ginning and cotton pressing were also vital to the southern economy, and most plantations had gins to clean their cotton and "screws" to compress it into bales for local transportation. At ports and river towns mammoth cotton presses operated by slaves recompressed cotton bales for overseas shipment. New Orleans's Levee Steam Cotton Press with 104 slaves and Mobile's Factor's Cotton Press with ninety-five bondsmen were large enterprises in 1850. Such cotton gins were described by one observer as places of "eternal clamor, clangor, clatter, clang, jumping, [and] jarring." [51] The related industry of cotton seed oil extraction began to emerge as early as the 1830's, when fifty slaves worked two Black Belt oil mills and the Orleans Cotton Seed Company employed sixteen bondsmen.[52]

The southern mining industry ranked in importance with manufacturing and processing and also served national needs. Coal and iron mining were widespread, but the chief centers were near Richmond, throughout the Appalachians, in the Cumberland regions of Maryland and Tennessee, and in central Alabama and Missouri. In 1820, Virginia and Kentucky led the nation in coal extraction. By 1860, these coal mining regions still ranked with Pennsylvania and Illinois. The decline of coal-fired salt boiling and the use of charcoal by southern iron works and of wood by railroads and steamboats temporarily injured coal mining enterprises. But this industry was clearly reviving by the eve of the Civil War.

The southern coal and iron mining industry was greatly dependent upon slave labor and many mining companies invested substantial sums in bondsmen. By 1861, Virginia's twenty-two leading establishments employed 1847 slaves, Kentucky's thirty-three pits used 746,[53] and Maryland's mines probably stood third in the number of slaves used. In 1837, the Black Heath Coal Company spent $11,345 for Negroes; the Creek Company of Colliers owned thirty blacks. Though some coal mines preferred to hire slaves rather than to purchase them, nearly all mining entrepreneurs seemed to agree with one leading Alabama mining promoter that

> Every days experience confirms my opinion that it is next to impossible to prosecute my mining interest successfully with free labor. . . . No reliance whatever can be placed upon it. . . . I have now not a white man on my work. I own but six men indeed but 5 effective ones. Of these but 3 can be kept in the mines, two being required outside. While with a force of 20 hands 16 could be kept inside and 4 do all the outside work . . . . I must have a negro force or give up my business. . . .[54]

Gold was mined throughout the Piedmont and Appalachian regions largely with slave labor. North Carolina's gold diggings produced tens of millions of dollars of the nation's wealth until 1849, and the federal government depended upon Carolina gold entirely between 1804 and 1827. The gold discovery of 1828 attracted more than 6000 new diggers into the Cherokee region, where Auraria, Georgia, became a center of the rush. Soon, Dahlonega, Georgia, and Charlotte, North Carolina, housed federal mints. Between 1828 and 1861, Georgia and Virginia pits alone produced over $11 million for the Dahlonega and Philadelphia mints. California, which dominated gold production after 1848, had some mines worked by slaves, but the southern industry revived in the mid-1850's.[55]

All sorts of Southerners, famous and little-known, participated in the gold-mining industry with their slave labor. Senator John C. Calhoun, who sent several slaves to his Georgia diggings in the autumn after completing the cotton harvest at "Fort Hill," typified the wealthier gold miners. "Our own little colony . . . numbers, white and black, some 40 or 50 persons," explained a lesser-known Georgia gold miner, J. Belknap Smith. "We have plenty of excitement in looking at Saw Mills, Gold Mills, Carpenters Shop, Blacksmiths Shop, Steam Engines, and all sorts of rumbling, tumbling, Grinding, and Steam Blowing noises." [56]

Lead mining was another industry which employed many slaves; the federal government was dependent upon southern lead for the military. Lead mining began in southwestern Virginia and soon expanded into Missouri. In 1801, the famous pioneers Moses and Stephen Austin, like many other Southerners, migrated to the western lead district, accompanied by their twenty-one slave adults and six slave children. By 1819, well before the deposits reached their peak production, more than 1100 diggers, mainly slaves, worked the Missouri lead fields, while the Virginia mines, dug by blacks, still remained operational. [57]

Salt, the vital preservative, was produced with slave labor along the southern coasts, in western Virginia and eastern Kentucky, and in Arkansas. With "smoking boilers," "mournful screaking of the machinery, day and night," and their "half-naked and degraded" slave attendants, according to one visitor, seventy major saltworks in Kanawha county—Virginia's largest salt center—employed two hundred slave coopers and 440 slave laborers in 1829. At this time Virginia produced as much salt as the rest of the slave states combined. By 1854, the number of saltworks had declined to forty, but employment had risen to 1230 male and 67 female salt boilers, most of whom were slaves. In the 1850's, the eastern salt industry was being complemented by new production by slaves

Saltworks

at the Petit Anse salt lake in Louisiana. But in 1860, Virginia still ranked second in the nation in the production of salt.[58]

The forests of the South supported a lumber industry, including the logging and sawing of timber and the cutting of shingles and barrel staves, which was basic to American maritime power. In the 1850's, Georgia led the lower South in lumber production, while Kentucky led the upper slave states. By 1845, lumbering was so extensive in the Carolinas that Wilmington alone supported at least nine steam sawmills. The value of southern lumber production more than doubled in the last antebellum decade, when water- and steam-powered sawmills alone annually cut $20 million worth of timber.[59]

Slaves were used greatly to log the pine, cypress, and live-oak in the swamps and forests from Texas to Virginia and especially along the Gulf Coast. The largest sawmill in the

Pascagoula, Mississippi, area employed twenty-five slaves in 1850; about 110 Negroes—worth $138,850—belonged to another lumberman in Alabama. The prominent slavetrader Isaac Franklin operated his (appropriately named) "Angola" sawmill-and-steamboat woodyard with more than a hundred slaves, valued at $65,000. Like President Zachary Taylor's Louisiana lumber operation, hundreds of smaller sawmills dotted the slave states. By 1860, the southern lumber industry engaged about 16,000 laborers, most of whom were slaves.[60]

Equally as vital as lumbering was the turpentine extraction and distillation industry, which centered in the Carolinas and was entirely dependent upon slave labor. In 1850, North Carolina's pine forests alone yielded 88 per cent of the nation's naval stores; South Carolina and Georgia production followed behind. In 1845, the Carolinas together produced enough turpentine to supply eleven Wilmington distilleries as well as innumerable small stills and tar kilns dotting the piney woods.[61]

By the 1850's, the turpentine industry had become crucial to the southern economy and was advancing into the Gulf States. This westward movement was typified by the Grist family, one wing of which worked almost forty slaves as chippers, dippers, coopers, distillers, and teamsters in North Carolina, while another group worked almost a hundred slave turpentiners in Alabama. The small producers of the eastern district were represented by the Williams family, which owned thirty-seven blacks; Daniel W. Jordan, a wealthy Tarheel, worked 200 bondsmen. In 1847, North Carolina alone employed almost 5000 slave turpentiners; and by 1860, the naval stores industry throughout the South employed about 15,000 slaves.[62]

Slave-worked fisheries, like salt boiling, were vital to southern society. Fishing provided an important export commodity as well as a useful protein supplement to the standard Dixie diet of pork, corn, and molasses. In 1835, the Potomac River fisheries alone employed about 8000 slaves; fifteen years later, 5000 blacks worked along the Albemarle Sound.[63] The daily life of the fishery slaves, who numbered about 20,000 by 1861, was graphically depicted by one traveler as follows:

> As you approach near the [Chowan River, N.C.] fishery beach, the hum and song indicate business and good humor, especially when catching a plenty . . . . hearing the merry songs and pithy original jests and sayings of the workmen and attendants—seeing the two fine large boats loaded down with the sein rowing out to the middle of the river more than three miles wide to shoot it, that is, to drop it out into the river. First—the two boats row off in company and astern of each other, the leading boat, bow foremost, the hinder stern foremost, for the sein is astern. When they have gone out far enough, they separate, one boat going down, the other up the river, as far as they design, dropping out the sein as they separate and so continue until they reach shore on their return. Then while the sein is drawn up by mules and horses, the sein hallers sleep, eat, or otherwise amuse themselves until the sein comes ashore—then all hands— if it is discovered it is a large hall, the excitement, motions, and preparations are thrilling. . . . Loud orders & quick motions announce the crisis, their process of landing commences—a roaring now bursts on the ear that thrills the breast with pleasing and intense excitement. . . . The roar and thunderings and frequently the cheers that follow the landing of a big hall of fish may be heard to neighboring fisheries. . . . Now the shelters are crowded with the processors, the cutters &c . . . . I slept down on the beach amid the din, roar and song, jest and laugh. They halled all night as they do in a big run of fish.[64]

The network of transportation facilities constructed between 1790 and 1861 was necessary to southern economic growth. In the early period, turnpikes were opened, bridges built, canals dug, and waterways improved; later, steamboats, levees, plank roads, and railroads were the rage. Blessed with navigable rivers, however, the South lagged behind the North and the West in railroad development. In 1860, the slave states boasted about 11,000 miles of railroad track—to use but one index—compared with 20,000 in the free states.[65] But this southern mileage still represented a ninefold increase in twenty years, and in its own terms the southern transportation system was expanding. Although the southern network was not growing as fast as the northern, it adequately served the needs of a predominately agricultural economy.

Southern internal improvement enterprises were so dependent upon slave labor that virtually all southern railroads, except for a few border-state lines, were built either by slave-employing contractors or by company-owned or hired bondsmen. The Mississippi Railroad, owning sixty-two Negroes, the Montgomery and West Point, with sixty-seven, the South Carolina, with ninety, and the New Orleans, Jackson and Great Northern, owning 106 blacks, were typical slave-owning railroads. Investing heavily, the Georgia Railroad spent $48,925 for Negroes, and the Baton Rouge, Opelousas and Gross Tête line spent $115,000. Other railroads which shifted from slave hiring to direct slave ownership were represented by the Raleigh and Gaston Railroad, which appropriated $125,000 in 1861 to purchase blacks.[66] Altogether, southern railroads probably employed more than 20,000 slaves.

Most southern canals and navigation improvements were excavated by slave labor. Hirelings dug such canals as the Brunswick and Altamaha, the Muscle Shoals, and the Dismal Swamp. A hundred company-owned bondsmen built the Barataria and Lafourche Canal, while slaveowning waterway projects included the Rivanna, the Roanoke, and the Bayou Boeuf.[67] Like railroads, many canal companies that began construction with hirelings soon converted to direct slave ownership. The Cape Fear and Deep River Navigation Works and the Santee Canal, for example, both switched to slave labor, while the superintendent of the slave-employing James River and Kanawha Canal explained his preference for slave labor in the following terms:

> . . . I would respectfully urge on the board the propriety of purchasing a sufficient number of young men and boys . . . to keep . . . the canal in repair; for the following reasons: 1st because of the difficulty, trouble, and expense to the company of hiring them even at exorbitant rates . . . 2ndly because of the great savings to the company as an economical measure.[68]

Other southern transportation facilities were dependent upon slave labor forces. Private turnpike companies commonly hired slaves, but Virginia's Lynchburg and Salem Turnpike was one company that owned directly its work force.[69] Some plank roads, such as the Lewiston Company of Virginia, initially engaged slaveowning contractors, but they soon decided to complete the work with company-hired bondsmen to eliminate the expense of contractors.[70] Slaves often built and operated southern ferries: two bondsmen—Stephen and Stewart—manned Governor John A. Quitman's Mississippi ferry, while Moses Grandy, who later purchased his own freedom, operated ferries and canal boats in North Carolina. The entire crew, as well as the pilot and engineer, of a Norfolk ferryboat were blacks.[71] Similarly, many southern shipbuilders employed slave labor extensively. One Gulf-based shipyard used six bondsmen continuously from 1838 to 1856. Before he escaped, Frederick Douglass had worked as a ship-caulker at Baltimore yards in the 1830's, and other

Maryland boat yards continued to employ blacks down to the 1850's.[72]

Slaves hauled most of the heavy cargo along southern streets, roads, and waterways. As many as 9000 blacks lugged New Orleans's 3000 drays; one Mobile wharfinger alone owned 106 Negroes. "Those tugs and unwieldy boats . . . required twenty or thirty hands to work them," explained one traveler about the tedious work of pulling keelboats upstream. "I have seen them day after day on the lower portions of the Mississippi, where there was no other way of working them up, than carrying out a cable a half mile in length, in advance of the barge, and fastening it to a tree. The hands on board then drew it to the tree." [73]

By the 1820's, when steamboats were replacing most keelboats, slaves served as deck hands, firemen, engineers, and even pilots. Before he escaped and became a famous abolitionist, William Wells Brown had worked aboard two different steamboats, as did many other fugitive slaves. One early enterprise was the Steamboat Company of Georgia, which owned thirty-five slaves in 1821. By the last antebellum decade, almost 10,000 bondsmen manned Ohio and Mississippi River steamers, of which the *Uncle Sam*, hiring twenty-four bondsmen in 1860, was representative. "It was a fantastic and grand sight to see the energetic black athletes lit up by the wildly flashing flames," concluded one observer of Mississippi steamer slave stokers, "while they amidst their equally fantastic song keeping time most exquisitely hurled one piece of firewood after another into the yawning fiery gulf." [74] To round out the southern transportation system, slaves also erected the bridges spanning streams and rivers. Black Belt bridge builder Robert Jemison, Jr., for example, used many slave laborers and even employed Horace and Napoleon, two slave architects! [75]

Though studied little, the reliance of municipalities, states, and even the federal government upon slave labor to build public works throughout the South was important. As early as 1819, the New Orleans Water Works engaged six slaves; in 1861, Savannah's water department purchased two Negroes. The New Orleans Gas Light Company owned twenty-five blacks in 1840 and about fifty slaves, valued at $53,000 by 1860. The Charleston Gas Light Company used four bondsmen in 1859; as many as 487 slave firemen, including many black volunteers, manned Savannah's seven fire engines.[76]

Slaves commonly cleaned and repaired the streets of towns and cities, whose ordinances often permitted black prisoners to pay off their fines by fixing roadways. In 1828, Nashville appropriated $20,000 to purchase fifty Negroes for street work. Savannah bondsmen worked as garbage collectors and at drainage, sewerage, road repair, and waterway improvement projects. Mobile likewise purchased two slave scavengers. New Orleans's chain gangs of male and female Negro prisoners constructed municipal improvements. "We were much pleased to see the runaway negroes and city force [of slaves] busy in sweeping and purifying the streets of our city," editorialized the Natchez *Free Trader* during the yellow fever epidemic of 1837.[77]

From 1816 to the Civil War, southern state governments promoted public internal improvements programs, and some states required the annual service of slaves to build roads and levees and clear rivers and harbors. Other states purchased or hired slaves to construct state-controlled levees, canals, and railroads. Georgia's Western and Atlantic line hired hundreds of bondsmen, while Mississippi's Southern Railroad purchased 140 Negroes. Virginia's James River and Kanawha Canal used slave hirelings and the Mississippi River levee system engaged state-owned slaves.[78] "No great or valuable improvement can be accomplished without an effective [slave] force, and this too continually at the disposal of the State," explained one

North Carolina official. "The absence of such a force, would seem to account for the unsuccessful attempts already made, and promises no better result from any future enterprize until the cause be removed. To acquire this force," concluded the Carolinian, "but two methods can be suggested—by [slave] hire or by purchase." [79]

Agencies and departments of the federal government were deeply involved in the industrial use of hundreds of slave hirelings. Slave stone-quarriers and common laborers helped erect the first national Capitol at Washington; after the War of 1812, they participated in its reconstruction. "I am satisfied," reported one Florida road official, "that it would be to the interest of the Government for me to hire a gang of negroes . . . & place them under charge of an efficient Superintendent and commence opening the Road [from Tallahassee to St. Augustine] immediately." [80] Slaves also manned government dredge boats clearing Savannah's harbor, and according to another federal official, "the best plan for the government to insure the work [of constructing a Mississippi River levee system] for the least sum, would be to purchase negroes and provisions, and employ overseers." Federal fortifications, naval installations, and arsenals also frequently used slaves. As late as 1859, slaves labored at Fortress Monroe and Fort Calhoun, Virginia, to give but two examples. [81] The navy yards at Washington, D.C., and Pensacola, Florida, hired large numbers of bondsmen, while in 1848 almost one-third of the 300 workers at the Gosport (Norfolk) navy yard were hired slaves. Many slaves also worked as common laborers and artisans at federal arsenals such as Augusta and Fort Hawkins, Georgia, and Charleston, South Carolina. [82]

The federal government only reluctantly dissociated itself from its practice of employing slaves on public projects. Not until a conflict-of-interest scandal broke [83] did Congress, in 1842, compel government agencies to report the number of slaves they were hiring. The various Army departments admitted employing 687 slaves, including many coopers, carpenters, masons, blacksmiths, armorers, boatmen, teamsters, and hundreds of common laborers. "We do not hesitate to employ them [slaves and free Negroes] on any appropriate duty, when they [planters] offer to hire," explained the Chief of the Corps of Topographical Engineers. The Army Quartermaster added that he "was not aware of any regulation forbidding the employment of persons of color in such labor as they are capable of performing. In the unhealthy climates of the South," he explained, slaves "are preferable to white men as laborers, deck hands, firemen and cooks, and a regulation prohibiting their employment would be injurious to the service." [84] The Navy Department claimed that it used no slaves, "except only in some few cases, in which officers have been permitted to take [on board] their personal servants, instead of employing them from crews." But a later investigation revealed that the Treasury Department's revenue-boat service hired many slave crewmen. "It has been the practice ever since the Revenue Boats have been established in this district," summed up a Wilmington, North Carolina, federal customs collector, "through *all administrations*, to employ this class of persons [slaves], because white labor cannot be obtained at the monthly rate of compensation allowed, and if it could be, the service can be better performed as at present." [85]

The wide use of industrial slaves by state and federal agencies suggests not only the centrality of industrial slavery to the southern economy but also the extent of southern control of the national political structure. That private enterprise also relied greatly on slave labor suggests the dependence of the private economic sector upon slavery as well as the determination of Southerners to use that labor system most advantageous to their program of industrial development. However, the use of slave labor in southern industries raised many knotty questions. Was it not dangerous to subject valuable Negroes to hazardous industrial pursuits? Would not bondsmen create disciplinary problems which might inhibit the creation of an efficient, docile industrial work force? Was not slavery an unprofitable labor system which might retard the economic growth of the South? And would not slave-based industries create insoluble contradictions within southern society, if slave employers insisted on industrializing the Old South without changing its political, economic, and social relationships?

CHAPTER TWO

Working and Living Conditions

The employ of the plantation negroes is not by any means so fatiguing, and laborious, as those employed here; they can generally find conveniency to Skulk, more or less at their respective Jobbing about a plantation; a thing intirely out of the question here where every negroe is under the eye of the superintendant from before sun rise to after sun set, and the moment they slack or intermit their labour, it is perceived and the means directly applied to make him pull up: Added to this the work is of the most fatiguing kind; digging, Shovelling & wheeling dirt, tumbling large pieces of the Rock, where every muscle of the body must be strained, boring holes, and driving wedges, & fellows & Tongs with heavy Sledges; indeed the handling of the bits, sledges, crowbars, drills, Fellows & tongues &c is heavy work of itself, and requires a constant exertion of muscular power—

Robert Leckie to Commissioner of Public Buildings Samuel Lane, Marble Quarries [near Washington, D.C.], May 16, 1817, Commissioner of Public Buildings of the District of Columbia Letterbook, Vol. 7, 1815-33. (NA RG42)

For the bulk of the southern population—free and slave—engaged in agriculture, life was mean and labor was hard. Primitive tools meant long hours, whatever the season or the crop. Diet was monotonous, clothing inadequate, shelter damp in the summer and drafty in the winter, and sickness was common. Compared with most free farmers, North or South, however, most agricultural slaves lived a harsh existence and were limited to the bare necessities of life. They could hardly better their standard of living no matter how hard they strived, and they possessed little bargaining power with their masters. The lives of most free agricultural laborers were bleak, but by comparison most plantation slaves endured a greater degree of misery.[1]

The conditions under which industrial slaves lived and worked resulted from the inhumanity accompanying industrialization as well as from the brutality that was an integral part of bondage. In the early stages of industrial development and under any labor system most industrial work would have been hazardous; industrial life could hardly have been anything but "nasty, brutish, and short," to borrow Hobbes's phrase. Employers everywhere seem to have regarded their workers as capable of enduring even the worst working conditions. Negro slaves merely formed a special case within the general pattern, and the slave system simply compounded what would in any event have been a disagreeable process of industrialization for industrial workers.

For laborers—slave and free—engaged in southern industries, working conditions were usually worse than those for laborers engaged in southern farming, since industrial development often demanded longer and harder working days than did plantation agriculture. Industrial labor clearly posed greater hazards than did farming, because factory tools were in the early stages of machine development. Luckless or careless industrial bondsmen drowned in rivers, were struck by falling trees, and cut their feet with axes or hoes as commonly as did plantation field hands. Of course, slaves, like machines, were such valuable property that the interest of slaveowners encouraged good care to prolong productivity. But treatment also depended upon the intelligence, whim, and liberality of masters. Both free and slave industrial workers had little hope of improving their living or working conditions; but slave industrial laborers had no possibility of changing jobs when industrial conditions became intolerable. Industrial slaves could run away from their work, but their chances of escape were slight. The dangers and hardships to industrial slaves were therefore unique compared to plantation conditions, because of both the rigors of bondage and the hazardous nature of southern industries. How then did bondsmen themselves fare under industrial working conditions, and how did employers attempt to alleviate the dangers of industrial work?

The Hours and Hazards of Work

Even without any particular abuse, industrial work demanded intense expenditures of time, effort, and life itself. Few masters risked working their slaves 365 days a year, as one Louisiana railroad company did, but industries rarely followed the example of a Mississippi cotton mill where the eight-hour day and 300-day year were the rule. Most industrial slaves worked from "sunrise to sunset" or from "six to six," [2] and industries as a rule operated at least twelve to sixteen hours daily, with variations according to the season. Leisure was so rare that only a short lunch period broke the long work day. Industrial slaves commonly worked six days a week, every week of the year; only the Sabbath or an occasional holiday provided a respite from toil. [3]

If the majority of industrial bondsmen worked this normal span, many others labored even longer hours in such enterprises as internal improvements, fishing, steamboating, and sugar refining. One master noted that his blacks had been "constantly without intermission on the Levee and the Roads every night and day" for many days. The overseer of a Georgia river improvement project worked his slaves seven days a week through the summer and fall, and once awoke his hands in the middle of the night to secure the flats against a suddenly rising river. A traveler described how 300 slaves closed a Mississippi levee break in "four days and four nights of continuous work." [4]

The very nature of some enterprises occasionally compelled long stretches of intense effort. Fisheries usually operated during the spring months only, but during this time everyone suffered from a lack of sleep. Recounting his grievances, fishery worker Charles Ball complained, "we had to rise and lay out the seine, no matter at what hour of the day." Observing the operations of the North Carolina Chowan River fisheries, a visitor noted that "there are no delays. Success is in proportion to the promptitude and energy displayed in every department and from the beginning of the season to the end they are driving day and night without intermission. The powers of endurance . . . are heavily taxed. . . . The whole process takes from five to seven hours averaging four hauls per day of twenty-hour hours." [5]

The quest for quick profits or the necessity to meet deadlines at particular jobs often resulted in abnormally long working hours. "We are compelled to keep our work under constant press. . . . we cannot relax for a moment—even nights or Sundays," wrote one railroad overseer. Numerous slaves were "engaged night and day, excepting during the winter months," over a period of several years on the Potomac Aqueduct. The press of business was likewise the determinant of the nighttime operations of many textile factories, where slaves sometimes carded wool for several days and nights on end. "Boys are rather worsted from loss of sleep . . . let them take a nap . . . run all night again. . . . the boys [awake] a half night each," noted one proprietor. "Orders plenty & business brisk," confided another cotton miller, "the wagon is all the time going—Old F'nand wanted to knock up several times but I keep him constantly going." [6]

Though steamboat slave deck hands did not stand regular

Gold Miners

watches, they could still be summoned to work at any hour of the day or night. Most steamboat crews therefore did "beastly" labor for thirty or forty hour stretches, and seven days of uninterrupted work was not uncommon before slave crews obtained a "fair amount" of leisure to sleep, loaf, or gamble. On the other hand, firemen who stoked steamer furnaces did stand watches, working all day and part of each night for seven or more days in succession, until the boat touched port and the routine was broken.[7]

Southern mines commonly operated around the clock seven days a week with two gangs working twelve-hour relays. Virginia coal mines reportedly "worked day and night except Sundays—when the water is drawn [off] as often as necessary to keep the works below from being flooded." In tunneling operations the usual practice was for two slave teams to work three eight-hour shifts seven days a week. At the Blue Ridge Tunnel of the Virginia Central Railroad sixty slaves dug from each end on eight-hour shifts, while two sets of hands regularly spelled each other on another Virginia line.[8]

Round-the-clock operations frequently prevailed in milling and lumbering enterprises. Gristmills often had such a rush of business immediately after the harvest that they had to grind day and night. Coastal rice mills dependent on tidal power were, as one traveler observed, "obliged to work by day or night, at whatever time the water served to impel the wheel." Since cypress timbers could be floated out of Louisiana swamps only when the water was high, President Zachary Taylor ordered his sawmill on continuous operation. "From the quantity of the timbers you must have on hand the mill ought to be run night & day, otherwise it may become seriously injured before it can be cut into lumber," ordered the President. "You must have as many logs as you can saw in two years or more even should the mill be kept running day & night; besides which you must try and fulfill your contract for lumber in N. Orleans."[9] Even twenty-four-hour operation, using two shifts of slaves, occasionally did not satisfy industrial entrepreneurs. For instance, according to the manager of an Alabama coal mine,

> the plan of working double shift [has] not succeeded as well as we expected. One reason of it is, and it is the principal reason, the servants rely on stopping work at the stated time whether the complement of work is done or not. I endeavoured to make it operate all I could, the roof in the low room has been rather worse than commonly, if the room had a rock roof and there was no dirt

to send out double shift would probably do. They kept Ben tramming all night and only put out ten trams of coal.[10]

The outstanding example of an industry exceeding the normal twelve- to sixteen-hour work day was sugar milling, which was, however, a seasonal operation. Continual processing of the cane was necessary to forestall rotting, and the elaborate system of vacuum pans, boilers, and machinery could not be easily stopped once it had been started. Sugar refineries therefore operated twenty-four hours daily, seven days a week, from November to January each year. "This is the most interesting period of the crop," explained one sugar miller, "for after the knife is put to the cane, there is no respite." Sugar refining thus demanded so much work from bondsmen that Christmas holidays were frequently postponed until January or even February. Masters granted a day's rest only if machinery accidentally broke down or if cane cutters fell behind due to poor management.[11]

Efficient and continuous operation required sugar manufacturers to divide their slave work forces into shifts. Some divided their blacks into two relays, which spelled each other every twelve hours. Others employed one day shift and two night watches, each of which embraced half the force of the day shift. One sugar miller allocated his slaves as follows: "eight boiling-house hands, seven mill-house hands, twelve carters, and thirty-three cane cutters." This same miller explained that "to make this number [the sixty slave work force] answer, the field-hands at night must spell the Boiling-house and Mill-house hands." [12] Bondsmen at such sugar refineries could therefore expect to work all day and six hours nightly, for a total of eighteen hours a day. The rule of the sugar industry was unremitting toil for several months of the year, with illness or accident the only relief.

The hazards of industrial environments threatened slaves engaged in many different occupations. The wild animals, poisonous reptiles, and malarial mosquitoes of the southern swamps and forests made lumbering, shingling, turpentining, and canal digging dangerous callings for industrial slaves.[13] The absence of safety devices in the early stages of industrial development created even more serious danger for bondsmen in other occupations. Slaveowners often tended to gamble even with valuable human property, because safety precautions were either too expensive or unknown. Injuries and deaths from fires, explosions, drownings, crushings, scaldings, and manglings, as well as from breathing toxic gases and choking dust, were therefore everyday occurrences in southern industrial establishments.

Fire was by far the most common danger in mills, mines, factories, and steamboats; and carelessness or malice, particularly by slaves, exposed most industries to the hazard of conflagrations. Cotton gins and presses were especially susceptible, and the records abound with reports of fires. "Clear cold day. . . . This afternoon ¼ past 4 o'clock my two Gin Houses took fire, 'adjoining' and & in ten minutes or Less were one solid sheet of Fire. . . . the second Gin House I've had burnt. . . . a Loss of $8,000 or more," lamented one cotton ginner. Four slaves died and three others were severely burned at another typical gin blaze, as a swinging door knocked a candle from the hands of a black woman, igniting the lint room into an instant inferno.[14]

Fires were so common at cotton factory "pickeries" that cotton millers experimented with and advised special types of mill construction. "This room [the pickery] is in all the recently constructed factories," warned one promoter, "built off some distance from the main factory, from the number of fires which have originated in it, and caused the total destruction of the factory, cotton on hand, injury to machinery, etc. A connection is so arranged, that in the event of fire, this can be instantly knocked away, and the room and its contents abandoned to the fire." Though some advocated other precautions, such as single-story construction, which might help save valuable machinery and slaves in case of a fire, by the close of the antebellum period very few manufacturers had installed fire-fighting equipment, and fires had already taken a heavy toll in industrial and human property.[15]

Turpentine distilleries were notoriously inflammable; to protect their real and personal property manufacturers proposed strict legislation against setting fires near pine forests. One Tarheel publicly warned that "the evil consequence of getting a turpentine plantation on fire is so great as to justify the labor of hoeing around the boxes, so as to clear away all the grass and pine straw to a distance of four or five feet." Another fearful Carolina farmer sued to enjoin the erection of a nearby distillery on the basis of the following argument:

> . . . fires frequently happen in these distilleries, six and sometimes eight hours after the fires are extinguished, under the still, owing to the combustible nature of turpentine, and that the distilleries are necessarily surrounded with barrels of turpentine and Rosin, which are usually spread over the lot and around the still.—these barrels take fire very rapidly, are exceedingly difficult to extinguish, and would if the wind were favorable, carry the flames to considerable distance . . . .[16]

The operation of steam engines at mills and factories and on railroads and steamboats was also extremely dangerous to industrial slaves. The explosion of dredging machinery on a canal horribly burned, scalded, and dismembered one slave crew; as the boat burned, blood, limbs, and flesh hurtled through the air amidst parts of the engine.[17] The slave fatality rate on steamboats can be figured almost precisely, since the government and newspapers made many reports. Most steamboats carried a crew of about twenty-five slaves, and about eight bondsmen died in each disaster; therefore the chance of death was about one in four, while serious injury was almost certain. More than 10 per cent of southern steamboats suffered accidents each year, according to official records. Of 245 vessels based in Wheeling, Louisville, Nashville, and St. Louis in 1841–42, for example, sixty were damaged or lost—an annual mortality rate of 12 per cent. Thousands of slave crewmen thus lost their lives or suffered serious injuries during the antebellum period.[18]

Defective boiler construction and the carelessness of inexperienced captains and crews increased the risks of steamboat and railroad operation. The blame for disasters, however, usually fell upon the slaves themselves, whether they were responsible or not. The bursting of a locomotive on one slave-run railroad allegedly "occurred from the safety valve being held down by one of the negroes attached to the Car. . . . the negro who acted as fireman being incommoded by the unpleasant noise of the steam escaping through the safety valve," the company reported apologetically, "ventured on the expedient of confining it, by pressing the weight of his body on the lever-gauge of the safety valve, which experiment resulted in the explosion of the boiler." On the other hand, other observers blamed "the cupidity of a few reckless steamboat owners, whose occupation and habits of life are such as to lead them to place but little value on the lives of their fellow-men when brought into competition with their own pecuniary interests."[19]

Aside from boiler explosions, the operation of railroad and waterway equipment was naturally hazardous, and slaves often severely injured themselves or died working handcars, coupling trains, or loading cargo. Trainmen fell from moving cars or were crushed beneath them during derailments; cotton bales tumbling down long chutes from high river banks sometimes knocked boatmen overboard. Five slaves were severely maimed, two of them mortally, when a pile driver repairing a New Orleans wharf capsized.[20] Keelboat hauling was, according to one experienced Missouri riverman, as dangerous to crewmen as steamboat navigation:

> . . . I consider that stream one of the most difficult . . . I have ever seen to navigate; it is one of the strongest currents I have ever attempted to navigate, owing to the many sandy bars, logs, snags, roots, the changing of the channel, &c. You may find a dry beach to day, where the main channel was one week before; and from the frequent changing of the sand bars, falling in of the banks, the water becomes so muddy that it is impossible to see the many logs that lie concealed under water; and it is not uncommon for us to run fast on those logs, and with great difficulty we get off, and of great risk of our boats; and it is not uncommon for us to hear of boats being lost or much damaged . . . .[21]

The toll of slaves working on public waterway projects was great enough to keep southern legislatures busy with the petitions for compensation filed by owners of killed or injured Negroes.[22]

Lumbering operations caused a high casualty rate among slaves, and railroad reports abound with references to fatalities from falling trees. "Felling some trees & a tree fell on a boy named Washington & killed him instantly," ran a representative daybook entry. "The chosen tree is attacked at water level with an axe," observed a visitor to the Louisiana cypress swamps; "it is important for the Negroes to direct the fall of the cypress carefully, for it might crush them in its fall and many careless woodcutters have been the victims of their negligence."[23]

Slaves engaged in mining, tunneling, and quarrying operations often suffered casualties from cave-ins, explosions, fires, flooding, suffocation, and foul air.[24] The danger of entrapment in tunneling work was compounded by the use of rudimentary machinery, the seepage of water, and the shifting of soil. These risks were graphically described by the chief engineer of a railroad whose tunnels were being dug by slaves:

> We can hear the rocks falling from an unknown height upon the timbers under which the men are at work, with a rumbling noise resembling that of distant thunder . . . . So appalling were the difficulties I have but imperfectly described here, and which, as far as I know, have not been equalled by any tunnel on record, that it became with me a subject of serious consideration whether it should not be abandoned for some other plan . . . . As regards the main tunnel . . . the work became so very hazardous that many of the [hired slave] hands left it. This was the source of considerable delay at that end. . . .[25]

Mining operations produced many spectacular disasters which took a heavy toll in slave lives. One gas explosion at Virginia's Maidenhead coal pits killed 93 per cent of a slave work force; another disaster at the slave-operated Midlothian coal pits was depicted as follows:

> A terrific explosion occurred . . . by which thirty-four persons were instantly killed, and a number of others so badly burned that little or no hopes are entertained of their recovery. . . .
>
> Mr. Atkins [the agent] (who descended a shaft with a rescue party) describes the scene as heart-rending in the extreme. Some of the dead men, the flesh charred on their bones, held their shovels in their hands. . . . and Samuel Hunt, a small boy, who had been deprived of reason for the time, by the concussion, was calling loudly to the mule he had been driving to go along. Those who were not dead . . . begged earnestly not to be left, and

then prayed loudly for a few drops of cold water to quench their burning thirsts. . . .[26]

Foul air and flooding constantly menaced slave miners, and the old refrain that mines were "as dark as a dungeon and damp as the dew, where the dangers are double and the pleasures few," was entirely justified. Seven slaves drowned when the Midlothian pits flooded in 1856; twenty years earlier the James River had broken into an entire upper cavern of one mine. At another Virginia mine a shaft fire produced sulfurous fumes which caused the slave diggers to "stagger and fall" as they attempted to escape. The manager had great difficulty rescuing the hands, one of whom almost failed to recover. Similarly, the lead mines of Missouri were so "dark," "unwholesome," and "half full of water," according to one traveler, that slave diggers often suffered from chills and colds.[27] Ventilation at mines was usually so inadequate that bondsmen constantly breathed noxious gases and silicosis-producing dust. Trapped hydrogen endangered many coal miners, and a visitor to one coal mine reported that "carbonic acid was so strong that two of our lamps were extinguished, and the third, carried by the guide, was kept burning only by his holding it as high as possible." Missouri mines were reported to be "dangerous from foul air." [28]

Mine owners frequently failed to shore up their excavations properly, and they often forced the slave diggers to work under hazardous conditions. Gold mine operators in particular, eager to make quick profits, sometimes made slave hirelings dig directly into hillsides without propping up the roof. The earth often gave way and crushed the workers, whose full value the employer was compelled to pay to the owner of the slaves.[29]

Slave lead-miners were often forced to dig lying flat on their backs, and, according to one traveler in 1837, "the dragging of the loaded corves seemed to be heavy and oppressive labor. Each man has a chain fastened by straps around his breast, which he hooks to the corve," the observer explained, "and thus harnessed, and in a stooping posture, he drags his heavy load over the floor of rock." A visitor to a gold mine complained that "the rough footing, the stooping posture necessary for getting on, and the confined air were so disagreeable that I had never before known . . . how to sympathize fully with those who . . . are condemned to the mines. . . ." [30]

Such dangerous working conditions, compounded by the recklessness of many operators, made many masters reluctant to rent their bondsmen to mining enterprises even when the best precautions obtained. As early as 1832, slaveowners required even respected North Carolina railroad contractors to include in hiring bonds the stipulation that slaves "shall not work . . . in the goldmines." In the 1840's, some mines began to replace Negro tramdraggers with mules or oxen, due to pressure from slaveowners. In 1858, both the Black Heath Mining Company and the Richmond *Dispatch* assured masters that the coal diggings were free from flooding. Another company advertised for sixty slaves, stressing that only "surface work"—railroad, boat, and coal-yard duties—would be required and claiming that "the above mines are entirely free from inflammable gas, and no accident from any cause involving life or limb has occurred therein for the past SEVEN YEARS. . . ." [31]

Heavy industries such as mining and transportation were certainly the most hazardous of all, but light industries such as manufacturing were also dangerous. The dusty airs of cotton gins, cotton presses, textile factories, and sawmills were serious threats to slave health. Ropewalks were generally described as "miserably dirty and ill kept"; one Louisville establishment was reported to be "in a filthier state than any fac-

tory . . . in Great Britain." Frederika Bremer's sensitive ear
for the shrill noise of an Augusta cotton mill was matched by
her keen eye for its "dusty, unwholesome atmosphere." Most
visitors smelled only the sweet essences of tobacco factories,
but Miss Bremer astutely observed that the "laborious" work
"not infrequently produces diseases of the lungs, and costs the
laborer his health and life. I suppose they become accustomed
to the smell and the dirt which always prevails in a tobacco
manufactory, and which to me seems murderous," she concluded, "as they are employed in it from their very child-
hood." Her suspicions were confirmed by many slaveowners,
one of whom publicly warned that "servants who have once
worked in tobacco factories are, in a measure disqualified for
other employments . . . after they have been cooped up in
the unwholesome and destructive atmosphere of a tobacco
factory." Both travelers and entrepreneurs agreed that lead
smelting was "very trying to the health." As early as 1807,
Frederick Bates disclosed that "the only inconvenience attending this employment, and that by the bye, a pretty serious one
is the poisonous effluvia of the furnace. The smelters die not-
withstanding their precautions." [32]

Casualties among slave millers of all types were also high.
"I got one of my most efficient [slave] hands badly crippled,"
complained one Alabama sawmiller, "he was one of Daniel['s]
best negro men. One of his hands is entirely distroyed or
nearly so. it so torn up that he will never have much strength
in it. he got it caught in a fly wheel and it is a grate wonder
that he had not ben killed. . . ." Less fortunate was one female slave sugar miller who, trying to extract the cane from
a choked roller, had her hand and arm crushed and soon died.
"This melancholy accident," lamented her master, "has caused
myself and family the most sincere sorrow as we view our
Slaves almost in the same light as we do our children." More

tragic still was a slave turpentine distiller, whose fate was described by a physician attending numerous cases of cut legs, scalded limbs, and infected wounds:

> . . . I found the negro in a hopeless condition, his whole leg mortified to the knee, & he presenting symtoms indicating that the inflammation had extended along the large Bloodvessels of the thigh to the Abdomen. In such cases it is customary to amputate: in his case it was too late. . . . he must have continued to lose blood for eight days at least!—Poor creature, he presented a seane revolting to humanity—such a one as I hope never to witness again. . . .[33]

Food, Clothing, and Shelter

Most industrial slaves lived at a subsistence level; their food, clothing, and shelter were barely adequate to their everyday needs. Since the typical industrial slave lived in a rural area or a small town, not in a city, the assertion that urban slaves (and, by implication, industrial slaves) were better clothed and fed than rural bondsmen, and had an above-average standard of living, is dubious.[34] Urban slaves such as house servants and service tradesmen may have fared better than most plantation field hands; but urban industrial slaves did not necessarily live as well as urban domestic servants. In fact, the evidence suggests that most industrial bondsmen—rural and urban—had approximately the same standard of living as did the mass of agricultural bondsmen.

For rural and urban industrial slaves, as for plantation hands, the basic foods were corn, pork, and molasses. The usual weekly ration in industry, as in agriculture, was one peck of corn meal, three or four pounds of salt pork, and a quart of molasses. There were few significant variations from these allotments.[35]

Quantity, quality, and variety of food were not determined simply by rural or urban residency; deviations from the standard ration depended more upon particular locale, type of occupation, season of the year, or personality of masters. Industrial slaves rarely had the opportunities afforded urban domestic servants or plantation house slaves of enjoying food from their masters' tables. Skilled industrial slaves often ate better than common industrial slaves, just as plantation artisans fared better than field hands. Food was certainly as plentiful at rural plantations and industries as in cities, quite apart from bondsmen's opportunities of stealing from smoke houses, chicken coops, or corn fields. Provisions at isolated mining, lumbering, and transportation enterprises could be as different from those available at sugar, rice, and grist mills attached to plantations, as provisions in small-town cotton mills were from those at urban iron works. Most masters did what they could to assure adequate food, but since food was the largest maintenance cost, it was usually held close to subsistence standards. The self-interest of slaveowners often protected bondsmen from inadequate provisioning of food by slave-renters, but many industrial bondsmen, hired or directly owned, suffered from notoriously poor care.

Some industrial slaves received certain foods as supplements to the basic diet of corn, pork, and molasses. At rice mills the standard ration was complemented by broken rice, unfit for marketing; similarly, slave sugar millers managed to obtain an above-normal portion of sweets. Tidewater transportation projects, fisheries, and turpentine distilleries, where the basic fare might include shad, herring, and mackerel, provided an above-average protein diet.[36] Slaves working near transportation facilities, where certain foodstuffs were in greater supply, enjoyed more varied fares than bondsmen isolated from routes and centers of trade. The Savannah River improvement project, for example, furnished salt and fresh beef, bread, crackers,

beans, rice, butter, onions, flour, potatoes, and fish [37] to complement the standard ration of pork and corn. Slaves working
in areas where cattle and swine were abundant enjoyed larger
portions of meat. The Cumberland River Iron Works in Tennessee, for instance, ordinarily provided nine pounds of pork
weekly, three times the customary ration.[38] Industrial enterprises closely linked to plantations sometimes furnished above-
average amounts of certain foods. Slaves raised staples, aside
from their industrial tasks, at the Roswell cotton factory in
Georgia, for example, while William Weaver's blacks raised
cattle and crops near their iron works, which sometimes supplemented the standard fare with fresh meat, green vegetables,
and flour.[39]

Moreover, some industrial occupations demanded such
strenuous exertion by slaves that efficiency necessitated above-
average allotments of food. "You ask would not the common
allowance that Negroes receive . . . on the plantations in
the neighbourhood be sufficient for the quarry negroes?" responded one slave-employing builder. "I answer decidedly no;
and for the following reasons: the employ of the plantation
negroes is not by any means so fatiguing, and laborious, as
those employed here. . . . From the above statement it is
obvious that the same ration of feeding would not do, in Cases
so dissimilar, and it would be bad policy to try it. . . ." In
this sense, some industrial slaves in especially arduous occupations may have received more food than typical plantation
hands, suggesting that feeding practices did not always follow
a uniform pattern when greater nourishment was required.[40]

At many industrial establishments slaves periodically suffered from food shortages, which apparently resulted from
mismanagement by employers. At William Weaver's iron
works, for instance, bondsmen almost completely lacked meat,
flour, and corn in the winter of 1828; flour that did arrive was
"so very bad" that it had to be returned. Soon slaves ate only

corn and, reported the superintendent, "complain very much." A year later, the manager repeatedly requested prompt delivery of flour, but three months passed without it. "We are living on corn pones at present," he complained the next summer; "we want about six Bbls Flour, our Hands have not had any for some time past," was the report the following winter.[41]

Weaver's slaves again suffered acute shortages of meat in the spring of 1859:

> we have no meat in the Smoke house now. . . . The hands are complaining very much on a/c of the beef—it spoils before the week is out—warm weather—I am afraid if we are to push through your two hhds—we will lose our white force—We only lost about 75 lb & that was last week—It spoils after issuing—I mention this so you can form your own judgment in ref. to sending *beef or bacon* one of which we want *this Week*. We want *this* week ½ *load of chopp* ½ *load of corn.* . . .

"It is taking all our management to get off that beef and to keep them in good humor," reported the superintendent, when supplies failed to arrive for another week. "John Purely sent us word privately that the hands at the [ore] bank would leave if they did not get bacon—they are sending it back as fast as we send it to them. . . ." Despite subsequent improvement, the situation again deteriorated in July, 1859, when the manager reported: "we are out of Bacon . . . last week & this. there is a good deal of complaint about bad meat." Nine months later, when food shortages recurred, the slave hirelings became so restless that the superintendent reported: "Our hands are here today wanting flour, coffee & tobacco. I have for the past month been putting them off—I am afraid they will leave in a body & throw us behind. . . . We by all means should have something to satisfy them if we wish to keep them." Yet, shortages continued into the summer of 1860.[42] Thus even William Weaver, who raised crops and cattle nearby his iron works, undermined slave living standards by chronic mismanagement.

Many masters carefully watched food prices and varied the kind and amount of provisions accordingly. The director of a waterway improvement project ordered his overseer to furnish fresh beef two or three times weekly only if the meat was inexpensive, "that is at the lowest market price." A sugar miller advised his overseer to grow more corn, and added: "I am glad that you have cut down the rashions as pork will be $20 p bbl here [in New Orleans] before two weeks. tis now $17.12. You will do well to let them Fish. . . ." [43] In this way, substantial savings could be realized in slave maintenance costs, since food was one of the largest expenses.

Some slaveowners deliberately stinted food rations either to reduce costs or to stretch short supplies. Such cutbacks ordinarily affected meat allotments and corn made up the deficiency. The proprietor of one iron works admitted that "by bad management [the Negroes] had had a short half allowance of meat"; one "progressive" rice miller similarly wrote: "I purchase only what is required to keep the plantation in a sound state. I adopt the principle of buying only the best food, —that is corn, for you will perceive that the issue of meat is very small, being on the Hopeton gang . . . net 25 lbs per annum each or 1 oz. per day, or ⅛th the usual issue in the south western states and upper counties. . . . The issue of corn is only that which the negroes have received for 50 years," he added, "and is no more than they require with the small allowance of meat." [44]

Industrial slaves were ordinarily about as poorly clothed and shod as agricultural bondsmen, contrary to the assertions by some historians that urban slaves were better dressed than rural bondsmen. To be sure, many travelers reported that city slaves

were well-dressed, but they usually had been observing the
Sunday or holiday wear of domestic servants. Slave week-
enders and celebrants certainly wore colorful cast-off finery,
but as one visitor astutely observed "on working days the case
is altered, for then they return back to their labour and dirty
clothes again." [45] The average industrial slave thus acquired
basic articles of clothing—a shirt, a pair of pants, and a pair
of shoes—twice annually. Winter clothing was somewhat
heavier and coarser than summer gear, and "drab" was the
most common description of slave apparel. Bondsmen normally received caps and jackets once a year, and blankets every
second or third year; depending on occupation, some slaves
also received coats and boots. Such allotments were usually
sufficient to maintain bondsmen at a subsistence standard of
living.[46]

Most enterprises probably met the minimum clothing needs
of their bondsmen,[47] but evidently some employers deliberately stinted on clothing allotments just as they did on food.
"Many of the Oxford [Iron Works'] servants are suffering
for cloaths," privately admitted the owner one winter. "The
practice . . . of giving to the Negro everything he may want
to desire is one wh. must prevent the growth of any industrious habits," warned one rice miller. "I have therefore, as
has been seen, only supplied what I consider absolutely necessary for his health & endurance." "The Boys were returned
entirely naked and I had to furnish them with clothes as soon
as they came home," complained an owner of tobacco-factory
hirelings. "I never saw any servants returned in such condition." [48]

Some industrial establishments were as incapable of providing sufficient slave clothing as they were of furnishing adequate food. Again, William Weaver was as troubled with
clothing shortages at his iron furnaces as he was with food.

Shingle Maker

"Our Sole leather is the same [entirely exhausted] & a good many boys barefooted. I will have to give them new [costly] shoes," unless leather arrives to repair the old ones, complained the manager in the winter of 1859. "What are we to do for shoes?" he pleaded throughout the spring and summer of 1860. "Three of the Blk [black] & some of the White hands at [the ore] bank are entirely out. . . ." Twelve pair of shoes were requested in September, because those that had arrived did not fit; several weeks later the manager reported:

Some four or five of our Blk hands are entirely out of shoes. I will be obliged to buy 4 par in town. Spott is laying up at Bank for the want of a par. The bank is very wet, it is so rough they cannot work without them. There was only 2 par of the last lot that would fit the negroes—they went to the bank. Two of the Car's boy is barefooted, they will be layed up if they are not shod. . . .[49]

Employers of slave hirelings often attempted to stint on clothing allotments so that slaveowners tried, without guarantee of success, to bind them to contracts requiring a minimum of good wearing apparel. "My Negroes told me they had not got all their clothing, their hats Blankets & c," complained one master to a turpentine manufacturer. "If convenient [I] would prefer your giving them shoes early in December, & made of thick strong materials to fit well having a view to their service & not looks & they will go through the winter," wrote another slaveowner to a tobacco manufacturer. For their part slave employers tried to convince slaveowners that good clothing had been properly provided, since employers sought to retain the same hirelings from year to year. This desire sometimes led them to supply clothing shortly before the Christmas recess, when the slaves returned home. "We will want a good many shoes before our hands start home," requested one ironmonger of his factor just before the commencement of a holiday season.[50] The bondsmen would appear well-shod for Christmas at least.

Most industrial slaves lived in cabins, shanties, shacks, or tenements. Crude, poorly constructed dirt-floored cabins, without shutters or doors, were typical in rural areas; multistoried wooden structures characterized urban housing. Slaves usually cooked their meals in an open pit at the center of the shack; smoke rose through a hole in the roof, since few dwellings had chimneys or fireplaces. The evidence thus suggests that urban industrial slaves lodged no better than plantation bondsmen, and that rural industrial slaves were housed no better than their urban counterparts. Urban house servants usually had quarters that were superior to those of rural field hands, but backcountry shanties and cabins differed little in quality from backyard shacks and tenements in towns. If anything, slave quarters were comparatively airier and cleaner in the countryside than in the cities.

Housing conditions seemed to vary more according to type of industry, particular locale, and personality of master than from urban or rural residence. Bondsmen tended to be more comfortably lodged at permanently located factories and mills than at temporary lumbering, canal digging, and railway construction camps.[51] Louisiana sugar mills had brick cabins made from readily available clay; owners of coastal rice and sugar mills built substantial structures (some of which are still standing) from "tabby," a sea shell cement. Industrial slaves at large establishments tended to live more comfortably than those at small ones, since wealthier entrepreneurs sometimes provided better-than-average housing facilities. At William Aiken's huge Jehossee Island rice establishment, for example, slave cabins had doors, windows, and brick fireplaces, and were whitewashed inside and out. At R. F. W. Allston's somewhat smaller rice estate each Negro house was, according to one visitor,

> 22 ft by 19. 10 ft high, with a foundation 3 ft & consists of a living room (a hall) and 3 bedrooms, and a loft above for store-room. Each person and each married couple have a bedroom, & each 2 children the same. As frequently as possible only one family occupies a house, wh conduces to peace & good morals. The houses are framed, with weather boards & shingles, & the floors are of matched boards.[52]

Most permanently located or large industrial enterprises did not provide such above-average accommodations, since most industrial slaveowners were not as "progressive" as Aiken and Allston. One traveler was so disgusted by the condition of the quarters at one rice mill that she left this graphic description of slave degradation:

> Those [Negroes] that I passed to day, sitting on their doorsteps, or on the ground around them eating, were the people employed at the [rice] mill and threshing flour. As these are near to the settlement, they had time to get their food from the cookshop. Chairs, tables, plates, knives, forks, they had none; they sat on the earth or doorsteps, and ate either out of their little cedar tubs or an iron pot, some few with broken iron spoons, more with pieces of wood, and all the children with their fingers. A more complete sample of savage feeding I never beheld. . . . I went into the house, and such another spectacle of filthy disorder I never beheld.[53]

Urban industrial slaves lived mainly in tenements attached or nearby to factories or mills; sometimes they resided inside the establishment itself. Slave lodging in manufacturing towns was more congested than the sprawling quarters of rural or plantation-based industries. Some Louisville hemp factory hands slept in six two-story tenements close by the main buildings, while a Mississippi cotton mill's ninety bondsmen dwelled in three large brick boarding houses. Bondsmen belonging to the New Orleans Gas Company, the Bell textile mill, and the Tredegar Iron Works lived in tenements within the walls skirting the perimeter of the plant. Rather uncomfortably, Lexington hemp factory slaves slept on a "long table," or bunk, which extended along two sides of an apartment next to the noisy spinning room. The Tredegar company admitted, moreover, that "our present arrangements are not at all equal to the wants of our people," and it suggested enlarging its housing facilities.[54]

Sleeping quarters for rural industrial slaves were more primitive and transient than those for urban ones. "No permanent fixtures are made at the mines for the accommodation of the workers," observed one visitor to North Carolina diggings in 1828. "They all encamp out of doors, each little company of three or four by themselves, sometimes under temporary coverings, made by a few boards, or formed by stretching a few blankets over poles set up for that purpose." According to this traveler, the slaves were, however, "more often without any other protection from the dews of the night than shelters made by the boughs of trees." The typical coverings at lumber and fishing camps were, according to one visitor, rude lean-tos "barely wide enough for five or six men to lie in, closely packed side by side—their heads to the back wall, and their feet stretched to the open front, close by a fire kept up through the night." In these transient shelters, the traveler continued, "The roof is sloping, to shed the rain and where highest, not above four feet from the floor. . . . The [wood] shavings . . . make a bed for the laborers." [55]

Similar housing conditions—unpleasant at best—prevailed at rural transportation projects. Bondsmen on the James River and Kanawha Canal ate and slept on barges; steamboatmen usually slept on cotton bales or other cargo above or below deck. Slaves on one steamer dozed on bunks attached to the engine-room wall, amid condensing boiler steam and the stench of expectorated tobacco juice. Bondsmen on another steamboat boarded in the hull, where their bedding was always damp.[56] Railroad companies ordinarily threw up temporary shanties, the quality of which was revealed in the course of a North Carolina suit involving twenty slaves who had been forced to sleep on rough boards in the crowded structure described as follows:

Lumber Camp

. . . a square pen, made of pine poles, with large cracks, through which one might thrust his double fists. . . . no shutter to the door; the top would not shed water; . . . no chimney and no floor, no bed clothing and no cooking utensils, and the fire was in the middle of the house. . . . another [shanty was similarly constructed, but with] . . . loose planks laid down for flooring; that along the centre . . . logs were placed . . . and earth . . . between them as a place for building fires; . . . no chimney, but . . . an aperture, three feet wide, at the top of the roof. . . . this shanty had a door to which there was a shutter. . . . other shanties . . . made of cross ties . . . placed on top of one another, to the height of some six feet, on three sides, . . . one side entirely open, . . . and were nothing like as good as the ordinary stable. . . .[57]

Such shelter—even at its worst—seemed hardly to trouble those slaveowners who bitterly complained about inadequate food and clothing provided by slave hirers. Throughout the antebellum period, neither masters nor employers substantially improved the quality of living or working conditions of industrial slaves. No doubt these conditions were largely responsible for the poor health suffered by many industrial slaves.

Health, Medical Care, and Insurance

Travelers, industrial promoters, and even some entrepreneurs claimed that the health of slaves in certain industrial occupations—shingling, turpentining, and sugar milling, for example—was better than in others. "With all their exposure, the laborers are remarkably healthy and almost entirely free from the autumnal fevers that so severely scourge all the surrounding country," declared Edmund Ruffin, famous for his scientific observations, after a visit to the Dismal Swamp in the 1830's. "It is said that no case has yet occurred of a shingle-getter dying of disease in the swamp—nor did my informants know that any one had been so sick as to require to be brought out." [58] Twenty years later, the often perceptive Frederick Law Olmsted claimed that "the turpentine business is considered to be extremely favorable to health and long life. It is sometimes engaged in by persons with pulmonary complaints, with the belief that it has a remedial effect." One highly respected agricultural journal held that turpentining "is considered a very healthy employment" for the workers. "The labour of grinding a cane crop has been frequently represented as injurious to the negroes," declared one sugar miller. "The reverse has been the case here," he insisted. "During that period the hands are cheerful and at its termination they have improved in general appearance. At no period of the year is there so little sickness, or disposition to avoid work." [59]

However, business records from the very occupations in which health conditions were allegedly superior tend to contradict such claims and make the conclusion inescapable that many travelers (and some who have drawn upon them) were victims of inaccurate observation or misleading promotional literature.[60] For the tendency to drive industrial slaves to the utmost, and to feed, clothe, and shelter them at subsistence levels, as well as the inadequate medical knowledge of the time, contributed to a tragic incidence of disease and fatality in virtually all industrial occupations.

Lumbering enterprises exposed slaves to numerous swamp-based diseases. In the summer of 1838, the Dismal Swamp Land Company officially confirmed that "the weather is so intensely hot & the flies so numerous in the Swamp, that few hands are at work in the Swamp & they get comparatively but few [shingles]. . . ." At the same time, a business agent reported to the firm's president: "I regret to inform you that One of the Co. Negroes died last week with inflammation & obstruction of the bowels. . . ."[61] Nor does the evidence confirm the alleged salubrious character of turpentining. From May to October, 1856, a typical period when compared to other years, twenty-three slaves belonging to one turpentiner lost a total of 218 out of 3000 work days from illness. Afflicted slaves lost between one and twenty-five days and averaged about eleven days each—a morbidity rate of 7 per cent. This rate seems greater than that for other types of industry, but comparable to plantation averages.[62]

Surviving records of Louisiana sugar mills reveal that the long working days, nighttime operation, and seven-day work weeks led to exceptional slave fatigue, debilitation, and disease during the milling season. One year, Maunsel White's sugar mill began grinding on December 11 and did not stop until February 19. The slaves worked seven days a week, eighteen hours a day, and had only one holiday, January 27.

Not surprisingly under such conditions, White wrote on February 5: "all hands trying to finish Rolling. Many sick . . . from severe Cold, & pains and sleepless nights. . . ." During the round-the-clock routine at another mill in 1855, the owner recorded: "more sick now than any previous time this year." [63]

The most poignant picture of sugar-milling conditions at their worst comes from R. R. Barrow's plantation journal. Even before the grinding period had begun, Barrow's blacks had been driven every day and part of each night during the harvest. "All hands at Rest, and for the first time in the last 6 weeks [.] we have also worked evry night until 10, 11 & ½ 11 oclock with a view of getting ready for Rooling—," wrote Barrow's overseer on Sunday, November 8, 1857. During the grinding season, which began on November 14, Barrow drove the slaves day and night, seven days a week for eight weeks, until, on January 11, 1858, the crop was wholly processed. Observing neither Sabbaths nor the standard week-long Christmas vacation, the overseer wrote on January 14, "We are taking our Christmas today so all hands are at rest."

Exceptional incidence of illness (in what was an unhealthy area of the South anyway) resulted from Barrow's driving of his slaves. On October 4, measles, influenza, and "Bilious" fever were reported; on October 8, twenty-five of seventy slaves were hospitalized; on December 13 and 14, respectively, eighteen and twenty-five cases of measles were recorded. "I fear the MEASELS will much retard the progress of our Rooling," wrote Barrow's manager. With only two births balancing twelve deaths in 1857, he reported on January 1, 1858, "we have lost much of our labour last year. . . . 1717 days work lost by sickness in the year 1857. . . . We have worked encluding the Rooling to date 183 nights in 1857." Though Barrow never appeared to understand that such long working hours accounted for the extraordinary amount of sickness, when he reckoned sugar production at a mere 175 hogsheads, he confided to his journal, "there is something wrong in the management of this plantation." [64]

Exposure to the elements—on top of inadequate nutrition, clothing, and shelter—took a toll of slave lives that tended to interfere with efficient industrial operations. One spring a Virginia railroad builder reported that

> the weather lately has been so changeable & severe. I fear it will be bad on your hands from this climate. Our people at this time are suffering very much from numonia. . . . or Pleurisy which I dreaded when our hands went. If they can stand it till the season of the spring fully settles I hope they will be safe. The only chance we have to escape in this climate in such changeable weather is not to expose the hands more than we are obliged to do. . . .[65]

"They complain very much about their sleeping quarters (being in the hull of the boat) and say it is killing them," reported a steamboat hiring agent to a slaveowner. "Nothing serious seemed to be the matter with any of them, but all of them wer out of health—all had had colds and looked badly." When the master ordered an investigation, the doctor confirmed that the damp bunks and bedding were causing illness, and added, "were they my negroes I should remove them at once, as I am sure their health is in danger from such a life." [66]

Hot summers afflicted industrial slaves with disease-bearing insects, sunstroke, and unusual fatigue. "Sunstroke . . . is quite common among the hands," reported a Louisiana railroad early one summer, while a nearby line reported that "the heat of the climate and the dread of sickness prevent many laborers from continuing through the warm season." [67] Mosquitoes, which were responsible for yellow fever and malaria—particularly virulent near swamps and rivers—were a continual menace during southern summers.[68]

A dramatic instance of the hazards of industrial work occurred at the construction of the Central Railroad from Natchez to Washington, Mississippi, in the spring and summer of 1836. Samuel Smith Downey of North Carolina had hired fourteen male and nine female slaves to the line's contractors in January. The contractors promised to "furnish each negro with the usual bed clothing, find them with plenty of good & wholesome food, employ physicians when necessary and . . . provide good & comfortable Houses for said Negroe slaves to live & sleep in." [69] Joseph Hicks, Downey's agent, transported the slaves from North Carolina and was supposed to watch over them in Mississippi. In February, upon his arrival in Natchez, Hicks reported to Downey, rather optimistically, that "I am very pleased with the appearance of this city and can see no cause calculated to produce disease. It has the reputation of being one of the healthiest places in the States." [70] However, by March, half of the blacks had already come down with diarrhea; by the middle of May, Hicks reported that he was spending virtually all of his time attending the sickly slaves. "We have been fortunate in not loosing any of them—the hearse has been running regularly . . . bearing dead bodies from the negro Market to the publick Cemetery." [71] Though the contractors had just begun to build shanties for the slaves, who were being fed spoiled meat and given little clothing, Hicks failed to associate the blacks' ebbing health with their poor living conditions. By the end of June, eight slaves, over one-third of the force, were sick; Reuben had been severely injured by a fall from the loft of a shanty. "I was sent for to see him and could not get a Doctor, and had to stay with him all that night. . . . I have my hands full, to walk three miles every day to see that they are attended to," reported Hicks. By the middle of July, one slave was dead, Moses complained of pains, Washington's foot was so sore that he could not walk, and a half dozen others were still sick:

The weather here is very warm, too warm for our hands to work all the day without killing them up—the exercise of walking a little, makes the sweat roll off from any one in large drops. . . . All our negroes seem to be dissatisfied here. Such Shantees as they have will not do in the winter—the Mosquitoes torment them almost to death in the night time—the meat they use is very salty and a little spoiled. . . . My task is a very hard one, I have to stay by the sick ones and give all their medicines day and night without any white person to assist me—railroads are very bad places for sick people. They have not proper articles of food for sick people. . . .[72]

Late in August, as the sickly season subsided, Natchez natives congratulated Hicks on his small losses! "The wonder among the people here," wrote Hicks, "is that so few out of so large a number of unacclimated hands should have died." [73]

Of all epidemic diseases, cholera—which swept the South in 1832, from 1848 to 1852, and again in 1854—seemed to strike industrial slaves hardest. When cholera threatened the Gosport Navy Yard and Richmond's tobacco factories in 1832, fearful slaveowners sought releases from their hiring contracts to remove their slaves from the sickly cities to the healthier countryside.[74] In 1834, when cholera struck one rice mill for the second time in two years, several children and twelve adults died, including eight prime hands and four of the most valuable artisans—Billy, the miller and head carpenter; Toney, a carpenter; and Aleck and Charles, the coopers. During the summer of 1854, various diseases, including typhoid and "fits," killed seven more slaves; eight more died of cholera in November and December, out of a total of twenty-six afflicted. During the height of the scourge, the rice miller removed healthier slaves to a piney-woods camp and thus lost thirty-five days' labor during the milling season.[75]

Measles, mumps, and dysentery, though less lethal than cholera, were so contagious and endemic that they posed perplexing problems for employers. "Sickness to an alarming extent prevails at 'Gowrie'—disease '*Measles, superceded by dysentery*' the latter having proven fatal in its effects upon two Women & a girl," reported a rice mill manager in the summer of 1848. Touring Europe at the time, the master advised medical care for the slaves, but stipulated that doctors not be called unless they were absolutely necessary.[76] During January, 1848, one textile mill reported fourteen cases of measles and was forced to curtail operations. Mumps and measles plagued another cotton mill throughout 1847, incapacitating as many as thirty-five workers and resulting in at least three deaths. By March, 1848, the owner reported "great distress. More than half of our people were out of the factory sick with the measels." [77]

Filthy, crowded slave quarters encouraged contagions such as pneumonia, typhus, typhoid, and tuberculosis, while elderly hands died of "dropsy" or "rupture of the heart." Afflictions such as scarlet fever, diphtheria, apoplexy, pleurisy, "marasmus," hepatitis, diarrhea, and "angry looking biles" were also endemic.[78] Infant mortality, children's diseases, and pregnancies were also serious problems. But the most serious epidemic diseases by far (after cholera) were yellow fever and malaria, which in 1847, 1853–55, and again in 1858 struck deep-South regions on spectacular scales.[79]

Masters met the ravages of disease with a myriad of medications, many of which now seem pathetically inadequate and ineffective. To complement the standard practices of bleeding, blistering, cupping, catheterizing, purging, and emetics, one rice miller administered "okra, coffee, molasses and gruel, and other nourishment when required." During the measle and dysentery disaster of 1848, one rice mill manager administered arrowroot, cream of tartar, mustard, paregoric, gum camphor, and gum arabic, as well as a half-gallon of brandy; he also prescribed flax, sage, and various other teas. Fishermen plagued by "ague and fever" received tartar, salts, calomel, jallap, and castor oil—five very common medications. Within two months one sugar miller ordered a bottle of wine, eight boxes of sugar, one barrel of flour, two quarts of coffee, and ten bottles of whiskey for his clinic. Among other similar remedies, an iron works doctor applied magnesia, "assafoetida," oil of turpentine, spirits of nitre, lavender, and peppermint, senna, and pitch plasters to ailing slaves. Senator Henry Clay prescribed salt, mustard, calomel, and rhubarb for his hemp factory slaves, who complained of the violent abdominal pains symptomatic of cholera. Clay claimed that this concoction had been successfully used at a Lexington bagging factory.[80]

Some owners vaccinated their slaves against smallpox, used quinine for malaria, realized the importance of cleanliness, and attempted to quarantine sick slaves. Such practices led by the logic of grim experience (not from a knowledge of the germ basis of disease) to the building of slave hospitals and more sophisticated medical treatment. First used in the eighteenth century, vaccination was widely practiced in the nineteenth so that smallpox seldom victimized industrial slaves.[81] Some of the more progressive industrialists who recognized the wisdom of cleanliness, began to whitewash slave cabins annually or during "sickly seasons" and to prescribe bathing and clean bedding for their infirmaries. At one rice mill's "airy," steamheated hospital the mattresses were refilled with straw and the pillow cases and blankets were washed each month. The wards were swabbed weekly and the entire building was whitewashed annually.[82]

Gradually, small enterprises began to build crude clinics, many of which resembled slave shanties but did at least separate healthy from sick slaves. Meanwhile, the wealthiest sugar and rice millers erected larger, cleaner, and, by contemporary standards, more modern infirmaries, the best of which probably resembled closely the one described by a visitor as follows:

> . . . a neat tabby building . . . shaded by several large oak trees. . . . the nursery and hospital . . . are in one building. They were remarkably neat and clean, well ventilated, and heated altogether by steam, which produces a more equal temperature throughout, then could be attained by fireplaces. . . . the hospital is an airy and warm building 80 feet by 24, with four wards, an entry which answers as an examining room, a medicine closet, a kitchen, and a bathing room. One ward is for lying-in women, another for women, and two others for men. . . . The accommodations for the sick are a cot for each person, with a straw matrass and pillar, a pillar case, 2 blankets and a coverlid, with benches. . . . A Daily account is kept of the names of the sick, their diseases and the remedies applied. A nurse and two small girls attend to this department.[83]

Since nursery and maternity wards were in the same building that housed the sick slaves, and since bedding was not changed after each patient, even such advanced institutions as this had obvious shortcomings.[84]

In the last antebellum decades, some cities began to build medical facilities especially for slaves. As the cholera scourge of 1832 swept up from the Virginia Tidewater, Richmond tobacco manufacturers began seriously to consider building Negro hospitals. Two "comfortable" slave clinics were quickly fitted out, while the city's Board of Health announced that bondsmen with "malignant cholera" could be hospitalized for five dollars the first day and three dollars daily thereafter. However, the epidemic was so infectious that hospitalization proved inadequate and the *Enquirer* urged tobaccories to shut down until the disease abated.[85]

By 1860, Richmond had permanently established an allegedly "airy," clean, and quiet "Hospital for Slaves." It accommodated as many as forty patients, attended by four physicians who paid "the most rigid attention . . . to cleanliness . . . a *sine qua non* for health under any circumstances." By the same time, other cities, like Augusta, Georgia, had begun to build slave hospitals, while the federal government had constructed marine hospitals to serve boatmen—free and slave—at Norfolk and Louisville. Other federal facilities were projected for Paducah, Vicksburg, Natchez, St. Louis, and Napoleon, Arkansas.[86] Despite these advances, the number of industrial slaves receiving adequate medical care, even by the primitive standards of the time, could not have comprised more than a fraction of those in need—a fact which helps explain the practice of insuring the lives of industrial slaves.

Studies of slavery have usually ignored the extent or significance of slave life insurance. Scholars have concluded that slaveowners "as a rule carried their own risks" and that slave life insurance "was very rare." [87] They have also assumed that the practice of insuring slave lives was an innovation of the late antebellum period, when, actually, slave underwriting dated back to at least the turn of the nineteenth century. Since slaves represented substantial investments, it was logical for masters to insure Negroes against the hazards of industrial work.[88] Slave life insurance thus increased as slave-based industries developed, and the growth of insurance reflected the toll that industry was taking in slave capital. Insurance was beginning in the 1840's to become significant for the future stability of industrial slavery.

Surviving evidence suggests that industrial slave life insurance was becoming increasingly common in the nineteenth century. As early as 1811, for example, the life of Jacob, a slave boatman, was insured; by 1835, the Virginia legislature had incorporated the Kanawha Slave Insurance Company, and slave life insuring was becoming established in the upper

South and was not unknown in the lower. By the 1840's, many southern and a few northern insurance companies had begun to warrantee the well-being of industrial bondsmen. The North Carolina Mutual Life Insurance Company of Raleigh, the Greensborough Mutual Life Insurance Company of North Carolina, the Albemarle Insurance Company of Charlottesville, the American Life Insurance Company and the Valley Insurance Company of Richmond, Virginia, typified southern enterprises. The Nautilus Life Insurance Company of New York engaged a Louisiana agent in the 1840's; the United States Life Insurance Company of Philadelphia underwrote Virginia and Louisiana industrial bondsmen in the 1850's. According to *Affleck's Southern Rural Almanac*, most southern insurance companies were willing to risk insuring slaves.[89]

The number of insured industrial slaves was infinitesimal compared with the total slave population in the last antebellum decades. Indeed, only about 3 per cent of all industrial bondsmen were insured in any year of the 1850's. Most warranted slaves were either skilled artisans or engaged in mining, steamboating, and waterway improvement projects, the most hazardous occupations of all. U. B. Phillips's conclusion, that "in practice the lives of a few slaves engaged in steamboat operation and other hazardous pursuits were insured, but the total number of policies taken on their lives . . . was very small," is therefore technically correct.[90]

However, by the 1840's, those employers who operated such dangerous industries as mines, riverboats, and internal improvements were becoming increasingly interested in slave life insurance. By spreading slave losses among large numbers of slave users, life insurance promised to underpin valuable investments in industrial slaves. Life insurance may have been relatively insignificant in the 1850's, but if slavery had survived past the 1860's, life insurance would have tended further to stabilize slave-based industries.

By the last antebellum decades, many industrial enterprises already understood that slave life insurance could protect valuable investments. One master warranted a carpenter for $1250, half his value; a North Carolina miner and tanner insured at least seven of his blacks; and George, a slave rented to the steamer *David White*, was underwritten for $700. The famous Mobile physician Josiah C. Nott publicly reported that "most of the negroes presented to me for insurance [examinations] have been deck hands of steamboats," who worked under hazardous conditions.[91] However, the Cape Fear and Deep River Navigation Company, which heavily invested in slaves, probably purchased life insurance policies more frequently than any other enterprise. Almost all of the forty Negroes purchased in 1855, for instance, had their lives insured for one-year terms and had their policies renewed annually.[92]

As the value of slaves rose in the last antebellum decades, industrial slave employers increasingly offered insurance to induce reluctant owners to hire out their bondsmen, while life insurance companies competed for slaveowning clientele. Lumber companies assured "indemnities," turpentine distilleries tendered "inducements," and railroads promised to guarantee hirelings against accidents. One Virginia coal mine repeatedly advertised that "the lives of slaves hired . . . can be insured at a reasonable premium, if desired by the owners [of hirelings]." Another coal mine nearby announced that "these pits are now considered so entirely free from danger, that an insurance can be affected at reasonable rates if desired. . . ." In 1857, the City of Savannah resolved to guarantee owners of regularly enrolled slave firemen injured at fires the assessed sum of damages. "It will be out of my power to hire hands unless I could express to the owners what kind of work & c they are to be put at," warned one railroad hiring agent. "They are unwilling they say to put their hands on any Publick work unless there is a Guarantee for the value of the slave in case he should come to his death by being on such work, and further a Guarantee for the safe delivery of such a slave at the end of the year. . . ." Generally, by 1854, promoters of canals and railroads were including insurance expenses when they estimated the total cost of their projects.[93]

Though during epidemics the demand for slave life insurance increased dramatically, companies sometimes raised their premiums or became reluctant to issue new policies or to renew old ones. After fears subsided, however, the insurance business accelerated. "The Richmond Fire Association, (in consequence of the disappearance of cholera,) have resumed Insurance on the Life of Slaves, at the former rates of premium, *without the extra charge*," reported the Richmond *Dispatch* in 1854. "Since last summer, when the cholera swept off hundreds of our slaves," concluded the Richmond *Enquirer* with unintentional tragic irony, "insuring their lives has become a very general precaution with owners, and there are now three or four offices in our city where risks are taken. The present is a good time to insure. . . ."[94]

Even though the livelihood of some slaves may have been improving slightly, by 1861 the daily working and living conditions for the vast majority of industrial slaves remained barely tolerable at best. Long hours, hazardous work, subsistence living levels, sickness, and inadequate medical care—all these contributed to a heavy toll in slave health and life itself. Undoubtedly these conditions in turn contributed to the unrest which pervaded the institution of slavery. Thus, employers still had to solve the problem of pacifying their industrial-slave work force.

CHAPTER THREE

Patterns of Resistance and Repression

> The whole South is like one of her own cotton-steamers—
> such as I have just left, filled from the hold to the topmost
> deck with the most inflammable matter; everything heated
> up to the burning point, and a furious draught blowing from
> end to end, and a huge high pressure boiler in her belly
> pressed to bursting. . . . On such a volcano is based the in-
> stitution of slavery. . . . The remedy proposed for this state
> of things is repression, severity. . . . Terrorism does not pac-
> ify a people. It only changes complaint into conspiracy. . . .
>
> James Stirling, *Letters from the Slave States* (1857), pp. 59, 301.

Whether slaves were content with their living and working
conditions, lacked concepts of freedom, developed "infantile"
personalities, or otherwise accommodated to bondage are con-
troversial questions. Some historians have argued, for example,
that slaves working in industry or living in cities were happier
than those on rural plantations. Others have alleged that such
industries as tobacco manufacturing, lumbering, and sugar
milling were virtually free from slave unrest. Slave artisans
and industrial workers, who had privileged or personal relationships with masters, were allegedly more faithful than typical slave field hands.[1]

Though the most sophisticated theories of human behavior
can be used to support such assertions, few records reveal the
thoughts and feelings of the industrial bondsmen themselves.

Their emotions, intentions, and personalities can reasonably be inferred only from the records of their masters, that slave testimony which has survived, and the blacks' own overt activity. Such patterns of behavior do, however, reveal that apparently most industrial bondsmen grudgingly acquiesced in their condition and did not seem to present masters with insoluble disciplinary problems. On the other hand, though some masters were able to control their workers more effectively than others, the records also clearly indicate that no enterprise, industry, occupation, or region repressed slave resistance entirely. In fact, there was always a substantial number of industrial slaves who clearly demonstrated all of the varieties of resistance to servitude, ranging from passive to violent protests, exhibited by plantation bondsmen. Moreover, industrial slaves as a group resisted enslavement as frequently as did agricultural slaves, and individual blacks sometimes rebelled against slavery with great courage. Artisans and industrial slaves generally became leaders of those insurrections—industrial and agricultural, urban and rural—which occasionally occurred. But paradoxically, industrial slave leaders often sullenly accommodated themselves to slavery as did many of their black brethren.

If industrial slaves were discontented with long working hours, hazardous working conditions, and subsistence living standards, they could be expected to protest against industrial routines and the slavery regime. Not surprisingly, most resistance by industrial slaves stemmed chiefly from resentment at the brutal extortion of labor, from humiliation at personal indignities, and from general dissatisfaction with bondage. Human beings innately resented inhuman treatment, and human aspirations for a better life could not be eliminated entirely. Despite isolation, division, terror, and subtle forms of discipline of the slave workers, discontent remained one of the most perplexing problems faced by industrial employers.

Slave dissatisfaction expressed itself in two basic ways. Many industrial bondsmen, aware of the virtual impossibility of overthrowing their masters or escaping from the South and terrorized by the system of slave controls, passively acquiesced in slavery's labor requirements and feverishly enjoyed its occasional rewards. Other industrial slaves were not so cowed that they were incapable of protest. Their dissatisfaction led them to make attempts to control more of their own time, to make some of the decisions affecting their daily lives, or occasionally to make spectacular assaults on the institution of slavery itself. Between these extremes lay numerous other manifestations of opposition to bondage.

Industrial Slave Resistance

The most subtle forms of slave protest were negligence, slowdown, feigned sickness, outright refusal to work, and pilferage. Such behavior often expressed itself as thoughtless carelessness, resulting from the lack of respect for property and work engendered by enslavement. These actions did not always represent conscious resistance, but they did reflect underlying discontent with industrial work routines and the restrictions of bondage. Whatever the cause, negligence, laziness, and thievery were in any case manifestations of blind or reasoned hostility to slavery, which often disrupted industrial routines.

Slave laziness and carelessness may have stemmed from fatigue or fatalistic protest, but they certainly perplexed employers much of the time. George Washington called his carpenter a "bungler," while an overseer lamented that James, a cobbler, was insufferably idle: ". . . this is the . . . time when he should exert himself to be a good workman, but he will not do what is proper . . . he is capable of finishing Six pairs of Shoes a Week and he seldom does more than three." [2] Such slowdowns seemed to bother many industrial enterprises.

Another measure of protest—conscious or unconscious—was a slave's flat refusal to work. This situation occurred at one Alabama coal mine when slave Jack was assigned the task of pumping water from the pits and refused to co-operate. Jack's manager reported that he "lay there on a plank and went to sleep insisting that it was not necessary to haul any more, and in fact did not haul any more." Similarly, hired slaves often refused to return to employers after Christmas recesses. Isaac expressed "such an unwillingness to return to you," wrote one owner to an iron manufacturer, "that I feared should I send him over he would runaway." Apparently by concerted plan, several hirelings refused to return to work for a railroad contractor whose hiring agent reported that the slaves complained of whippings and other harsh treatment, a lack of sufficient food, having to cook for themselves, overwork, and having to wash their clothes on the Sabbath. The agent closely interrogated each bondsman separately and satisfied himself that they were misrepresenting their working conditions and engaging in a conspiracy to avoid work. He concluded that Charles, the ringleader, was a "no account scoundrel . . . and if he had been beaten with sticks, clubs & c as he states, I expect he deserved it." [3]

Because such outright refusals to work could become risky ventures for bondsmen, slaves often resorted to subtler stratagems such as feigned illness. A fugitive related how two slave distillers got drunk one night and faked sickness the next day. A gold miner complained of drowsy and drunken bondsmen; a turpentiner was upset by a drunk, disobedient, and foul-mouthed Negro; and the chief engineer of a North Carolina river-improvement project lamented the "excessive losses of time by sickness *real* or *feigned*." [4]

Pilferage was also a perennial problem pervading most industrial enterprises. Since bondage left slaves with little respect for property or their work, thievery was a more or less conscious form of protest. Industrial slave thieves usually sought either the fruits of their own labor for their own use and satisfaction, or resentfully tried to cripple their industrial work places. Rice millers were especially vulnerable to such losses. One overseer confided to his employer that "I can never think that Stephen [the rice miller] acts perfectly honest with the rice in the mill." Another rice miller's suspicion that his rice "had been much exposed to plunder" was paralleled by the *Southern Agriculturist's* report that pilferage was a major problem for many rice millers. Moreover, any manufacturer who, like William Weaver, lacked adequate supplies of food and clothing was liable to harassment from slave thieves. "I had a notion of Comeing down tomorrow evening," wrote Weaver's distraught manager, who was compelled constantly to remain at the furnaces, ". . . but I am afraid if I leave here they will steal the place. They come very near it while I am here." [5]

Some industrial bondsmen were in more favorable positions for stealing than others. Tobacco factory thefts were such constant sources of aggravation that Richmond and Petersburg newspapers daily reported them and claimed that tobacco manufacturers were losing more goods to thieves than any other businessmen. One slave left a factory after cleverly concealing tobacco in his coat sleeve and casually throwing the garment over his arm. According to an anonymous "One Who Knows," blacks frequently boarded the Raleigh and Gaston Railroad's cars, and "running in the night as slow as they run . . . could in conjunction with other negroes throw off what they choose." While railroad agents were sleeping, the informer continued, other slaves "take off what they wanted, even to a Hhd of sugar & I have no doubt but hundreds of Dollars worth of lost goods go in this way." As a fire consumed storehouses and shanties of another railroad, slaves somehow managed to save "nearly all their plunder," while

allowing the company's tools, supplies, and property to burn!
Blacksmith Jacob stole provisions from a smokehouse by
means of a false key, which he himself had forged. Carpenter
Frank stole $160 worth of gold and silver from his master by
the same "art & cunning." [6]

Industrial slaves stole both for their immediate gratification
and for the illicit "black market" which developed within
factories, mills, and towns. Thomas Mosby, a slave, robbed his
factory of wool, which he exchanged for snacks and drinks,
while slave Charles made off with a piece of Tredegar bar iron,
which he traded for liquor at a grog shop. A group of Virginians accused the local slave gristmillers not only of being
dishonest and deceptive, but also of forming "a sort of link of
communication" between other slaves and free blacks in the
neighborhood. Eager white and free black peddlers and merchants so encouraged slave thieves that the Richmond *Dispatch* reported that "Many of the manufacturers have adopted
stringent regulations, with the hope of breaking up this trade,
but until they can ensure the recovery, conviction, and punishment of the buyers, they will not be able to break down the
system of illegal traffic, which has proven so injurious to themselves and ruinous to their servants." [7] Some slave thieves even
specialized in stealing only valuable articles, apparently to meet
the demands of their market. One slave stole a clock from his
brickyard, two others stole money and a traveling bag from a
train, an iron worker stole a gold watch and silver tableware,
and two workers in a lumberyard even attempted to carry off
nine hundred pounds of iron. Undoubtedly the most clever
slave thieves of all were those gold miners who, according to
Niles' Register, daily concealed substantial amounts of gold
dust in their hair! [8]

Pilferage, slowdown, and negligence by bondsmen bewil-
dered many masters. A "well-informed capitalist and slaveholder," interviewed by Frederick Law Olmsted, perhaps best

summed up the naïve responses of many masters to passive protests:

> We have tried reward and punishments, but it makes no difference. It's his nature and you cannot change it. All men are indolent and have a disinclination to labor, but this is a great deal stronger in the African race than in any other. . . . We must always calculate that they will not labor at all except to avoid punishment, and they will never do more than just enough to save themselves from being punished, and no amount of punishment will prevent their working carelessly and indifferently.[9]

Servile protests sometimes assumed more extreme forms, ranging from arson to escapes and from assaults to rebellions. Though fires were common occurrences at many southern factories and mills, many manufacturers suspected that not every fire was accidental, and newspapers often expressed suspicions of arson. "It was supposed to be the work of an incendiary," reported the Charleston *Courier*, after Senator Henry Clay's bagging factory burned in 1845; Clay's building "was set fire to by some unknown villain," confided one Kentuckian to another.[10] Concrete evidence of arson was sometimes found, however. A Texan charged that his blacksmith had burned the shop; the court sustained the claim. A tobacco worker threatened to burn down the factory if his master did not dismiss his overseer. Such slave behavior so perplexed some manufacturers, millers, and ginners that they began arming themselves against slave incendiaries. "I expect to kill someone about it yet," vowed one cotton ginner upon the smoking ruins of his gin.[11]

When appropriate opportunities arose, industrial slaves attempted to escape. "Isaac, my carpenter, ranaway wednesday, & is probably now in S. Carolina," lamented a prominent Georgia builder with the use of a political metaphor. "He has seceeded. & I do not know when he will return to the Union. He left me at an inconvenient time." Other masters professed surprise when even their most trusted, faithful, or privileged bondsmen departed.[12] Slave absences created serious problems at industrial enterprises, since there was always a small but active minority of industrial slaves who ran away.

The primary motivation of runaways, aside from slavery's inhumanity, seemed to be the natural desire to avoid the drudgery of industrial routines. The majority of fugitives remained absent only for a short time before returning voluntarily to their jobs. Church, for example, ran away from his forge in Virginia for four days in 1830; Adam left for five days the following year, and three hirelings ran off together for about a week in 1844. Mack, who was continually troublesome, was "off on a spree a couple days last week," reported the manager of one iron works. Comparatively more fortunate were one sugar miller whose slave blacksmith left one morning and returned that night, and another sugar mill, which in the late 1850's counted only eleven fugitives, all of whom—except one—were absent only a week. The runaway problem became more critical at one rice mill, where, in the winter of 1860–61, George the carpenter and Hector the boatman escaped together, and Jimmy the engineer absconded for a week. Altogether, this rice miller lost for the season the services of five indispensable bondsmen.[13]

Absenteeism was evidently highest during the late summer and autumn months when industrial operations peaked and production pressures mounted. Virginia flour miller Big Phill absconded a week before threshing began one year; six years later, he robbed corn from his master's mill and fled with some friends during the height of the milling season. Escapes at Louisiana sugar mills ordinarily occurred during the grinding season, when round-the-clock operations began and there were few work breaks.[14]

Slaves frequently ran off to visit their families or loved ones. "Jacob has been at me the past month to let him go . . . and see his wife," recalled one gold miner after the bondsman had fled to Savannah. "I would rather to let you have Mathilda than to here of Luis running away," wrote one turpentiner to another. However, some hirelings who ran home to their own- ers or "wives" created trying circumstances, an example of which befell the overseer of a river-improvement project. After his bondsmen had been working for about six weeks, they requested permission to visit their families. The overseer refused, and after haggling for several weeks, six slaves left anyway; their action forced him to allow the remaining crew- men to see their wives for a couple of days. Eventually all hands returned and the work continued without incident.[15]

The threat or infliction of punishment often precipitated slave escapes. "Turner got careless and lazy after I went to supper," reported a coal mine manager. "I went over to the Pit right away with the intention of correcting him, but prob- ably he saw me approaching the Pit, for the other negroes said he was there a few minutes before, he is in the vicinity of the mines I presume." [16] On the other hand, many bondsmen ab- sconded for no apparent reason whatsoever.

If flight and other protests were any indication of slave dis- affection, runaway advertisements, business records, and slave narratives contradict the theory that urban bondsmen and industrial slaves were more content than their rural agricul- tural brethren. For such evidence suggests that industrial bondsmen—in both urban and rural locales—absconded as fre- quently, in proportion to their numbers, as did plantation hands. The argument that it was more difficult for a slave to escape from a factory than from a farm also seems dubious; [17] industrial slaves working in rural or small-town environments could slip into the woods almost as easily as plantation field hands. Urban industrial bondsmen could choose between fleeing by water, escaping to the countryside, or losing themselves in alleys, attics, cellars, or the maze of city life. Fading into forests or dodging into doorways required little imagination; eluding rural patrols or avoiding urban guards demanded little luck.

Permanent escape within the South or to the "free" states, however, necessitated courage, cunning, and a great deal of intelligence. An ingenious means of escape was developed by one literate Louisiana carpenter who, caught selling forged passes to friends, successfully escaped by writing himself a pass. Slave Manuel, who had been entrusted to transport turpentine down river, bought a certificate of freedom from a friend, escaped to Philadelphia under an assumed name, and persuaded an abolitionist to purchase his children. Though many runaway advertisements requested steamer captains to search for stowaways and cautioned them against employing fugitives, slave boat hands and woodyardsmen had little difficulty reaching northern shores, just as three slave hirelings who worked the *Sophila* easily jumped ship at Liverpool, England.[18]

Southern swamps—the Dismal, Pasquotank, Great, Okefenokee, and the bayous of Louisiana—were favorite refuges for slave desperadoes fleeing nearby industrial sites. If bondsmen safely reached these wastelands, their capture was virtually impossible and they were almost as secure as in Canada. Swamp slaves even transformed their hide-outs into fortified enclaves from which they pillaged nearby plantations and surrounding turpentine, shingle, lumber, and fishing camps. Aware of this threat, aggravated masters warned lumbermen not to employ fugitives and vigorously attempted to prevent bondsmen from secreting themselves in the solitude of the swamps. "I found he had dodged off and fearing he might get into the Dismal Swamp, when I should never get him, I concluded to sell him to W. Clark who owns his Wife," confided one owner to a turpentine manufacturer. "William Clark has a negro man, who has been in the Swamp for the last three years, and lost another in there some two years since, who was runaway. I thought it best for all concerned to sell him. . . ." Similarly, lumberman Jim's master became so fearful that he would remain permanently in Pungo Swamp that he was rented out in a more secure area.[19]

Some antebellum travelers discovered that swamp refugees often earned livelihoods (in a curious inversion of the slave system) by working for lumbermen—white or black. Desperadoes "live by woodcraft, external depredation, and more frequently . . . by working for the task shingle-makers at reduced wages," reported one correspondent. "These employees often return greater quantities of work than could by any possibility have been produced by their own labor, and draw two or three times the amount of provisions necessary for their own subsistence. But the provisions are furnished, the work paid for, and no questions are asked." This traveler was so fascinated by the Dismal Swamp's refugees that he set out from a lumber camp and "crawled and struggled on" until he was nearly exhausted:

> At length my attention was arrested by the crackling sound of other footsteps than my own. I paused, held my breath, and sunk quietly down among the reeds. About thirty paces from me I saw a gigantic negro, with a tattered blanket wrapped about his shoulders, and a gun in his hand. His head was bare, and he had little other clothing than a pair of ragged breeches and boots. His hair and beard were tipped with gray, and his purely African features were cast in a mould betokening, in the highest degree, strength and energy. The expression of the face was of mingled fear and ferocity, and every movement betrayed a life of habitual caution and watchfulness. . . .[20]

Other industrial slaves challenged their masters more directly, and fights between industrial bondsmen and their superiors were thus not at all unusual. One Saturday evening a furnace manager commanded Anthony to return to work the next day, but by ten o'clock Sunday morning the slave had not yet appeared. The overseer finally found the slave, who explained that Sunday was "*his*" day and that he was not going to take it up going to your place." Infuriated by such impudence, the manager collared Anthony, who resisted and struck back; thereupon the manager smashed Anthony's head with a rock.[21] Anthony was not killed, but other fights sometimes resulted in homicide—either intentional or unintentional. William Jackson, a young tobacco-factory overseer, attempted to chastise Jordan Hatcher, a seventeen-year-old bondsman, for the allegedly inferior quality of his work. In the ensuing scuffle Hatcher fatally struck Jackson with a poker and the slave fled. Hatcher was soon captured, convicted of murder, and sentenced to hang. After much publicity, the Governor of Virginia commuted the bondsman's sentence to deportation, on the grounds that he had acted without malice in merely trying to escape punishment. The Jackson-Hatcher Affair so outraged the Richmond *Dispatch*, however, that several weeks later, after another slave threatened an overseer, it editorialized:

> We think that full protection should be guaranteed to the overseers in the different tobacco factories, by law, against the attacks of turbulent hands. If a negro is to be discharged with the trivial punishment of ten lashes . . . then, indeed, is the life of an overseer and a white man at the mercy of a parcel of turbulent black ruffians, to be granted at their discretion. . . . the negro merited a back-warming such as would have lasted him for a year to come.[22]

Lumberman

Industrial slaves often took dramatic advantage of the circumstances of their occupations to resist their superiors. Two slave railroad workers hurriedly jumped off their hand car, failing to warn their overseer riding with them that a locomotive was unexpectedly approaching. A slave sugar miller attempted to dump his overseer "into one of the kettles full of boiling juice." Frank, cane knife in hand, threatened "with intent to kill" his master and overseer. He was shot. A rice miller sincerely believed that his "exceedingly lazy . . . although quite smart" slave carpenter (named Jack Savage) "was always giving trouble & ever appeared dissatisfied . . .

[and] was the only Negro ever in our possession who I considered capable of murdering me, or burning my dwelling at night. . . ." [23]

Repressing the most spectacular forms of slave resistance—organized conspiracies and rebellions—presented masters with more difficult problems than quelling individual acts of violence. Revolts raised the specter of servile retribution against masters and mistresses, and they threatened the injury of valuable property and breaking the chains of bondage forever. The slave insurrections which did occur clearly revealed dissatisfaction with bondage, just as the frenzied panics which periodically swept the slave states were symptoms of the fear permeating the minds of whites in the Old South.

The black insurrections and white panics which surfaced occasionally between 1790 and 1861 have been studied elsewhere in some detail,[24] but the striking fact that almost all rebel leaders and many followers actually were, or were thought to be, artisans or industrial slaves has not generally been made explicit. Gabriel Prosser, organizer of the Henrico County conspiracy of 1800, was a blacksmith, who planned to base his rebellion upon Richmond's industrial-slave population. Five hundred slave sugar workers, armed with cane knives, reportedly marched on New Orleans in the little-known Louisiana revolt of 1811. Denmark Vesey, leader of the Charleston conspiracy of 1822, was a free Negro carpenter. But Vesey's co-conspirators were mostly slave draymen, sawyers, stevedores, ricemillers, ropewalk workers, and artisans: Peter Poyas was a "first-rate" ship-carpenter, Mingo Harth and Tom Russell were mechanics and blacksmiths. Monday Gell was a harness maker who "hired out" his own labor and kept a workshop in the center of Charleston. Even Nat Turner had been trained as a carpenter and wheelwright, before he became a slave preacher.[25]

Fearful of insurrectionists like Prosser, Vesey, and Turner, white Southerners naturally blamed later uprisings and conspiracies on industrial slaves. Some panicky Virginians, for example, associated Nat Turner's rebellion of 1831 with Buckingham County's slave gold miners. Four years later, the sight of seventeen slaves marching together down a Virginia road with pickaxes raised over their shoulders and a rumored plot of slave iron workers in the Cumberland River region of Tennessee made some whites conclude that nearby gold miners or iron workers had revolted. This panic subsided only after troops had been mustered and it was discovered that the suspected blacks had simply been going to work on the local roads. In 1853, slaves working on the Manassas Gap Railroad were reported to have "actually revolted." Bondsmen at turpentine, fishing, or lumbering enterprises probably participated in the eastern North Carolina conspiracy of 1860.[26]

The little-studied conspiracy of 1856[27] was especially significant, since it involved industrial slaves almost exclusively. The unrest seemed to begin in the early autumn among Louisiana slave sugar millers, Arkansas salt boilers, and Missouri lead miners and iron workers. Rumors of revolts quickly spread from west to east, finally crystallizing in areas of Tennessee and Kentucky, which employed large numbers of industrial slaves, and where whites had been fearful of slave revolts ever since Turner's insurrection a generation before. Bondsmen at the various iron works along the Cumberland River seemed the most deeply infected with the spirit of revolt. Sixty-five slaves were arrested at Senator John Bell's iron works; nine of them were eventually executed. A black coal-miner was shot near the Louisa Iron Works, and nineteen iron workers were hanged at Dover, Tennessee.[28] From the Lafayette Depot of the Memphis and Charleston Railroad came the following dispatch indicating the extent of involvement of industrial slaves in the Tennessee conspiracy:

. . . a negro girl of Mr. G. W. Vandel, who is engineer at Mr. R. Glenn's steam-mill, three miles below this, informed her mistress that she had been told by one of the negro men at the mill, the night before, that the negroes all intended rising on the day of the election; and that their plan was to take advantage of the absence of the white men on that day, and while they were all from home at the polls voting, to kill all the women and children, get all the money and arms, and waylay the men on their return home from the election and murder them; then make for the railroad cars, take them and go to Memphis, where they could find arms and friends from up the river to carry them off to the Free States if they did not succeed in taking this country. . . .[29]

Characteristically, white Southerners blamed the slave unrest on outside agitators such as the Black Republicans who were running for the first time in the 1856 national elections. "The Great excitement during the presidential canvass about abolition was well calculated to create such an attempt among the Blacks," confided one Southerner to another. The Richmond *Dispatch* expressed "no doubt that white men, Northern abolitionists, were the instigators of the insurrections." [30] Despite such delusions, the reality of slave dissatisfaction remained to haunt the mind of the South.

The involvement of Negro artisans and industrial slaves in conspiracies and rebellions indicates that they were greatly disaffected and that they were also the natural leaders of agricultural and industrial slave workers. Indeed, such insurrectionary leaders tended to confirm the fears of many Southerners, such as South Carolina Senator James Henry Hammond, who believed that when slaves were employed in industries they were "more than half freed" and soon would become "the most corrupt and turbulent" members of their race. However, since some Negro artisans and industrial slaves often accommodated to their bondage instead of resisting it, in effect they undercut those industrial slaves who were sincerely struggling to overthrow the slave regime or to escape from it. In any case, slave resistance generally confronted employers with a serious dilemma: could slave protests be repressed and could a stable work force be created without undermining either industrial work routines or the slave system itself?

Disciplining Industrial Slaves

Slave repression and discipline took many forms, ranging from persuasion to coercion and from the subtle to the brutal. Merciless suppression of slave protest was probably effective in the short run or in such extraordinary circumstances as conspiracies or rebellions. Still, severity involved the risk of injury to valuable slave capital and, as James Stirling noted, produced desperate, vengeful, and conspiratorial bondsmen. The most intelligent masters therefore necessarily experimented with more sophisticated means of controlling their slaves and increasing their productivity, which were probably more effective over the long run. However, most masters had occasion at one time or another to deploy the full range of disciplinary measures at their disposal.

The most common disciplinary methods were the routinizing of daily work, religious indoctrination, the total mastery of living and working conditions, and the pass and badge system. Masters continually directed overseers to follow work schedules strictly. "Two leading principles are endeavored to be acted on," advised a Georgia rice miller in his instructions to his overseer. "1st, to reduce everything to system; 2d, to introduce daily accountability in every department." Accordingly, the slaves received specific tasks, a black driver was responsible for each gang, and every evening the slave drivers and foremen reported to the white overseer in the owner's presence.[31]

Masters discovered that slave singing not only helped to routinize industrial work, but it regulated and increased production. Many travelers interpreted the singing of industrial slaves as an indication of their contentment, and singing could be a means of slave communication and cultural self-expression. But singing had actually become a calculated disciplinary device used by masters. A visitor to a Lexington hemp factory observed the slaves singing and "at the same time walking backward and forward about their spinning, with great regularity, and in some measure keeping time with their steps." The manager of a Richmond tobacco factory confided to poet William Cullen Bryant that "we encourage their singing as much as we can, for the boys work better while singing." [32]

Many employers considered Christian indoctrination an effective means of controlling industrial slaves. Through religious instruction bondsmen learned that slavery had divine sanction and that disobedience was an offense against God as well as against their masters. Slaves received the Biblical command that servants should obey their superiors. They also heard of the punishment awaiting insolent slaves and of the salvation rewarding faithful service. "My plantations are visited by . . . Episcopal clergymen . . . each Sunday," disclosed one rice miller. "I have found the greatest advantage from this, & I know many [slaves] who perform their service for me as a religious duty." An itinerant preacher at the Midlothian coal mines "was gratified to learn from the managers, that many of them [the slave miners] are orderly and consistent in their deportment, and that generally there is a marked difference between the conduct of those who profess and those who do not profess religion." [33]

Large slaveowning industrialists sometimes built chapels at their establishments and hired clergymen to preach to their slaves on Sundays. Some sugar millers and rice millers held regular Sunday services, especially during the milling season. One North Carolina cotton miller occasionally allowed preaching, revivals, and baptisms. A Virginia coal mine permitted a circuit rider to preach to the slave colliers during a work break down in the pits; later, this company built a church for its black miners.[34] Thus, while under certain circumstances religion could have a liberating effect on bondsmen, employers were convinced that it served mainly as a means of control.

The distribution of food and clothing was carefully controlled to discipline industrial slaves. Moses Austin divided his slaves into several "messes," each of which received a precise portion of food. The "forge hands eat in one kitchen collectively, its being so convenient we can oversee the whole," reported an iron manufacturer. A rice miller explained to his overseer his disciplinary procedures:

> It has always been my plan to give out allowance to the negroes on Sunday in preference to any other day because *this* has much influence in keeping them at home that day. Whereas, if they received allowance on Saturday for instance Some of them would be off with it that same evening to the shops to trade & perhaps would not get back until Monday morning. . . .

A gristmiller in his "Memo for 1857" wrote: "Don't give Booker any summer shoes because he stole Monroes [in] 1856. . . . Don't give John & Charles any summer shoes, because they killed a shoat."[35]

Industrial housing arrangements were often planned to prevent slaves from escaping, in contrast to plantation slave quarters, where few such precautions were taken. The New Orleans Gas Company's fifty bondsmen inhabited tenements inside the plant, which was surrounded by iron gates and

brick walls fifteen feet high. At Richmond's Tredegar Iron
Works slaves slept in tenements near the rolling mill, where
they were also fed by the company. "The whole of our concern is surrounded with a brick wall ten feet high," wrote the
manager of an Alabama textile mill, which lodged its slaves
within the grounds; "no one is admitted after work hours
except the watchmen or one of the owners." [36]

To facilitate identification and to minimize escapes, industrial bondsmen were required to wear badges or to carry
passes when they left their work places. Badges were manda-
tory in most urban centers, passes in rural areas and in some
towns as well. Thus, to one traveler the management of Dismal Swamp slave lumbermen was "interesting and instructive.
. . . Early in February—they go into the swamp in gangs,
each gang under a white overseer. Before leaving, they are
all examined and registered at the court-house, and 'passes,'
good for a year are given them, in which the features and
marks upon their persons are minutely described." The use
of passes was apparently so great that the New Orleans Gas
Company used printed forms.[37]

Neither passes nor controlled living arrangements could
substitute for close, personal supervision by responsible whites.
Slaves working by-the-piece had to be carefully watched and
their work correctly counted to prevent them from cheating
their employers. One master only suspected his slave rice
miller of improperly filling the barrels. Other masters were
particularly vexed by slave woodcutters. "You will please
have them [barrel staves] counted by some one you can depend on after they are hauled down," wrote a North Carolina
fishery-owner to his overseer, "for I suspect your Negroes
might give you an account of more than they cut & I know
that my Coopers will not account for all that are carried down
if the counting is left to them." [38]

Another means of disciplining workers and increasing their efficiency was the system of rewards and incentives associated with industrial slavery. Such indirect controls consisted of the simple device of granting holidays and the more sophisticated one of paying money or commodities to slaves. Holidays were not merely an obvious way of resting the hands, but an integral part of a subtle system of supervision of slave labor. Rest periods were less a slave's right than a master's privilege, because employers granted recesses or denied them according to whether the slaves had worked well, refrained from resistance, or remained healthy. The dates and lengths of holidays were varied, so that activities of Negroes were carefully regulated and their expectations enhanced.

The timing of holidays varied according to industry and master, but almost all industrial slaves, except sugar millers, enjoyed a few days' relaxation at Christmas. This recess coincided with the long-established hiring period for tobacco, hemp, and iron manufacturers and for others who interrupted operations late in December to rent slaves.[39] Though most hired slaves thus received a vacation at the end of the year, owners sometimes requested employers to detain slaves during the recess if it was inconvenient for them to return home. "I am quite willing . . . that they [the hirelings] should remain with you during the Christmas holidays," wrote one master to a turpentine manufacturer. "It can do them no good to come home. It is an unpleasant season of the year and the time of their stay will be so short, that they cannot expect to enjoy themselves much." [40]

Once the custom of returning hired slaves to their masters for the holidays was broken, bondsmen were entirely at the mercy of their employers, who often compelled them to continue work. Five slaves were thus forced to remain aboard the Savannah River dredge boats during the Christmas recess as punishment for infractions of discipline. Other bondsmen had their rest periods spoiled when they were compelled to stand on the hiring block. On the other hand, some hired slaves enjoyed longer vacations than those employed by their owners. The Charleston and Savannah Railroad's hirelings, most of whom came from Virginia and North Carolina, annually made a three-week steamboat excursion to visit their owners and friends.[41]

Most enterprises, except sugar mills, shut down on Sundays; for good work, slaves might enjoy half of Saturday as well. A North Carolina gold mine observed all Sundays, as well as Easter Monday, Whitmonday, July 4, September 29, a five-day Christmas, and designated "Negroes day," when slaves mined gold for themselves or to share with their owner. Some employers granted occasional holidays to deserving slaves or permitted relaxation at the end of arduous work periods. Several slave wool manufacturers got one afternoon "to take a rabbit hunt," another afternoon to go to a circus, and a wintry morning to skate with their master, who usually, however, drove them long hours, sometimes several days and nights in succession.[42] At a cotton gin slaves who had been promised a four-day vacation after the crop was ginned considered this insufficient compensation for their unusual exertions and succeeded in extracting an extra day's rest. "The negroes interrupt me at this moment, with clamors that I must give them tomorrow, (Monday) as an additional holiday, which they have had since last Wednesday evening," wrote the ginner to his brother. "I wanted them to wait until all of yours came up; but they prefer the present, & I have consented for them to take it." [43]

The entire pattern of holidays was askew in the sugar industry, where refining of the crop often remained unfinished by Christmas or New Year's Day. Variables such as ripeness, the weather, the health of the slaves, the number of runaways,

Tar Kiln

and the condition of machinery inevitably contributed to the delays that compelled most sugar millers to celebrate Christmas early, late, or not at all. One mill observed Christmas December 6 through 8 one year, while another mill waited until February 16. For various reasons, but usually to punish slaves for inefficient work or bad behavior, some refiners eliminated recesses entirely. One sugar mill skipped Christmas holidays in 1852, 1853, 1854, and 1856—a common pattern at other refineries.[44]

Masters consciously used holidays both to control their industrial slaves and to increase their productivity, and they clearly had no intention of liberating their bondsmen. One rice miller instructed his overseer to slaughter a steer and to distribute extra allotments of bacon, molasses, corn, and rice during the milling period—but only if the slaves behaved themselves. A turpentine manufacturer who had given his slaves two hogs, a barrel of flour, and potatoes for their Christmas dinner promised that "I shall due my very Best to keep the negroes all strat & satisfyde. I hope that they will behave well." Another rice miller attempted to reduce the number of slaves feigning sickness during the arduous milling period by promising each slave who did not lose time an extra bushel of rice. "It should be taken into view that a great quantity [of sugar] has been consumed by the negroes [during the grinding season], for when we begin to harvest every one eats," admitted Thomas Spalding in a passage on "Expenses" in his widely read *Observations on the Sugar Cane*.[45]

What industrial slaves themselves thought of holiday periods can be inferred from their behavior and fragmentary surviving opinion. Such evidence indicates that most slaves used holiday periods feverishly to relish extra allotments of food, as a time for merry-making, or as an opportunity to catch up on lost sleep. Indeed, in the opinion of at least one industrial slave, the Baltimore ship-caulker Frederick Douglass, holidays kept bondsmen "occupied with prospective pleasures within the limits of slavery. . . . These holidays are conductors or safety valves to carry off the explosive elements inseparable from the human mind, when reduced to the condition of slavery."[46]

Holidays were often festive occasions when masters arranged dinners, dances, games, and "marriages." Extra allowances of rice, flour, or corn were doled out; beeves or hogs might be killed; molasses, vegetables, or tobacco were sometimes distributed; and clothing, trinkets, or money were occasionally handed out to the slaves.[47] Since these gratuities were presented not only at Christmas but on other occasions as well, however, they comprised part of the complex system of discipline-by-reward. Thus another part of the disciplinary procedure was the payment of money to industrial slaves.[48]

That many bondsmen were actually paid money has been

interpreted by some historians as a developing wage system which was supposedly an innovation of the last decades of the pre-Civil War period. It has been held, moreover, that such cash payments indicate that the institution of slavery was undergoing radical structural transformations easing the black man's bondage. Slaves receiving money were, it is said, in effect being liberated or placed in a realm of "quasi-freedom," a "shadow-land" between bondage and liberty. Money payments were therefore subverting slavery from within. "The payment by industries of extra money to . . . slaves for their personal use," argues one historian, "was an incipient stage of wages. . . . Also there was developing . . . a tendency to rely more and more on the incentive motive instead of on force and thus liberalize to some extent the 'peculiar institution.' " [49]

An examination of the manner, timing, effects, and tradition of cash incentives suggests, however, that they were not a step toward emancipation, but rather a technique of slave control which had long existed and which supported the slave system. Industrial slaves received money for many different kinds of work. Some were paid for raising foodstuffs, fabricating clothing, or collecting useful materials in their spare time. Others were paid for working overtime—"overwork," as it was ironically called—at specific tasks, while still others received what was sometimes known as "Sunday money" for "extra-work"—odd jobs done at night, on Sundays, or on holidays. The form of payment was also important: some bondsmen received direct payments in cash or kind; others worked for credits, against which they drew cash or goods.

"Overwork" payments were common to almost every type of southern industry. A tobacco manufacturer paid slaves from one to three dollars overtime weekly. At a turpentine distillery, which paid cash for production above the required task, slaves annually earned sums which ranged from $2 to

$14 and averaged about $6. One year, slave iron workers at one forge each received 50 cents, while the Tredegar Iron Works in Richmond permitted its slaves to earn about 50 cents per month in extra money for odd jobs and for cleaning or stoking furnaces and mills. A Tennessee turnpike company annually paid each of its slaves between 40 cents and $3, called "Stimulant & Reward money." [50] (By comparison, free white workers in the South between 1800 and 1861 earned on the average about one dollar a day—$310 per year.)

Many industrial slaves earned "extra-work" payments by collecting commodities or cultivating crops in their spare time. One master annually paid one or two dollars to each of twenty-two slave sugar millers for raising corn. The federal government permitted slave dredge boatmen to sell driftwood collected from the Savannah River. A tanner kept a "List of Bark from different Negroes," which recorded sums owed slaves for gathering bark. Miners bought gold retrieved by bondsmen in their spare time, and iron manufacturers and rice millers also paid cash to slaves. [51]

Many enterprises adopted the credit system of payment. At one Tennessee iron furnace slaves worked forty or fifty Sundays, chopped wood, and hauled cargoes to earn "extra allowances" of about $20 in credits. The company kept a written account for every slave upon which could be drawn shoes, winter and summer suits, shirts, overcoats, tobacco, knives, and flour. At the end of the year, the value of goods obtained was subtracted from the accumulated credits; the slaves received cash for the remaining credits (usually about $7 worth) or carried them over to the next year's account. [52]

Extra payment for night, Sunday, and holiday work was widely practiced by such industries as sugar mills, sawmills, railroads, and turpentine distilleries which required extra services or extraordinary quantities of items such as wood. The Cape Fear and Deep River Navigation Works, under both private and public ownership, paid hired and state-owned slaves small sums (averaging about one dollar monthly) for burning charcoal, hauling supplies, cooking food, pumping boats, unloading stone, and assisting blacksmiths on Sundays, holidays, and at night. The Savannah volunteer fire department's several hundred bondsmen each received 12½ cents per hour for fighting fires. The slave who reached a blaze first won a reward of one dollar, while the next two slaves to arrive got fifty cents each, and all were eligible for merit awards ranging up to thirty dollars per fire.[53]

The available evidence suggests that the incentive system was neither a late-antebellum innovation nor an indication that slavery was undergoing internal transformations leading to freedom. Indeed, business records reveal that money payments were as common in the late eighteenth and early nineteenth centuries as in the 1850's. From 1796 to at least 1802, for example, slaves at the Cumberland Forge in Maryland did various chores at night and on holidays in return for small sums of money. From 1798 to at least 1808, both the Redwell Furnace and the Pine Forge in Virginia followed the same practice. As early as 1794, Georgia lumberman Alexander Telfair distributed bonuses, while from 1806 to 1823, Stump and Ricketts paid cash to their slave sawmillers and gristmillers in Alexandria, Virginia.[54]

Not only did the cash rewards system function fully in the early nineteenth century, but many masters used it for long periods of time. Tobacco manufacturer Robert Leslie made money payments from 1827 to 1852, ironmonger William Weaver from 1827 to 1857, Ebenezer Pettigrew, the North Carolina shingler, turpentine distiller, and planter, from 1803 to 1854, and Telfair from 1794 to 1860.[55] Such evidence therefore indicates that cash incentives had, at least as early as the 1790's, become part of the slave system. If such rewards were ineffectual, would not masters have abandoned them, and if cash incentives were radically undermining bondage, should not slavery have collapsed long before the 1860's?

Entrepreneurs who consciously used cash incentives to control their industrial bondsmen and to increase slave productivity clearly had no intention of "liberating" their slaves. A Tennessee iron manufacturer, for example, kept account of breaches of discipline and subtracted them from his slaves' credit sheets. Sam Talley, a slave, thus lost $10 for twenty days' runaway time, young Reuben Jackson was charged $7.50 for ten days' absence, and Anderson Trotter was docked $2 for his "interest in [a] stolen bag." [56] In his account books Ebenezer Pettigrew also carefully balanced the extra work of his blacks against their infractions of discipline. Pettigrew's slaves automatically forfeited their credits or had their accounts closed for thievery, absconding, or other annoying activities. Though one slave lost his money for "infamous behaviour" and another lost his for "outrageous conduct in many ways of 5 years," Pettigrew indicated that well-behaved bondsmen eventually received their money. "Settled with Tom, George, Cromwell & Lewis for their ditching in the 9 feet ditch," he wrote. "This settlement is nothing more nor less than presents for their good behaviour while working in it." [57]

Owners and employers of hirelings, who certainly would have opposed the incentive system if it was liberating their slaves, approved of money payments because they improved discipline. Two slaveowners who rented blacks to the Cape Fear and Deep River Navigation Works, for example, explicitly requested that their bondsmen be paid about a dollar monthly. "Deducted $6.00 for 3 Days allowed Tom by his master this amt paid Tom and not included above [in the bill of hire]" was the notation next to one master's account.[58] Similar approval by employers of the bonus system was probably best summed up by the director of construction of the Gosport Navy Yard, who required masters to pay their hirelings a ten-cent "bounty" and steadfastly refused to rent slaves from masters who declined to pay. "All the negroes employed on that work [the navy yard] had 10 cents a day allowed them on our rolls which was paid over to them by their masters," he explained; "but if their masters refused to pay it over, we dismissed the blacks from our employment." [59]

Though employers almost unanimously approved of the incentive system, how the slaves themselves reacted to rewards is another important question, for which outside observation provides some evidence. "They [the slaves] work with as much steadiness and cheerfulness as the whites, and the fear of losing their ten cents, if they are lazy or inattentive, saves all the expense of overseers," insisted one employer. "Every man and boy in this establishment . . . has his 'steint' to perform, and each one is paid for what he does beyond it," reported a visitor to a Lexington, Kentucky, ropewalk. "This keeps them contented and makes them ambitious, and more labor is obtained . . . than could possibly be forced from them by severity. I saw no overseer in any of the rooms where the labor is performed," he added.[60]

The behavior of slaves in industries making incentive payments over long periods of time is further evidence of the overt response of the slaves themselves to the reward system. At William Weaver's iron works, which made money payments for more than thirty years, for example, slaves who chopped wood and hauled coal in their spare time each received about twelve dollars a year. Yet there is no indication that slavery was breaking down or being transformed into freedom at Weaver's establishment. Weaver's bondsmen certainly enjoyed spending their earnings, but slave resistance, to use one indicator, troubled Weaver no more in the earlier period than in the later, and his bondsmen seemed as firmly enslaved in the 1850's as in the 1820's. Satisfactory discipline also obtained at Pettigrew's establishment, which also made money payments over several decades.[61]

In the context of the holiday and incentive system, money payments were not an incipient form of wages; like other rewards, they were given for extra work, not for required work. Bonuses were not usually given regularly, but at random. The amount of payment was not fixed, but varied according to the liberality of the master. Indeed, the incentive system was so firmly under the control of the masters that it could be abandoned at any time without consulting the slaves, even though this might have annoyed the slaves. Bondsmen may have enjoyed spending their money, which certainly did not leave them unaffected, but masters never seriously regarded cash payments as a slave's right. Incentives continued to be regarded as a master's exclusive prerogative.

Since bonuses never accrued until after the slave's required day's tasks were completed, masters also insured that a certain amount of work would be done *before* overtime outlays took effect. In this way productivity tended to be increased. Money payments enabled masters to obtain food, clothing, and supplies, as well as additional labor, at nominal cost. Slaves were kept at work and out of mischief during what would otherwise have been their spare time. Masters recouped their outlays, since bondsmen usually bought supplies from company commissaries. To be sure, a few industrial slaves saved their bonuses to try to purchase their freedom, but self-purchase was never very common and was declining in the late-antebellum decades.[62] Finally, the incentive system tended to weaken the slave's temptation to escape and to improve discipline. For, as a visitor to Lexington, Kentucky, hemp factories observed, "the stimulus of wages is applied behind the whip, of course the prime motor." [63]

Employers of industrial slaves maintained control in part by creating and exploiting divisions within the slave group. As human beings, slaves did not differ innately from other workers, but the problem of control was made considerably easier for masters because of differences in color, age, and capability among the bondsmen. Thus, as plantation practices were transferred to industrial settings, slave managers were trained both for their skills and to help discipline their black brothers. In this respect, industrial slave managers resembled plantation house servants and slave drivers, whose accommodationist role has long been suggested [64] even if little analyzed.

Industrial slave managers had a dual role regarding resistance and control. On the one hand, as has already been shown, slave artisans and industrial workers were the natural leaders of most organized resistance movements. On the other hand, they frequently became their masters' most faithful agents to control the other blacks. Even though slave managers themselves might have had aspirations to freedom, they often misled their fellow workers. Indeed, a paternalistic relationship sometimes developed between masters and slave managers, revealing the accommodationist function of the industrial slave managerial group.

Slave managers willingly assumed responsibilities, supervised complex industrial enterprises with little guidance from their employers, and responsibly directed workers—black or white—under their charge. "In all of these [rice milling] departments," observed Olmsted of one such manager, "his authority was superior to that of the [white] overseer. . . . His responsibility was much greater than that of the overseer, and Mr. X. [the owner] said, he would trust him with much more than he would any overseer he had ever known." [65]

Such capability, loyalty, and responsibility earned some slave managers their employers' genuine respect and their

Salt Worker

masters' paternal esteem. Concerning a bondsman directed to escort a slave mechanic from a neighbor's iron works, one master confided,

> I . . . apologize for sending upon this business, a man of colour, but this can be no objection to a man of sense . . . he is my founder at Oxford [iron works]—has been raised there from childhood, and supported an unblemished character. for his integrity, good understanding & talents, from his infancy to his gray hairs—the utmost confidence may be given his communications— his honor and integrity untarnished.[66]

Sandy Maybank, the head carpenter at the Reverend C. C. Jones's extensive plantation and rice mill typified the paternalistic relationship which could develop between masters and slaves. Since Jones was often absent, he placed Maybank in charge of all mill construction and usually communicated instructions to the slave by personal letter. Indicating the responsibility placed in Maybank, Jones wrote him and the white overseer separate instructions, the tone of which further reveals Jones's fatherly respect for the black head carpenter. "Dear Sandy," Jones began one letter,

> As I wished to have some work done I thought it would be best to write you a letter that you could keep and so have it by you, that you might not forget anything. . . . You can attend to this work as soon as you can & Porter & William will assist you in it. Am glad to hear that you have been generally well all the season & hope you may continue so . . . . Tell Mary howdye for me—and your children. . . . Your mistress sends howdye for you and for Mary. I trust you are holding on in your high profession of the Gospel of our Lord & Saviour Jesus Christ. A Christian to do well must trust in the Lord Jesus Christ at all times, and constantly watch and pray. . . .

The master extended Maybank further privileges, including permission to answer his master's letters, to marry, and, when Jones's rice mill was not too busy, to hire his own time at nearby plantations and mills.[67]

Similarly, other slave managers helped maintain industrial discipline, for which they also won their masters' paternal affection. Horace, a slave architect and civil engineer, built bridges throughout the Black Belt for Robert Jemison, Jr., a wealthy central-Alabama contractor, planter, sawmiller, and manufacturer. In fact, Jemison and Horace's owner were so pleased with the bondsman's performances that at the opening of the 1845–46 session of the Alabama Legislature they had a bill introduced to emancipate the slave. The bill passed both houses, and a few months later, Jemison sent Horace "the promised certified copy of the act of our last Legislature. . . .

I have had it made out on Parchment thinking it most suitable & that it would be most agreeable to you in this form." Thereafter, Jemison frequently consulted Horace about construction projects, wages, and other business and personal matters. Horace evidently answered Jemison's queries, though, unfortunately, none of the ex-slave's letters survive. The tone of Jemison's correspondence with Horace suggests, however, the cordiality existing between the two men. "Dear Horace," Jemison always began:

> Some two days ago Mr. Williams wrote to you [about] Columbus Bridge, Miss. If you can attend to this you will very greatly oblige both Mr. Williams & myself. . . . Will you answer at yr earliest convenience whether we can get yr services and about what time will suit yr convenience best and we will endeavor to arrange things to suit.
>   In Haste. yr friend R. Jemison jr.

Finally, when his former master died, Horace erected a gravestone, which he inscribed: "IN LASTING REMEMBRANCE OF THE LOVE AND GRATITUDE HE [Horace] FELT FOR HIS LOST FRIEND. . . ."[68]

Many industrial slave managers had aspirations to a better life as well as concepts of freedom which exceeded their extraordinary privileges and made their accommodationist role ambiguous. Simon Gray and Jim Matthews, slave hirelings of the Andrew Brown Lumber Company of Natchez and New Orleans, for example, responsibly rafted lumber down rivers, negotiated with woodyards men along the way, collected and disbursed large sums of money, and supervised both black and white crewmen. Simon Gray was undoubtedly one of the most highly privileged of all southern slaves—one historian considers him "almost free"—yet his vision of freedom clearly exceeded his exceptional status. Once, Gray subtly bilked the lumber company by rafting logs for his personal profit; sometimes he purposely missed the earliest boat back to Natchez to gain additional time for amusement in New Orleans. Indeed, even though escape was difficult from the deep South, Gray and other privileged slaves attempted to flee when opportunities arose. William Thompson, a literate slave fireman in Brown's sawmill engine room, eventually forged a pass and escaped to Canada. (There he composed a personal letter to his friend Jim Matthews, wishing him good health and sending his "best respects" to other friends and former employer alike!) Matthews, whose responsibilities and privileges almost equalled those of Gray, lacked an opportunity to flee until the Union triumph at Vicksburg in July, 1863, when the company records indicate that he successfully escaped. Simultaneously, Simon Gray's name vanished without explanation from the company's rolls, suggesting that he and Matthews probably fled together.[69] Thus, while they helped to control their black brothers, even the most privileged industrial slave managers resisted their bondage.

Since subtle methods of discipline could never guarantee perfect slave behavior, virtually all masters necessarily mixed persuasion with coercion. Incentives could increase production and make supervision easier, but force was necessary to forestall or to punish infractions of the routines of industrial slavery. The use of slave managers could turn black against black, for even such overseers sometimes resorted to force. Bondsmen were never quite certain whether terror would not follow closely upon reward, since the whip was, after all, "the prime motor."

Whipping was such a common punishment that industrial records abound with references to floggings, while advertisements for runaways minutely describe bodily scars and marks.[70] According to the engineer of one railroad, slave punishment consisted of

. . . whipping with a long cowhide whip with the culprit's shirt on or off according to the severity desired. Sometimes a more terrible weapon was used—a big hardwood paddle pierced with augur holes and administered on the bare skin of the culprit as he bent over a log. A half dozen strokes of this paddle was cruel punishment.

Similarly, a sugar refinery overseer punished slaves with a short-handled whip, loaded in the butt. The mate of an Ohio River packetboat reportedly "always carried a heavy cane made of hickory and . . . frequently used it with telling effect on the Negro deck hands." [71]

Bondsmen were beaten for major and minor offenses, or for no apparent reason whatever. Severity of punishment was generally at the employer's discretion, despite legislation prescribing the number of lashes. For instance, Alfred was thrashed "very severely" for running off a third time from a sugar mill; four skilled slaves were mercilessly flogged for the suspected murder of their master. "Sam lost one day by whipping for playing Cards and fighting," disclosed the Graham Forge time books,[72] while the proprietor of another iron works prescribed the following treatment for three unruly boat hands:

I must confess, I never before experienced such infidelity even in the worst of our Black Servants as . . . Peter, Aaron & Lewis——I presume Peter will not make his appearance any more at Oxford——If he does you must inflict the law upon him—39 lashes on his bare back—you may in company with . . . some of the most respectable black people seize upon Aaron & Lewis, carry them with ropes round their necks to the boat landing where the load was lost & there have them stript naked & 39 stripes inflicted well placed on the bare backs of each of these scoundrels——I confess I was completely deceived by this rascall Peter . . . . You are to seize upon Aaron & Lewis at once & punish them as they deserve—if they get notice of your intention they will abscond & merit double punishment—you are to give some of my trusty servants half a dollar for whipping each of those rascals provided they do their duty. give neither of them any new cloaths.[73]

The conflict of authority between owners and employers of hirelings was so common that hiring contracts usually required renters to treat slaves "with humanity." Since legal prohibitions against cruel and unusual punishment were rarely followed, however, many owners preferred to discipline their Negroes in person if possible. "His conduct . . . I know is almost unpardonable," admitted one master to an employer after personally meting out punishment to a hireling who had returned home and was being sent back to work. "But as I have chastised him severely for it myself, if you will pass it over in silence I will esteem it as a favor so long as I live—— As his principle complaint seemed to be lodged against your overseer, I will thank you . . . to put him to cutting wood." [74] Other owners who occasionally accused overseers and employers of unjust or cruel punishment warned renters to take better care of their blacks. One such master, who demanded that his slaves be disciplined separately from other hirelings, had his bondsmen returned by the contractor with the explanation:

. . . I cannot keep, in my service, negros to be treated differently from my own & others in the same service. All my hired servants must be subjected to the same treatment & submit to the same discipline. . . . I regret having to adopt this course but you will upon a moments reflection, see the impolicy of keeping amongst a gang of negroes a portion to be more favored than the rest. It would prevent all just and efficient discipline.[75]

Punishments sometimes became so brutal that they resulted in death. A wealthy tobacco manufacturer who whipped a fifteen-year-old slave girl to death, as his wife applied a hot iron to sensitive parts of her body, was brought to trial and acquitted. He later beat two other bondsmen to death but was never convicted of a crime. A tobacco factory overseer who shot a bondsman three times for two days' absence was publicly commended by the Richmond *Dispatch*. Railroad companies had sometimes to compensate owners of slaves who died from overseer abuses.[76]

Slaveowners often pursued industrial bondsmen with dogs when other means of retrieval failed. Unable to apprehend two skilled artisans for several months, one rice miller finally brought in some hounds, who so thoroughly frightened the runaways that they returned within a few days. "I have a man nowe with big douges & I intend to keep him after tham untill he git tham," wrote one turpentine manufacturer. "Soe all running a way with ours is done," he reported, when the slave catcher returned. On the other hand, clever slaves easily eluded dogs by hiding in trees, swamps, or elsewhere. "Mr. Davenport and others hunting a Negro with blood hounds," recorded one sugar miller, "—did not catch him—little Jack found him in the fodder house at the Quarters in the evening." [77]

Tracking fugitives with dogs sometimes injured the bondsmen, resulting in expensive medical treatment. "Harrison has been so badly bitten by a dog, that he can scarcely walk. You must send Andrew up to take him home in the steam boat," reported a jailor to a sugar miller, who later paid a doctor a large sum to treat the Negro's wounds. On the other hand, brave bondsmen occasionally injured dogs, as was revealed in this report on an elusive slave coal miner:

> the dogs took his track in the orchard and run him about
> 400 yards and bayed him, when Peyton killed the main

dog—or at least the dog has not been seen since he bayed Peyton. Peyton then got in the woods and having but one negro dog and all of the hounds in Town coming to us, we were thrown off the track and by time this negroe dog would find the track—these other hounds would run in and confuse the dog. So at last after running him till twelve o'clock at night, we gave up the chase. . . . I think it would be best for you to come over and buy some good negroe dogs.[78]

Punishment often consisted of imprisoning or shackling obstreperous blacks. One outraged owner tried to "mortify" a slave who had refused to work in the coal pits by placing him in irons. A sugar miller handcuffed one slave, while a hemp manufacturer fitted an iron collar about the neck of another bondsman. Charleston's jail ground its cornmeal with a treadmill operated by slave prisoners, who treaded three minutes and rested three minutes, eight hours a day, while an overseer maintained discipline with a cowhide whip. If a prisoner tired, he was battered by the treadle.[79]

Other masters disciplined industrial slaves merely by threats of punishment or sale to southwestern states. A Louisiana lumberman said he was able to "govern" his slaves "without the whip, by stating to them that I shall sell them if they do not conduct themselves as I wish." Other entrepreneurs, such as James H. Couper, who, "for the incorrigible habit of running away," actually sold two rice millers, carried out the threat. "I have born with them for several years hoping that they would reform," confided Couper, "but as they are useless to the plantation and have become a nuisance to the community, it has become necessary to sell them, or keep them constantly in jail. Their example is also a very bad one to the whole gang." Couper hoped to purchase a new blacksmith with the sale's proceeds.[80]

Perhaps the most effective agents of repression were the

patrols which dispersed unauthorized black gatherings, apprehended fugitives, incendiaries, and thieves, and guarded cities, towns, and rural regions against slave conspiracies and rebellions. In the early 1820's, the Pineville Police Association attempted to apprehend fugitive slave desperadoes who, from a heavily fortified swamp camp, were interrupting commerce along a South Carolina canal. The difficult-to-approach hideaway was successfully surprised and several slaves were captured. Others retreated deeper into the swamp, but the patrol resolved to pursue them until they had been wholly dispersed.[81]

The white "patterollers," as the blacks called them, feared more than anything else slave conspiracies and insurrections.[82] As the insurrection panic of 1856 spread through Kentucky and Tennessee, authorities arrested many white men suspected or accused of "free soilism," while long-feared free Negro "agitators" of the slave community felt official wrath as well. White Kentucky vigilantes hung Sol Young, a free Negro preacher, and Tennesseans terrorized white "complicitors." Bearing the brunt of white retribution, sixty-five slaves at Senator John Bell's Cumberland Iron Works were tortured until they "confessed." Many bondsmen withstood hundreds of "stripes" before "fessing up" and at least one died under the lash. At the Louisa Iron Works white panic engendered a black counter-panic, and many bondsmen, fearing an indiscriminate slaughter, attempted to flee. They were soon recaptured. Such fears were also shared by some masters who reportedly "felt far more apprehension for their slaves than for themselves."

To put down the 1856 conspiracy many Tennessee and Kentucky communities strengthened their patrols, strictly enforced ordinances governing free blacks and bondsmen, and, like Clarksville, procured more weaponry. The citizens of Gallatin, Tennessee, where four slaves had been arrested and panic-stricken whites assembled to decide their fate, abandoned all legal pretenses, however. According to one reporter, "a larger and more respectable meeting" had never before been held in the town,

> . . . the question was, what shall be done with the four [slave] leaders now in jail? A number of voices said, "*hang tham at once*." On this a vote was taken, and one tremendous shout of "Aye" was interrupted by only three small voices. . . . The meeting then adjourned to the jail, and though the jailor did all in his power to prevent it, the aforesaid Sam, Jack, Ellick and Dick were taken out and executed. . . .[83]

Whether they lived in rural or urban settings, industrial slaves seemed discontented with their working and living conditions. Some blacks resisted passively, while others rebelled violently. A few slaves became leaders of organized revolts, but many sullenly accommodated to their bondage. Nonetheless, industrial entrepreneurs were still able to discipline slave workers and to create a fairly stable work force by means of sophisticated incentives, by creating divisions within the slave group and, when necessary, by brutal repression. Moreover, there were other reasons why employers preferred to use slaves rather than free labor.

CHAPTER FOUR

Conversion, Hiring, and Integration of Work Forces

Experience on the canal has proven that there is no portion of the work which cannot be executed by slaves. A few months teaching is only necessary to make them proficient in almost every part of the work. . . . I might go on to point out the advantages to the state at large of the employment of our own labor. *. . .*

Report of the Chief Engineer of the James River and Kanawha Company, Richmond, Virginia, November 18, 1850.

Since southern industries posed great hazards to slave property, and since slaves often resisted their bondage, employers might have been expected to prefer free white wage laborers to Negro bondsmen. Indeed, some employers were beginning to replace their blacks with white workers in certain occupations, such as stevedoring, ditch digging, levee building, and especially in textile manufacturing. However, such replacements were not the general trend, partly because the alternative free white labor available to the South was more troublesome and less economical than the slave force. The imperatives of the proslavery ideology also apparently convinced many employers to continue to use slaves, rather than whites, as their labor force. Slaves therefore continued to dominate most occupations, and many companies that experimented with free labor eventually converted back to slave labor.

Conversion

Free white workers—especially immigrants—proved unreliable on many counts; for example, whites often quit work for no apparent reason. "Can't trust them," fretted one gold miner after almost all of his Irish hands had run off. "We may try once more, but 'tis uncertain." If immigrants were not paid each night and comfortably boarded, he added, they would leave without a moment's notice. One North Carolina railroad which imported 580 Irishmen from the North soon lost all but sixty of them. Another Carolina contractor concluded that Irish laborers had "no regard for what is just and right; they have to be watched more closely than negroes." [1]

Unruly white workers sometimes disrupted industrial routines with their binges and brawls. Twenty drunk "Dutchmen" were barely able to work on the Mississippi Railroad. "I will not drink any whiskey if you ask it," revealingly promised an unemployed white iron worker to a prospective employer. He was hired. Immigrants sometimes brought their Old World ethnic and personal animosities to the United States, and their quarrels interrupted industrial work. The routine was severely disrupted at a gold mine when one Irishman stabbed another and fled without settling his debts; the Augusta, Georgia, federal stone quarries suffered similar troubles. Wade Hampton planned to build a railroad section with his own slaves exclusively, whom he considered "far preferable to engaging a company of turbulent Irish." [2]

Minor disputes among immigrants occasionally escalated into major riots which destroyed industrial property, wasted time, and caused financial difficulties. In the 1830's, the Chesapeake and Ohio Canal Company hired Irish diggers after a disappointing earlier experiment with indentured immigrants and native whites. The Irishmen were so disorderly that nu-

merous working days were lost and federal and state troops
had to be used to keep the peace.[3] The Ocmulgee and Flint
Railroad of Georgia, unlike most others, engaged Irish laborers instead of slaves. During the depression year of 1843, when
food was short, money scarce, and the company hardly able
to furnish either, the immigrants rioted. A month's work was
lost, and the state militia had to be called to restore order.[4]
The Pacific Railroad had to ask for the Missouri militia to
break up a feud between rival Irish work gangs, and armed
guards thereafter had to police one section of the line, "The
Bloody Eighteenth." The resulting lost time and increased
expenses prevented the contractors from keeping within their
cost estimates and meeting their deadlines.[5]

To persuade free laborers to remain at industrial sites during
sickly seasons was very difficult. During a summer epidemic
in 1819, of thirty-two whites constructing the New Orleans
Water Works five quit, ten died, and six were chronically ill.[6]
Two cholera epidemics in the 1830's on the Chesapeake and
Ohio Canal dispersed one hundred white laborers who had
been imported from the North at considerable expense. When
they reached home they warned their friends not to take jobs
in the South.

The activities of organized white labor, especially strikes,
bothered employers more than anything else. Between 1815
and 1839, free artisans constructing the national Capitol repeatedly interrupted work to strike for higher pay. In the
summer of 1831, white workers on the Baltimore and Ohio
Railroad began tearing up the line when their wages were not
paid on time. In 1832, white workers struck the Gosport Navy
Yard, and in 1836 and 1837, Irish diggers struck the Brunswick and Altamaha Canal.[7] The 1850's were by far the most
troublesome decade for southern employers of white labor.
Free artisans struck Baltimore's railroad shops and iron foundries in February, 1853; a Nashville factory was shut down in

April, and Virginia and Maryland coal mines were hit later in the year and again in 1854. Irish workers struck a Carolina railroad in 1855; white miners walked out of a Ducktown, Tennessee, copper mine in 1857, and blacksmiths struck a Louisiana railroad in 1860.[8] Steamboats dependent on tight schedules were especially vulnerable to wildcat walkouts. But perhaps the most calamitous strike of all befell a Louisiana sugar miller, who had replaced his slaves with one hundred Irish and German workers. At the height of the grinding season the immigrants struck for higher pay, and the miller lost much of his crop.[9]

Despite their notorious unreliability, free laborers seemed to be making some inroads into occupations traditionally dominated by industrial slaves in the 1850's. Travelers sometimes commented that slaveowners were becoming less willing to employ increasingly valuable blacks in dusty textile mills, mosquito-infested marshes, and on dangerous dikes, when cheap and expendable immigrants were available. According to visitors to such port cities as New Orleans and Baltimore, immigrants (specifically the Irish and Germans) were beginning to compete with black dock workers and teamsters. Travelers also thought that immigrants were displacing slaves from canal digging and levee and railroad building in southwestern regions.[10] Most significant, the proportion of textile factories manned by slaves seemed to be declining after about 1845, as some textile manufacturers, typified by William Gregg, the proprietor of the factory at Graniteville, South Carolina, began to use native poor white workers instead of slaves.[11] "Under pressure of white craftsmen, Negroes were pushed out of one line of work after another," argues one historian. "If slaves and blacks were still found in many of the better crafts in 1860, they had been pushed out of many of the lesser-skilled jobs. . . ."[12]

The available evidence indicates, however, that such

changes in employment patterns have been exaggerated, and that even in the industries where slaves were supposedly being displaced, many entrepreneurs were actually converting from free to slave labor. For example, some textile manufacturers only contemplated converting from free to slave labor, and never did so. After one cotton mill in Columbus, Georgia, had been operating for some time with whites, and company affairs had begun to deteriorate, one investor confided to another that "the more I reflect upon it, the more I am convinced of the good sense of your own plan, of slave labor involving only the expense of cotton." Other textile millers actually shifted from free to slave labor. After employing whites for many years, in 1841 the Tuscaloosa Manufacturing Company of Alabama bought slaves, whose value quintupled during seventeen years of reproduction. In 1852, the Woodville Manufacturing Company in Mississippi replaced its ninety white immigrant laborers with slaves who operated the mill profitably thereafter. As late as 1858, a New Orleans ropewalk and textile factory reportedly converted from free to slave labor. Indeed, many low country textile mills (as well as some upcountry ones) continued to use slaves and did not convert to free labor.[13]

Even though the evidence suggests that the conversion to free labor by textile mills was far from universal, why such slave displacement was occurring at all should still be analyzed. Some investors still believed in the myth that slaves were not fit for manufacturing enterprises and should be confined exclusively to agriculture. There was an increasing recognition of the desirability of bringing poor native whites into the mainstream of southern society, from which they had been largely excluded. Especially in the upcountry regions many whites—particularly the wives and children of poor whites and yeoman farmers—were available for work. Finally, the demand for slave labor in agriculture and on internal improve-

Scraping Turpentine

ments was often so great that textile millers were forced to turn to the available free labor, even though they may have preferred to use slaves.

As in textile manufacturing, employment patterns on southern docks had not yet crystallized by the 1850's, and immigrants had not yet displaced black stevedores and teamsters. In fact, some employers began to abandon white dock workers when they proved less dependable than slaves, so that a reversal of the slave-displacement pattern may already have begun. In 1856, for example, when Savannah's immigrant longshoremen, who had previously staged periodic work stoppages, struck for higher pay, local merchants arranged "to dispense altogether with this foreign aid, and employ slave labor in their stead." [14]

Though some conversion to free labor may have occurred in textile mills and on the docks, it is clear that slave labor continued to be used on most waterway projects. Indeed, when white workers were unwilling to endure hazardous and unhealthy southern working conditions (as they often were), many waterway enterprises experimenting with free labor reconverted to slave labor. As early as 1822, for example, the Roanoke Navigation Company employed slaves exclusively when northern white masons refused to work beyond the month of June and when the whole white crew fled after one worker became sick. The James River Canal achieved a stable work force with slave hirelings, only by abandoning its expensive, untractable German diggers and Scottish "mechanics." [15] In 1855, the Cape Fear and Deep River Navigation Works resolved to purchase forty thousand dollars' worth of Negroes, when contractors and immigrants foundered. [16]

Like waterway projects, many southern railroads reconverted to slave labor after unsuccessful experiments with free labor. In 1833, after hundreds of white workers had died in an epidemic, New Orleans's Pontchartrain Railroad purchased about thirty blacks and hired eighty-four more. Anticipating that slave ownership would create a "well regulated economy," the company's directors "thought it proper to adopt this means [slave ownership] of reducing the heavy expenses that have weighed upon the company from its origin. For when it is considered that more than $50,000 of wages have been paid since five years, it will be seen how useful it would have been to increase their [the slaves'] number, and how advantageous it would have been to have bought from the beginning the number [of Negroes] required by the wants of the Compy." [17]

Because uneven profits in the 1840's and 1850's caused several railroad companies, which had bought slaves in the 1830's, to sell their slaves and employ free labor instead, some historians have implied that conversion to free labor was the general trend.[18] Actually, in the last antebellum decades many railroads were replacing free labor with slave labor, and many others either purchased or hired slaves as they had always done. South Carolina's Northeastern Railroad hired slaves, after white workers fled during the unhealthy summer of 1855. When restless whites disrupted work, the Wilmington and Weldon line hired slaves, while the Raleigh and Gaston Railroad successfully petitioned the North Carolina legislature to purchase $125,000 worth of blacks. "Last year some of the Railroad Contractors refused to give the going prices for negroes, and attempted to supply their places with Irish and German laborers," reported another North Carolina railroad in 1855. "The attempt proved an utter failure, and has put them far behind in their contracts. This year they are compelled to have slave labour." [19] Between 1845 and 1860, the South Carolina Railroad purchased eighty-nine Negroes, after white immigrants and contractors proved unsuccessful.[20]

The president of the Central of Georgia line, which converted to slave labor almost entirely, after a three-year trial with immigrants, explained this decision:

> . . . A few weeks since, some disturbances originating from sectional differences among the [white] laborers interrupted for a short time the harmony which had previously prevailed throughout the line; this has led some of the contractors to resort to the employment of blacks and I am much pleased to perceive a disposition on the part of several of the planters residing along the line, to engage in contracts; I have no doubt the effect will be, to enable us for the future to keep up a more uniform scale of operations during the whole year, than if the labor were performed by strangers.[21]

Like transportation enterprises, many mining, construction, and lumbering companies also converted from free to slave labor. As early as 1812, the Wilt-Herzog Missouri lead mining company switched to slaves. As late as 1854, the Midlothian Coal Mining Company of Virginia and the Washington Mining Company of North Carolina followed suit.[22] According to one shipbuilder, the federal government employed northern white shipbuilders in the 1790's, "but after some experience they dismissed them and employed only Negroes." In 1817, after first trying white labor, the Dismal Swamp Land Company purchased $5500 worth of Negroes, who (along with slave hirelings) cut shingles until the Civil War. "I am now decidedly of the opinion," wrote this lumber company's director in 1818, "that if the proprietors . . . had adopted my proposition of appropriating part of their Dividends towards purchasing Negroes, and cultivating their lands, they would have found their interest in it at this time." As late as 1857, a Mississippi sawmiller, who had been advised earlier that whites worked better than blacks, replaced his white sawyers with slave hirelings.[23] One Alabama coal miner, who decided to purchase bondsmen only after a costly trial with free laborers, perhaps best summed up the feelings of other businessmen in extractive industries:

> Every days experience confirms my opinion that it is next to impossible to prosecute my mining interest successfully with free labor. That labor is not in the country (and ought not to be) & when introduced, the employer is constantly at its mercy. No reliance whatever can be placed upon it. It will quit you when you most need it and there is no supply at hand to replace it; and you are driven to seek it abroad again at expensive outlays, & in the meantime to suffer severe embarrassments & loss. The consequence often is that I am forced to submit to gross imposition rather than discharge hands who know and will abuse their power over my interest. . . . The Ala Coal Mg Co. have tried the experiment of free labor pretty thoroughly and it has contributed to the disastrous results of their operations. I believe they are going to make an effort to raise a negro force. Certain it is if they do not they may as well abandon their work. . . . I must have a negro force or give up my business. . . .[24]

The most dramatic conversion from free to slave labor occurred at Joseph Reid Anderson's Tredegar Iron Works in Richmond, Virginia. Anderson had always preferred to employ bondsmen rather than wage laborers, for, in 1840, as director of the Valley Turnpike, Anderson had hired slaves, because, as he said, "I dont wish to rely on white labor." Two years later, Anderson had become the "commercial agent" of the Tredegar works, which with its nearly all-white labor force was having difficulty weathering the current depression. As a result of this crisis, the directors of the company requested Anderson to formulate a plan for the "curtailment" of their expenditures "without injury" to the company. In response, Anderson proposed to contract skilled white iron workers who were willing to train a crew of slaves for the most skilled and high-paying positions in the establishment. "It has always been considered an object of primary importance in our Country to introduce slave labour generally in the several branches of Iron manufacture," Anderson explained to his directors. "The difficulty has been here that certain operations, as Puddling, Heating, Rolling &c are known only to foreigners and a few Americans who have been from interest opposed to imparting this knowledge to negroes. The present depressed state of business has modified their notions somewhat," he continued, "so that, seeing themselves cut off from employment here and but little prospect of being taken in at other establishments, some of these men . . . have been induced to . . . instruct such persons, hired men, apprentices, or servants as may at any time be placed in the establishment."

Anderson went on to explain that all of the white workers currently employed had been discharged, except those who agreed to sign a five-year contract to train Negroes. He felt that the terms and cost of these special agreements were "reasonable," considering the "financial sacrifices" such whites would encounter "should they be shortly discharged by this Comp. and before the excited feeling and hatred of their fellows shall have had time to subside, which it is believed might forbid their safe entrance into any other establishment." Finally, Anderson estimated that either hiring or purchasing slave apprentices would result in substantial savings to the company; he personally recommended purchasing slaves rather than hiring them. So appealing were Anderson's proposals that Tredegar's directors resolved to implement them.[25]

Exactly five years later, when the slaves had been trained, when the contracts with the skilled whites were due to expire, and when he had become proprietor of the Tredegar Company, Anderson proceeded with the plan to place the newly trained slave "puddlers" in a new rolling mill. The white puddlers now resolved, however, to reject Anderson's decision, and they went on strike. The strikers stated: "We . . . do pledge ourselves that we will not go to work, unless the negroes be removed from the Puddling Furnace, at the new mill. . . . Gentlemen—You need not light up the Furnaces Monday, nor anytime, until you comply with our resolution." The puddlers later explained that their sole objective was "*to prohibit the employment of colored people in said Works.*" Anderson claimed that he "had not designed to get negroes to puddling at the Tredegar works, but that now I should be compelled by your quitting my employment to do so. . . . You have *discharged yourselves.*" Anderson explained further, in a statement to the Richmond *Enquirer*, that his conversion to slave labor was motivated as much by the ideological imperatives of a slave society as by the general prerogatives of Capital:

> . . . those who enter into his [a manufacturer's] employment must not expect to prescribe to him who he shall be at liberty to employ; and that he would not consent to employ men who would unite and combine themselves into an association to exclude slaves from our factories. It was because the late workmen asserted such a pretension that he determined that their employment should cease. . . . In that aspect, he regarded it as a matter in which the whole community was concerned; it must be evident that such combinations are a direct attack on slave property; and, if they do not originate in abolition, they are pregnant with its evils.

Anderson defeated the white strikers after a brief confrontation,[26] and within three years he was using about one hundred slaves alongside 150 white iron workers.[27] The most significant struggle over conversion of labor forces thus ended in a resounding victory for Slavery.

Such conversions from free labor to slave labor suggest that many industrial entrepreneurs clearly understood the advantages of slavery after unsuccessful experiments with free labor. Businessmen also believed that the proslavery ideology dictated the continued use of slaves in industry. Since slaves were more tractable than available white workers, many employers were willing to trouble themselves to change from free labor to a slave labor force.

Slave Hiring

Many employers either began operating with slave hirelings or eventually converted from free labor to hired slave labor, rather than to direct slave ownership. The practice of slave hiring thereby became widespread in southern industries and an important phenomenon in its own right. Each year, between Christmas and New Year's Day, employers seeking labor rented slaves belonging to masters with spare bondsmen. At county courthouses and in towns and cities slaves were hired through newspaper advertisements, personal solicitation, or on public auction blocks. Some slavetraders also rented out slaves as an adjunct to their regular business affairs. Others, like the Hill Brothers of Richmond, Virginia, became specialized slave-hiring brokers.[28]

The tenure of slave hire was customarily from January to the following Christmas, but bondsmen could also be hired by the day, week, month, or season. Written contracts specified the period of hire, the type of work in which the slaves were to be engaged, and the employer's obligation to keep them well fed, clothed, and "medicinated." Payments were normally made annually or quarterly. Southern courts decided that if a slave ran away during the period of service, the employer, not the owner, suffered the loss of time. However, the death of a slave hireling released the hirer from paying for the unfulfilled part of the contract. Hiring brokers usually received a 6 per cent fee for their services. They charged additional sums for attending slaves in illness, guaranteeing the hire, collecting the payment, and checking whether employers were meeting their obligations.[29]

Masters rented out slaves for a variety of reasons. Some leased them to others because they were unable to use them profitably, to relieve or settle indebtedness, to fully utilize surplus slaves, or to dispense altogether with the troubles of managing slaves. "I have hired out a part of my hands on the Rail Road, and will probably continue to do so," confided a North Carolina clergyman, "as I am anxious to have less care & trouble in attending to them." Executors rented out slaves while estates were being settled or to earn income for minor heirs. Urban masters hired out "husbands" and children of their female domestics.[30] Owners of skilled slaves rented them to others at least part of the time in order to augment their incomes. One North Carolinian contracted his Negro to a white blacksmith on the condition that the hirer was to work the bondsman "at the Forge during the whole time and learn him or cause him to be learned the arts and mysteries of the Black Smith's trade." A few southerners, such as Bickerton Lyle Winston of Hanover County, Virginia, bought blacks solely to realize profits from renting them out to others.[31]

Though the demand for slave hirelings came from numerous sources, the great majority were employed by industries such as mining, lumbering, turpentining, and various kinds of manufacturing. Virginia iron worker William Weaver (like many of his neighbors) hired scores of slaves during a forty-year period before the Civil War; North Carolina turpentiner Daniel W. Jordan also rented dozens of bondsmen. In 1850,

Tobacco Twist Room

about 40 per cent of the slaves employed at Virginia's tobacco factories, where slave hiring reached its peak, were
hirelings. By 1860, over half of the slaves in the eastern tobacco manufacturing district were hirelings. In the last antebellum decades, probably about one-fifth of all industrial
slaves were hirelings; the rest, of course, were directly
owned.[32]

Southern transportation enterprises also employed hired
slaves to a considerable extent. A majority of railroads, canals,
and turnpikes preferred to hire bondsmen rather than to purchase them. Most companies recruited hirelings in the neighborhood of their work, but some deep South enterprises advertised for slaves in Maryland, Virginia, and North Carolina.
A typical advertisement ran as follows:

500 LABORERS WANTED!

We will employ the above number of laborers to work on Muscle Shoals Canal. . . . We will pay $15 until the 1st November, for 26 working days. After that time, we will pay the highest wages given on the line; or we will employ negroes by the year, or for a less time, as may *suit the convenience of planters*. We will also be responsible to slave holders, who may hire their negroes to us, for any injury or damage that may hereafter happen in the progress of blasting rock or the caving in of banks.

For information in regard to the health of the men, the fare, general treatment, we would refer all who may become interested in this matter, to John Craig, Esq. acting Canal Commissioner. . . .

J. R. & S. S. HENRY [33]

Since a divorce of management from ownership was inherent in the slave hiring system, conflicts between masters and employers of industrial hirelings occasionally arose. "The Doctors bill for attending Dennis was also rec'd and I could [not] but feel indignant at the manner in which you treated me after my placing such implicit confidence in you as a high minded, liberal gentleman," complained one master to ironmonger William Weaver. "I put it to you as a man of good sense whether or not $25 was a fair & just equivalent for the services of Dennis for twelve months, and then to bring in a medical bill reducing his hire to the pitiful sum of $15— 'Shame where is thy blush!' " [34]

To discourage mistreatment of their slaves, some masters carefully stipulated working conditions in their hiring agreements. A few expressly forbade their blacks to be worked in such hazardous occupations as railroad, turnpike, or waterway construction, as well as mining, sawmilling, steamboating, or turpentine distilling. Other masters required employers to "feed and clothe well and treat hands with the utmost degree of humanity in every other respect." Still other owners requested hirers to rent slaves in groups, "in order to have my hands all together," and preferred to hire to the same employer year after year, "rather than be moving from one to another." One master even asked a renter to keep his slave "from running about at night. Don't let him become disapated." [35]

Masters became most concerned for the well-being of their slave property during epidemics. "I am much concerned about my Boys & I should be extremely glad to have them near me during the present alarm, and would make any arrangement you might require as to allowance &c," a slaveowner informed a Petersburg tobacco manufacturer, as the cholera scourge of 1832 swept up from the Virginia Tidewater. "The amount of hire is of small consideration to the value of the negro and risk of life unless you will take the risk and responsibility upon your selves. . . . I should suppose the risk would be very great to the owners of such property," he concluded, "by allowing negroes to remain exposed to the consequences, as it would be hardly possible for the owners of the Factories to give suitable attention to the sick, and [I] think they would be safer with their masters." Similarly, hiring bonds occasionally required employers to furnish extra clothing or shoes when slaves worked in industries that were hard on their apparel.[36]

By the 1850's, many slaveowners had become reluctant to rent their Negroes to certain dangerous industries. "Servants who have once worked in tobacco factories are in a measure disqualified for other employments," publicly warned a "Farmer." "At least it takes some time to make them efficient laborers for other purposes, after they have been cooped up in the unwholesome and destructive atmosphere of a tobacco factory." A hiring agent repeatedly reported that he was doing everything in his power "to do away the existing prejudices now existing against hands being put on public works." Within the space of two years, two masters independently objected to the abuse of their bondsmen at a Virginia iron works. "Davy Says that working in the furnace is Injurious to his eyes," complained one of the slaveowners. "Therefore I do not wish him to work there against his Will." A traveler observed that masters only grudgingly hired slaves to iron furnaces, because

> they were worked hard, and had too much liberty, and were acquiring bad habits. They earned money by over-work, and spent it for whiskey, and got a habit of roaming about and *taking care of themselves;* because when they were not at work in the furnace, nobody looked out for them.[37]

Other masters were reluctant to rent slaves for work in distant or dangerous places. One Carolinian feared that his hirelings at a railroad would "be exposed in the mud and water and it is too far from home, for if they were to get sick they might die before I could have an opportunity to do anything for them." A Virginian decided not to rent his Negro to an iron works, because the slave had "left no doubt on my mind, but he would make an effort to reach the State of Ohio, and by being placed at your Works it would greatly facillitate his Object." A Georgia rice miller refused to let his black carpenters leave the county, because "they are away from their families—generally uncomfortably lodged—away from restraints and exposed to temptations of various kinds—are much upon the road going and returning home on visits—& consequently in the way of colds & sicknesses—and if they are *taken sick*—we cannot be with them—they are left to strangers —and Doctors' Bills consume all they make." [38]

Despite such apprehensions, most masters rented slaves to

industrial enterprises with little apparent concern for their well-being. Only a few hiring contracts actually stipulated precise working conditions; only a minority of masters refused to permit their slaves to work in certain hazardous occupations. Indeed, in the 1850's, many slaveowners anxiously solicited employers to hire their bondsmen, and the slave hiring system seemed to be expanding and flourishing. "I am quite willing that you should take my hands for another year and that they should remain with you during the Christmas holidays," ran a typical letter from an owner to a turpentine manufacturer in 1851.[39]

That the slave hiring system emerged only as the South industrialized, and that slave hiring (like incentive payments) was leading to the breakdown of the institution of slavery has been argued by some historians. "There had been ceaselessly at work for at least two decades a slow and subtle erosion of the base of the institution," declares one scholar. "The growing practice of obtaining the service of slave labor by hire in stead or by purchase was invisibly loosening the bonds of an archaic system." The slave hiring system was expanding because of the growth of industry, he continues, "and as industry . . . increased in the South the rigidities of slavery were forced to yield. The hiring system contributed to this result by giving greater freedom and higher status to the hired slave. Indeed," he concludes, "the industrial occupations were the very points at which slavery was showing signs of breaking down."[40]

Actually, the evidence indicates that slave hiring dates from the early beginnings of slavery, and throughout the slave period it was nearly as common on plantations and farms, and in domestic servitude, as it was in industries.[41] Southern industrialization may have accelerated slave hiring, but slave hiring antedated the emergence of industries. More important, slave hiring (like rewards) gave little promise of transforming slavery into freedom. The divorce of management from ownership inherent in the slave hiring system did not necessarily mean that the hireling was less a slave. That slave hirelings "bargained" with their employers or chose their masters freely is an exaggeration, and there is little evidence that most hirelings obtained any more freedom than those employed directly by their owners. In general, as one authority has concluded, "the hired slave stood the greatest chance of subjection to cruel punishments as well as to overwork," and slave hiring remained essentially "a systematic method of controlling and exploiting labor." [42]

Since many slaveowners eagerly sought to rent their slaves to industries in the last antebellum decades, the theory that slave hiring was transforming the institution of slavery into a wage labor system seems doubtful. Instead, such evidence demonstrates that slave hiring was profitable and convenient both to slave owners and to slave hirers. The dramatic rise in prices paid for slave hirelings in the 1850's also confirms that the demand for, and popularity of, hired slaves was increasing.[43] If anything, slave hiring permitted employers to obtain labor without making heavy investments in Negroes. Slave hiring thus extended the benefits of bondage to non-slaveowners and thereby strengthened the institution of slavery as a whole. Slave hiring suggests how an allegedly rigid institution—slavery—could adapt to the needs of southern society.

Similar to, but essentially different from slave hiring was the practice by a small number of slaveowners of permitting a few of their bondsmen the privilege of "hiring out their own time"—that is, permission to find work for themselves. Unlike hirelings, these bondsmen did enjoy considerable mobility and were probably in a "twilight zone" between bondage and freedom. Required to pay their masters a fixed sum of money each year, they could save or freely spend whatever they earned above that amount. But permitting slaves to hire out their own time should not be confused (as some historians have done) with the practice of slave hiring.[44]

Concentrated in upper South cities, almost all of the slaves who hired their own time were skilled artisans who cherished their privileged status. "I would . . . be much obliged to you if you would authorize me to open a shop in this county and carry it on," wrote one slave blacksmith to his master. "I am satisfied that I can do well and that my profits will amount to a great deal more than any one would be willing to pay for my hire." This black man's wish was granted, as was that of Daniel, a slave cooper, who from 1832 to 1856 was permitted to hire his own time to various Richmond flour millers and coopers, including James Simms, a free Negro! "I was to be allowed all my time; to make all bargains for work; to find my own employment, and to collect my own wages," recalled Frederick Douglass; "and, in return for this liberty, I was required, or obliged, to pay . . . three dollars at the end of each week, and to board and clothe myself, and buy my own calking tools. A failure in any of these particulars would put an end to my privilege. This was a hard bargain." [45]

Unlike slave hiring, the practice of permitting slaves to hire out their own time was neither expanding nor flourishing in the last antebellum decades. Actually, by 1860, it was clearly declining and it had been made illegal in many areas. As early as 1822, South Carolina had, by penalty of forfeiture of the slave, declared self-hiring unlawful. As late as 1860, South Carolina was tightening its codes, while Mobile had, according to its code, forbade "slaves to hire their own time, or to be hired by other slaves and while so hired living apart from their Owners or Agents, and thereby lessening their value, corrupt their habits, and render them absolutely turbulent and insolent, as well as in many instances furnishing places of concealment for absconding slaves." [46] Also unlike slave hiring, the practice of self-hire was being bitterly attacked both by slaveowners and non-slaveowners alike in urban councils and leading periodicals throughout the South.[47] Thus, while efforts were being made to extend the fruits of slavery by encouraging slave hiring, attempts were also being made to curtail those abuses—like self-hire—which threatened to undermine slavery itself.

Integration

Though many southern industrial enterprises employed slave labor exclusively, a few of them employed both whites and slaves at the same factory, mine, or transportation project. In a limited sense, therefore, some enterprises were "integrated." At such establishments, to a striking extent, whites often worked alongside or in close physical proximity to slaves who were laboring at similar tasks. Such "integration" suggests that slavery was an important means of "race adjustment" while serving primarily as a labor system. Moreover, "integration" indicates the versatility of the slave labor practices in Old South industries.

To be sure, even at integrated industrial enterprises slaves were sometimes assigned to all-black work gangs, segregated into non-white areas of factories, or supervised by white overseers and artisans. Discrimination against slaves and differential working conditions were common. Prejudice and the pro-slavery argument helped to make some white workers personally antagonistic toward bondsmen. Competition for jobs created racial hostility between native white craftsmen, immigrant laborers, and slaves. Nevertheless, historians have exaggerated the extent of these antagonisms, for many white and black workers labored together without friction.[48] Also, the very nature of slavery necessitated some interracial association in order for white men to oversee closely the lives of bondsmen to maintain social order. Slavery thus created its own unique patterns of personal toleration and physical contact between the races.

Integrated work forces were especially common in extractive industries, such as lumbering, salt boiling, and mining.[49] Integration at southern mines resulted partly from the employment of skilled foreign miners, but mainly because common laborers of both races frequently dug side by side. One integrated coal mine was Virginia's Midlothian Company, which employed (and publicly advertised for) slaves, free blacks, and "many white laborers." A visitor observing the Midlothian's two hundred miners, "made up of Americans, English, Scotch, free blacks, and slaves," concluded, with the use of a mining metaphor, that "though politically and naturally there is a difference in these operatives, yet every tub here stands on its own bottom." A visitor to Georgia's gold mines observed "a most motley appearance of whites, Indians, halfbreeds and negroes, boys of fourteen and old men of seventy—and indeed their occupations appeared to be as various as their complexions, comprising diggers [and] sawyers." Indeed, the extent of integration at such gold mines was suggested by these lines composed by a Georgia poet:

> Of people, we've of every hue
> Some white, red, yaller, *black and blue:*
> Others with dirt, so covered well,
> What color they, I could not tell.[50]

Upper South transportation enterprises commonly utilized integrated work forces. Several black and several white chainmen and axemen surveyed a North Carolina railroad, while more than a dozen slaves, twenty free Negroes, and thirty whites together quarried rock for a nearby line. White and slave firemen and engineers operated trains on several Virginia and North Carolina railroads, whose repair shops were also staffed by slave artisans working side by side with white mechanics.[51] Slave boatmen, quarriers, and carpenters labored together with white workmen on the James River Canal; work forces of both races jointly repaired Kentucky's waterway projects, as well as at least one of its turnpikes. "A motley crew [of] Negro, Indian & white men" manned an Arkansas steamboat, according to one traveler, while five whites and three Negroes together piloted a Baltimore harbor boat.[52]

Deep South transportation enterprises sometimes employed integrated work forces. In South Carolina sixteen slaves and five whites together quarried at the Blue Ridge Railroad's "18 Mile Creek Work," while twenty-five slaves and fourteen whites constructed a nearby line. The Greenville and Columbia Railroad's slave firemen assisted its white engineers, while brakemen—free and slave—together operated Mississippi Central equipment.[53] Negro deck hands complemented Irish firemen on one Mississippi steamer; however, a Mobile steamer employed Irish deck hands and Negro firemen. Four whites and seven slaves together manned a Savannah dredge boat; six Louisiana pilotboats combined sixteen slaves with thirty-five whites.[54]

Some tobacco factories, hemp factories, and brick works, as well as wood-working enterprises, used integrated work forces, even though such industries usually employed slave labor almost exclusively.[55] According to one visitor, "a due admixture of whites and blacks assemble[d] together" to process tobacco in one room of a Louisville tobacco factory; "niggers and whites re-pick[ed] the fibres out more carefully" in another compartment; while "swarthy descendants of Ham" turned the screw press in still another room. Slave hirelings and whites, including several "Dutchmen," together worked a Louisville hemp factory; nine other Germans and six hired slaves jointly manufactured bricks in Texas. For twenty years, a dozen whites and slaves together built boats at a Gulf Coast shipyard; native whites, slaves, and "imported tutors" fabricated furniture in South Carolina.[56]

Slaves and whites were sometimes integrated at southern iron works. Twenty white Pennsylvanians assisted forty local bondsmen at a Kentucky furnace; sixty-eight whites and fifty slaves worked a Virginia forge; and, in 1861, eighteen blacks and about fifteen whites chopped wood at a nearby furnace.[57] Slaves comprised almost half the work force at the Tredegar Iron Works, but the greatest extent of integration occurred at Tennessee's Cumberland River iron works, where in the 1850's almost four thousand whites and slaves operated nineteen furnaces, nine forges, and two rolling mills.[58]

At least a dozen southern textile mills successfully used integrated work forces. Some textile factories totally integrated the two races; others worked whites and blacks either in separate rooms or at different tasks. Half of a Tennessee textile factory's 120 hands were free and half slave; a North Carolina mill employed both white girls and slave girls. A Georgia factory combined twenty-five whites with an equal number of slaves; a South Carolina mill combined many slaves with five poor white apprentices.[59] A Kentucky woolen mill complemented one hundred whites with a score of slaves. In Camden, South Carolina, two-thirds of the DeKalb cotton mill's ninety-three hands were whites and one-third slaves. The same state's Vaucluse Company combined thirty whites with twenty bondsmen, who reportedly were "equally apt and skilful in every department, except the weaving." An Alabama cotton mill added one slave family to its all-white labor force; by 1858, it was reported that "negro labor is much employed by them."[60]

Integrated textile factories fascinated the British traveler James Silk Buckingham who visited a Richmond, Virginia, factory where one hundred whites and 150 slaves together were busily weaving and spinning. Buckingham also found whites and blacks working "indiscriminately together" at another textile factory near Charlottesville, while near Athens, Georgia, he observed three cotton factories:

> In each of them there are employed from 80 to 100 persons, and about an equal number of white and black. In one of them, the blacks are the property of the millowner, but in the other two they are the slaves of planters, hired out at monthly wages to work in the factory. There is no difficulty among them on account of colour, the white girls working in the same room and at the same loom with the black girls; and boys of each colour, as well as men and women, working together without apparent repugnance or objection. This is only one among the many proofs I had witnessed of the fact, that the prejudice of color is not nearly so strong in the South as in the North. . . .[61]

Integration was, of course, far from complete in antebellum southern industries; racial antagonisms attested to that. Segregation of blacks was common, but it resulted less from public legislation than from ingrained personal prejudices, the desire to avoid hostilities, or slaveowners' fears that whites would corrupt, harm, or agitate their Negroes.[62] Wagoners—black and white—often slept overnight at the same taverns on the National Road, even though, according to one historian, "a separate table was invariably provided for the colored wagoners, a custom in thorough accord with the public sentiment of the time, and seemingly agreeable to the colored wagoners themselves." "So far as convenient they [the Negroes] were kept at work separately from the white hands; and they were also messed separately," observed a passenger on an Alabama steamer hiring slave and Irish crewmen at the same wage rates. According to the foreman of a Louisville hemp factory that

Carting Shingles

employed sixteen slaves and ten whites, "there were six two-story dwellings in a row for the slaves, [and] a large frame building, two-stories, put up as a boarding house for the white people." A Georgia railroad publicly assured owners of hire-lings that their slaves would be "worked separately and at a distance from any white laborers who will be employed in the same line of work." [63]

Such segregation was partly an expression of underlying racial hostility which sometimes dramatically surfaced, as at the Tredegar Iron Works in 1847, when white puddlers re-fused to work with blacks. The hiring of a few Negroes by the New Castle and Frenchtown Turnpike-Railroad (virtually all of whose workmen were whites from Delaware, Maryland, and Pennsylvania) created such "apprehensions" of racial conflict that the blacks were discharged. During the Depression of 1837–43, the apprenticing of slave Frederick Douglass to learn caulking at a Baltimore shipyard, where white and black craftsmen previously had worked together without any serious friction, precipitated a near-fatal attack on Douglass by four white artisans.[64] In the 1830's, the Gosport Navy Yard's integration of about one hundred slave common laborers with 130 white day laborers so incensed some white stonecutters that they petitioned the Navy Department, the President, and the Congress of the United States to exclude slave hirelings from federal projects. Despite such protests, however, the Yard's chief engineer continued to employ an integrated work force, convinced that blacks worked as well as whites and were better suited physically to the tasks.[65]

Racial hostilities occurred, of course, but they were much less significant than the striking extent of interracial co-operation among workers at most integrated industries. Whites were openly antagonistic to blacks only occasionally at integrated work places, yet the absence of racial conflict is surprising considering the racist foundations upon which slavery rested.[66] For instance, little violence was reported as Irish dock workers, deck hands, and diggers worked side by side with slaves. Racial antagonisms subsided once such enterprises as the Tredegar Iron Works had been successfully integrated. A Georgia poet penned the following verse, suggesting the depth of racial tolerance at southern gold mines:

> Wend you to the Cherokee? . . .
> Where . . . "chuck-luck" boxes loud are rattling;
> Where gin by the barrel full is drank,—
> And whites and blacks are all the same;
> Where no respect is paid to rank,
> But every one's of equal fame.[67]

Moreover, newspaper editors,[68] travelers,[69] and southern businessmen [70] who might have been expected to report racial hostilities seldom did so.

A study of those racial antagonisms which did emerge suggests that they fall into several patterns. Conflict between white workers and slaves was greatest when the southern economy was most stagnant. White artisans attacked Frederick Douglass during the depression of the late 1830's, for example. Most racial friction seemed to occur in Maryland, Virginia, and Delaware—that is, in upper South areas—even though integrated work places were common in other southern regions, including the deep South. Most racial hostilities occurred when integration was first attempted—as on the New Castle and Frenchtown line or at the Tredegar Iron Works. Racial hostilities were more severe at industrial establishments in the border slave states than in the deep South, perhaps because of large influxes of impoverished immigrants who competed against blacks for work. However, racial conflict seldom materialized when both races were working together under normal circumstances—as at Buckingham's textile mills and the Midlothian and Georgia mines.

Racial antagonism at integrated work places was partly subdued, because during most of the antebellum period southern economic prosperity reduced competition for jobs between whites and slaves and created work opportunities for both races. Racial tensions diminished further because slaves were, after all, a distinct caste firmly fixed in bondage so that whites hardly felt threatened. Moreover, the proslavery argument convinced most non-slaveowners that economic advancement came through slave ownership, not through the abolition of slavery. The proslavery arguments were effective enough so that virulent racist ideologies, upon which those opposing integrated work forces could rely, were unnecessary. Racism was, to be sure, common, but it hardened only after emancipation raised the specter of freedmen openly competing with whites. Neither legal proscription nor virulent racism was necessary, according to one authority, so long as the status of black people was fixed by enslavement.[71] Indeed, segregation would have seriously hampered the functioning of slavery, and thus some physical association between whites and blacks was required.

More importantly, slaveowners still had sufficient economic and political power to use slave labor or free labor however they wished. Since slave employers dominated the political economy of most southern regions, they had the power to use "integrated" work forces if they chose to. Those opposing the joint use of whites and slaves were less powerful than the masters, and their objections were largely unheeded. Thus, the extent to which employers were able to combine black slaves with free white labor, the widespread practice of slave hiring, and the many conversions from free labor to slave labor all indicate the versatility of industrial slavery. For after long experience with intractable whites, with the slave hiring system, and even with "integrated" work places, southern businessmen were convinced that slaves were the most stable industrial work force available. Besides, there were compelling economic reasons favoring the use of slave labor in southern industries.

CHAPTER FIVE

The Economics of Industrial Slavery

The Virginia and Tennessee Railroad ". . . though just commenced, is already exciting upon the public mind of that State in reference to turning a portion of its labor now entirely engaged in agricultural into other pursuits. . . . We really believe that this road is to be the *Moses*, which is to lead Virginia out of Egypt into a better land."

American Railroad Journal, 23 (1850), 147.

The economics of slavery is a subject in which scholars have long been interested. From the pre-Civil War period until the present day, historians and economists have offered theories and evidence regarding, in particular, the profitability of plantation slavery. After all, if slavery was not economically viable, would not slaveowners have abandoned their "peculiar institution?" And was a bloody civil war necessary if slavery was dying of its own weight? Obviously, the economics of slavery is important not only in its own right, but also in relation to the political development of the United States. Despite its political significance, however, scholars have devoted little attention to whether the use of slave labor in Old South industries was economically feasible.[1]

To study the economics of industrial slavery requires the consideration of several questions. The first is whether slave-employing industries could expect to earn reasonably profitable rates of return on their capital investments. In this analysis, profit rate means either the annual dividend paid on common stock or the annual net income expressed as a percentage of the net worth of the industrial enterprise. A reasonably profitable investment means at least a 6 per cent annual return on capital—the average rate of return on other forms of investment.[2]

The second question is whether industrial slavery was *generally* as efficient and as economical as an alternative labor system. Were slaves as efficient as free whites? Was slave labor —directly owned or hired—less expensive to employ than free labor? Did slave labor entail higher capital and maintenance costs than free labor?

The third question, related to the second, concerns the *specific* competitive advantages of industrial slavery—that is, how did the use of slaves enable Southerners to compete with the North and with Britain, where industrialization had progressed further? Specifically, did the exploitation of slave women and children, the training of slave managers, and the coupling of common slaves with skilled foreign technicians enable southern industries to reduce their costs and to raise their quality in order to become competitive in national market places?

The last question concerns the problems of capitalizing slave labor in industries. What were the sources of capital for slave-based industries? Did Southerners have sufficient investment capital to support industries? And, finally, did the funding of industries with slave capital have a detrimental effect on financial structures by reducing the flexibility of capital and the mobility of labor? [3]

At the outset, certain theoretical and methodological problems should be noted. While the above questions are obviously interrelated, an affirmative answer to one of them does not necessarily imply an affirmative answer to the others. Much confusion has resulted from a failure to distinguish the differences between the questions. Precise analysis of the economics of industrial slavery is also difficult, since information on the sources of finance, the capital cost and maintenance of labor, and the profits of enterprise is scarce. Available statistics are unsatisfactory because not all businesses kept records and only a few fragmentary accounts have survived. Those that have do not necessarily constitute representative samples of non-agricultural enterprises, since most records pertain to large establishments, and it is not certain whether small industrial operators were as successful as large ones. Moreover, the data on costs of labor and rates of profit is often unclear because of the peculiarities of antebellum accounting and the difficulty of finding long-term statistical series. Company reports tended to underestimate expenses and to exaggerate earnings to promote southern enterprise, while official censuses were haphazardly taken and must be used cautiously. Prices varied, while business cycles caused fluctuating profit rates and frequent bankruptcies. Variables such as location, luck, competition, and caliber of management also make computations of the profitability of industrial slavery difficult. Even so, it is worthwhile to explore the earnings, the efficiency, the competitive position, and the capitalization of those slave-employing industries whose records survive.

The Profitability of Industrial Slavery

Under normal operating conditions, slave-employing industries and transportation projects could expect to earn reasonable profits on their capital investments. Some enterprises failed, of course, but most industrial entrepreneurs employing slave labor enjoyed highly satisfactory rates of return on their investments. Most slave-employing enterprises whose records are available matched or exceeded an annual rate of return of about 6 per cent.

The records of southern textile mills employing slave labor

indicate that they usually earned annual profits on capital ranging from 10 to 65 per cent and averaging about 16 per cent. The DeKalb, Martin and Weekly, Roswell, and Tuscaloosa textile companies, to give but four examples, annually paid between 10 and 20 per cent. The Woodville mill, which went bankrupt with free labor, annually paid 10 to 15 per cent dividends after switching to slave labor. "The Saluda Manufacturing Company . . . is doing a flourishing business . . . [and] pays large dividends," ran a report of one slave-employing cotton mill.[4]

The available records of southern iron works employing slaves suggest further that substantial profits could be made in this industry. As early as 1813, one slaveowning iron manufacturer reportedly could "afford to work as cheap as others, and always do so but not at an under rate." From 1835 to 1845, a Mobile iron foundry made 25 per cent annually; during the 1850's, a South Carolina iron works earned 7 per cent yearly. The famous Tredegar Iron Company averaged annually better than 20 per cent returns from 1844 to 1861.[5]

Other kinds of manufacturing and processing enterprises employing slave labor evidently earned similar profit rates. One hemp manufacturer testified that he realized more than 42 per cent profits per annum in the 1840's. A tannery reported 10 per cent yearly between 1831 and 1845. A gas works also earned a 10 per cent return in 1854.[6] According to official reports, most Louisiana sugar mills earned better than 7 per cent returns in 1830 and almost 11 per cent in 1845. During the 1850's, a cotton press made 10 per cent; the Haxall Flour Mills of Richmond reportedly "made large fortunes for their owners for over half a century."[7]

Similarly, slave-employing enterprises in the extractive industries generally made handsome profits. Though one turpentine manufacturer "believed sincerely that no money can be made at the business while labour is so extremely high," in the 1850's, turpentine enterprises in North Carolina and Georgia did achieve satisfactory returns. In 1850, *De Bow's Review* proclaimed that "compared to other labor, this [turpentining] has, for the last ten years, been deemed the most profitable of all." The profitability of lumbering is suggested by one Louisiana woodyard that annually earned 12.5 to 25 per cent returns between 1846 and 1850. In addition, the Dismal Swamp Land Company reportedly "realized almost fabulous proceeds from the timber," while a Carolinian maintained that "I have no doubt from all I have heard . . . that more money can be made in this business [West Florida lumbering] than any other when [slave] manual labor is used." Fisheries usually earned at "a level with the ordinary industrial pursuits of the country," though "enormous profits" were "sometimes realized." [8]

Most southern mining enterprises employing bondsmen also earned substantial profits. As early as 1807, the Missouri lead-smelter Frederick Bates declared that "few labors or pursuits in the U. States, yield such *ample*, such *vast* returns—A slave, with a *Pick* and *Shovel* is supposed to do nothing, if the nett proceeds of his labor, do not amount, annually, to the sum of 400 dollars—the price which his master has probably paid for him." Later, Bates added: "You will see [in my letter to Albert Gallatin] the vast profits arising from the prosecution of this lucrative business." Official records indicate that between 1834 and 1845, several Key West salt works earned 8 per cent annually. Many southern gold seekers failed, to be sure, but scores of mines were as profitable as, for example, John C. Calhoun's which yielded nearly $1 million, and Samuel J. Tilden's which earned $4 million. The success of these gold miners confirmed the conclusion of the Richmond *Enquirer* in 1853:

> It is demonstrated beyond question, that gold mining, *as a business*, can be most profitably conducted . . .

Miners Descending the Shaft

with a proper outlay of capital in machinery & excavations. . . . Though worked thus rudely & superficially,
altogether by native labor and with little mining skill
or experience, they have all paid well.[9]

From the 1790's to 1861, the majority of transportation
enterprises employing slaves realized profitable returns. Some
southern railroads paid annual dividends as high as 20 per cent,
and most other lines averaged about 8 per cent. Some
canal companies, such as the Roanoke, did not do as well as
most railroads, but others, such as the Louisville and Portland
and the Dismal Swamp, paid nearly as well. Plank roads and
turnpikes, however, generally did not earn returns greater
than 4 per cent on the capital invested.[10]

A few unusually complete statistical series for such slave-employing enterprises as sawmilling, steamboating, and gold mining do survive to permit the further computation of the profitability of industrial slavery. As early as 1794, Alexander Telfair's sawmills made him one of Georgia's wealthiest citizens. The Hart Gold Mining Company yielded a similar fortune for another Georgian. The earnings of the *Thomas Jefferson* permitted a Virginia steamboat company to average acceptable dividends between 1833 and 1849.[11]

The surviving records of two rice mills are complete enough so that some idea of the profitability of this industry can be determined. Though it is impossible to separate the profits of rice planting from rice milling, James Hamilton Couper's Georgia rice estate annually averaged 4.1 per cent return on capital between 1833 and 1852, despite his financial losses from natural disasters and from long agricultural experimentation. However, Couper's 4.1 per cent return does not take into account personal expenditures to support his sumptuous living standard and the appreciation of his lands and slaves. Between 1827 and 1841, for example, the plantation appreciated in value as much as 26 per cent; between 1827 and 1845, the slaves multiplied from 380 to about 500—almost a 20 per cent increase on their original valuation.[12] Couper's average total annual return on capital was therefore greater than 6 per cent. Similarly, the records of the Manigault family's Savannah River rice mills reveal average annual returns of 12 per cent between 1833 and 1839, and 12.2 per cent from 1856 to 1861. The natural increase in the number and value of the Manigaults' bondsmen compensated for losses from three cholera epidemics, the absence of an experienced overseer between 1855 and 1859, a destructive freshet in 1852, and a devastating hurricane in 1854.[13]

The records of those industrial enterprises which hired bondsmen instead of purchasing them outright further reveal that reasonably profitable returns on invested capital could be earned. In such cases, of course, slave hirers computed only the cost of labor against their net income to estimate their profit rate, while slaveowners computed the amount of rent against their investment to estimate their profits for the year. In 1817, Ebenezer Pettigrew noted the expenses and earnings from a hired slave lumberman as follows:

Hire	$80.00
Clothing	17.00
Victuals	27.40
	$124.40

Net proceeds of said fellow geting Juniper Shingles is found to be $250.00

Moreover, from 1830 to 1860, the annual rates of return from slave hiring ranged, according to one study, from 9.5 to 14.3 per cent in the upper South, and from 10.3 to 18.5 per cent in the lower South.[14] Such earnings suggest that slave hiring was at least as profitable as direct slave ownership for industries.

Finally, it should be recalled that industrial entrepreneurs, like most other slaveowners, profited from slavery's intermediate product—marketable and productive slave offspring. Many industrial establishments owned slave women whose progeny could easily be sold, and both women and children could be employed in light and heavy industries. Slave women and children therefore gave competitive advantages to employers of industrial slaves.[15] It may therefore be concluded that industrial enterprises, which either owned or hired slave labor, earned profitable returns on their investments.

The General Efficiency of Industrial Slavery

It is possible that industrial slavery was an inefficient or uneconomical labor system, even though it was simultaneously profitable to most industrial enterprises. Slaves were so troublesome and so unwilling, according to some historians, that they were less efficient than free workers. After all, did not slaves have to be coerced, while free workers responded eagerly to wage incentives? Industrial slave labor may also have been so expensive compared to free labor that it was, objectively, an unviable labor system. Given these questions, it is necessary to examine further the general efficiency of industrial slave workers and the costs arising from their ownership.

The available evidence indicates that slave labor was not less efficient than the free labor available in the Old South. To be sure, the slave's indifference to his work and his resistance to bondage tended to diminish his productivity somewhat. But this does not necessarily mean that competent managers could not make industrial slaves work or would have found free labor more efficient to employ. Physical coercion, or the threat of it, was an effective slave incentive, and masters often gave bondsmen material rewards for satisfactory production. In addition, industrial slaveowners could exploit women and children more fully than could employers of free labor. The average industrial bondsman was disciplined more rigorously than the typical free worker. Slaveholders were not troubled by labor organizations and were not obliged to bargain openly with their employees. "These advantages," concludes one authority, "more than compensated for whatever superiority free labor had in efficiency." [16]

In theory, slave labor may be less efficient than free labor over the long run, but for this study the practical comparison is between southern Negro slaves and the alternative free labor —poor whites, yeomen, and immigrants—available to the Old South. If this comparison is made, then it may be seen that the available free labor—particularly the poor whites and immigrants—was less efficient than slave labor, since these whites were less tractable than slaves. [17]

Testimony from southern manufacturers who employed free labor supports the conclusion that it was not very efficient. White "hands had to be trained," admitted an associate of Daniel Pratt, the well-known Alabama businessman. "These [whites] were brought up from the piney woods, many of them with no sort of training to any kind of labor; in fact, they had to learn everything, and in learning, many mistakes and blunders were made fatal to success." Southern poor whites were not disciplined to sustained industrial labor, conceded the treasurer of William Gregg's Graniteville, South Carolina, cotton mill—another southern showpiece employing southern white workers.[18] Moreover, such testimony has been confirmed even by those scholars who argue that the level of productivity (that is, output per man) of slave labor was "low." "When white labor was used in Southern factories, it was not always superior to slave labor," admits one historian. ". . . [Southern white] productivity was much lower than in the North. . . . The use of whites did not guarantee a better work force than did the use of Negroes, for the South lacked an adequate pool of disciplined free workers."[19]

The efficiency, or total output, of slave labor compared to free labor can also be estimated by comparing the prices paid for slave hirelings with the wages paid southern free labor. From 1800 to 1861, white wages did not increase substantially; they remained fairly constant at about $300 per annum.[20] On the other hand, between 1800 and 1833, slave rents increased by about 50 per cent. Then, in the 1840's and the 1850's, slave hires again increased by another 50 per cent. At the same time, the value of slaves was increasing proportionately.[21] This suggests that both the productivity of and the demand for slave labor were increasing substantially during the first half of the nineteenth century. Thus, no matter how inefficient slave labor may have been, it was not less efficient than the free labor available to Southerners at the time.

It is often argued that the use of slaves entailed expenditures that were avoided by the employers of wage labor. The initial investment in blacks, the interest and depreciation on slave capital, the constant risk of financial losses from death, injury, disease, and escape, and the expense of maintaining slaves were all special expenses supposedly peculiar to slave ownership. These extra costs, according to some scholars, made slave labor more expensive and less economical than free labor.

It is clear, however, that these special costs did not make slave ownership more expensive than free labor. Many industrialists did not bear the cost of initial slave capitalization, since they had inherited their bondsmen or had shifted them from agriculture to industry. Interest on capital was a current operating expense only if bondsmen were purchased on credit rather than with cash. Depreciation of slave capital was not a cost for most slaveowners, since slaves were appreciating in value and were producing saleable offspring. The prospect of financial disaster from losses of bondsmen was beginning to be alleviated in the 1840's and 1850's as many owners began to insure the lives of their Negroes. Finally, industries that hired slaves rather than purchasing them did not bear directly the cost of initial capitalization.[22]

Yet, when industries did purchase bondsmen considerable expenditure of capital was involved, which should be compared to the costs of wage labor. The purchase of slaves entailed a different sort of expense than wages of free labor, since it was capitalization of future expenditures on labor and the payment all at once of a portion of what an employer of free labor would pay over a period of years. The cost of Negroes and their maintenance were, as one historian has argued, part of the wages an employer of free labor would expect to pay, and what masters were willing to pay for the right to fully control the time and movements of their workmen.[23] Slavery thus involved long-term capitalization of labor, while free labor involved the current expense of wages.

The surviving evidence also demonstrates that maintaining industrial slave labor cost much less than paying wages to available free labor. For directly owned industrial slaves the largest annual expenditures were for maintenance and supervision—specifically for food, clothing, shelter, medical care, and management, as well as such incidental expenses as taxes, insurance, and incentive payments.[24] The records of typical slave-employing enterprises reveal that the cost of important maintenance items and of supervision varied considerably. Suits of clothing, for example, ranged in price from $4 to $7, while shoes cost between $1 and $1.50, and boots from $1.50 to $2.50 a pair. Hats and caps sold for 50 or 75 cents, while blankets cost $1 or $2 each. Doctors ordinarily charged from $1 to $3 per visit; treatment of diseases such as syphilis cost from $5 to $15; medicine cost between 50 cents and $1 per illness. Life insurance ranged between $1.66 and $5 per hundred dollar valuation, but averaged about $2 per hundred, or 2 per cent of valuation.[25] Depending on self-sufficiency and locale, the annual per capita cost of food varied between $10 and $125; clothing varied from about $3 to $30 annually per capita, housing cost between $5 and $10, and management ranged from about $200 to $3000 a year.[26]

Despite such wide variations, industrial records indicate that between 1820 and 1860 food annually averaged about $50 per slave and clothing about $15.[27] Medical attention annually averaged about $3 per slave, housing probably cost about $7, and supervision amounted to about $800 per thirty hands, or about $27 per annum per slave. Incidental expenses annually cost little more than $5 per slave.[28] The annual average maintenance cost per industrial slave therefore amounted to about $100. Obviously this was higher than the maintenance of slaves on plantations, which were much more self-sufficient. But how did these expenses compare with the cost of free labor in the Old South?

In the antebellum South, the daily wages of white common laborers ranged from 75 cents to $2 and averaged about $1 a day, while skilled whites earned daily from $2 to $5 and averaged about $3. The wages of common white workers did not increase appreciably between 1800 and 1861.[29] Thus, for a 310-day working year, and depending on skill, white wages ranged from $225 to $1500 annually. But the bulk of unskilled white workers who figure in this study averaged only about $310 per year. Like slaves, wage laborers required supervision, but they ordinarily fed, clothed, and housed themselves, unless their board was furnished for them or they lived in company towns where their maintenance costs were automatically subtracted from their wages. The cost of free labor thus totaled about $335 per annum, including supervision. The annual average maintenance cost per industrial slave was therefore less than one-third the annual cost of wages and supervision of free common laborers.

The surviving reports from those "integrated" companies previously mentioned which used both slave labor and free labor simultaneously (or in succession) also reveal that slave labor was much less expensive than free labor. At the Cape Fear and Deep River Navigation Works white workers cost 40 cents per day to board, while slaves cost 30 cents. In 1849, the Jackson *Mississippian* reported that whites cost 30 cents per day to board, while slaves cost 20 cents. In the late 1830's and 1840's, the Graham Cotton Mill in Kentucky listed white board at from $65 to $71 per year, while slave board ranged from $35 to $50. The accounts of the Roanoke Valley Railroad for 1852–53 indicate that slaves were boarded more cheaply than whites, and the records of the Jordan and Davis iron works in Virginia for 1857–58 demonstrate that whites were boarded for $8 per month, while slaves cost $7.[30]

Similarly, in the 1820's, the proprietors of the Maramec Iron Works in Missouri (another such integrated enterprise) reported that slaves were cheaper than free workers. Whites cost on the average about $15 per month, *excluding* supervision and free housing. Slaves hired for $100 per annum; their supervision and maintenance ran no more than $80 per year. Maramec's proprietors also testified that the cost of labor per cord of wood chopped by slaves compared favorably with the cost when whites performed the task.[31] A Kentucky hemp manufacturer, who converted from free labor to slave labor, claimed that slaves reduced his costs by 33 per cent. In 1854, it was reported that Kanawha River, Virginia, slave miners produced $2 per day more than free miners at Pittsburgh, Pennsylvania, pits. The next year, the Virginia and Tennessee Railroad reported that slave labor cost only about $11 monthly while free labor cost $40 to $50 monthly. The manager of one South Carolina cotton mill estimated that in 1851 slaves cost less than half as much as whites.[32] Therefore, at such integrated industrial enterprises, where the only variable was the nature of the labor force, slave labor was very much less expensive to employ than free labor.

Unusually complete records of several other integrated enterprises provide additional evidence that industrial slave labor was much cheaper than free labor. The labor rolls of the Gosport Navy Yard reveal that in the 1830's slaves produced as much as white workers for two-thirds the cost—that is, the use of industrial slaves was, in this case, almost twice as efficient as the use of whites. This was partly because the daily rent of slave hammerers ranged only from 72 to 83 cents, averaging close to 72 cents. The daily wages of white hammerers ranged from $1.68 to $1.73. Of course, the cost of maintaining the slaves probably amounted to about 30 cents daily, which increased the cost of slave hammerers to about $1 per day. Even so, it was less expensive to employ slaves than whites.[33]

The account sheets for Robert Jemison, Jr.'s Alabama construction projects further indicate that in 1858 bondsmen were 26 per cent cheaper to employ than free laborers. In 1859, slaves were 46 per cent less expensive than whites. The accounts of the Graham textile mill in Kentucky reveal that from 1837 to 1843 unskilled slaves annually cost 26 per cent less than unskilled whites, while skilled slaves cost between 15 and 22 per cent less than skilled whites. As late as 1851, slave carders, weavers, and spinners still cost less than comparable whites. The records of the Woolley textile mill in Kentucky also indicate that, between 1856 and 1861, most skilled slaves annually cost 57 per cent less to employ than skilled whites. [34]

Another integrated industrial enterprise, Richmond's Tredegar Iron Works, offers an interesting example of the cheapness of slave labor. After commencing to hire slaves in 1848, Tredegar's proprietor, Joseph Reid Anderson, stated that slave labor "enables me, of course, to compete with other manufacturers." Competitiveness was achieved by combining slaves with white iron workers, which reduced the average cost of labor per ton of rolled iron. Between 1844 and 1846, *before* slaves were employed, for example, labor cost more than $12 per ton; from 1850 to 1852, *after* slaves were fully at work, labor averaged $10.59 per ton. The introduction of slaves thus enabled Anderson to reduce his labor costs by 12 per cent.[35]

A confidential report by the chief engineer of the South Carolina Railroad, which employed free labor at its Charleston terminal but used slave labor for its upcountry stations, offers additional evidence on the comparative cost of bondsmen and free workers. "It is a subject well worthy of enquiry whether the labor at the Charleston Depot could not be performed by slaves more economically than by whites," confided the official to the president of the line in 1849. "What cannot fail to strike you in the abstract of Depot expenses for August last is the fact that 1570 days [of] *white* labor at Charleston Depot cost $1,206, or 77 cts per day, while 1033 days [of] *slave* labor cost at the three *upper terminii* only $524 or 51 cts per day," he continued. "This statement also shows that it took 50 per cent more labor to load merchandise and unload cotton [at Charleston by white labor] than to load cotton and unload merchandise [in the upcountry by slave labor], or the cost of the former was two & a third ($2\frac{1}{3}$) times the latter." [36]

Similarly, an 1855 report by the State Engineer of Louisiana also reveals that slave labor was much less expensive than free labor. Since this report was based on detailed accounts and considerable experience with both slave and free labor, it is perhaps worth quoting at length:

> This department has employed for the last two years an average of one hundred and three negroes, at an average cost for provisions and clothing for the two years of $7,478.00. Nine of them have died in the meantime . . . so that . . . the State has lost but four per cent of its capital each year of that time. The account should stand thus, estimating the negroes at $1,200 each:
>
> Value of 103 negroes at $1,200 each $123,600
> Interest at six per cent on stock for one year . $ 7,416.00
> Loss on stock for one year four per cent 4,944.00
> Provisions and clothing 7,478.00
>   Total 19,838.00
>
> Total cost for each slave per year 192.60
> Cost per month 16.05
> One year's labor of 103 white men, at $35 per
>   month, including provisions 43,260.00
> Making a difference in favor of slave labor per
>   year 23,422.00

. . . There is, however, one item not taken into the account, and that is the fact that negroes in this climate will, for the year round, perform much more labor than an equal number of white men—I think the difference is about two to three—or that twenty negroes will perform as much hard labor as thirty white men, which would increase the difference in favor of slave labor from $23,422 to $37,475 per year. . . . The cost of superintending white and slave labor must necessarily be about the same. Another disadvantage attending the employment of white laborers is the fact that they are more difficult to control than the negro, and when they know you are most dependent on them they will either demand higher wages or leave you. . . .[37]

Whatever the capital costs of slave ownership, these hardly concerned the employers of slave hirelings. Slave hirers bore only the expenses of rent, maintenance, and supervision, even though other costs might be hidden in the slave rent. Slave hiring was thus similar to paying wages to free labor. Moreover, industrial slave hirelings, like directly-owned Negroes, were also more economical to employ than the free labor available. This is confirmed by comparing the total cost of hiring slaves with the cost of free labor. Throughout the slave states during the period from 1833 to 1852, the average annual rent of slave hirelings was $100; from 1853 to 1861, it was $150. During the same spans, per capita slave maintenance annually averaged about $100. The total cost of employing slave hirelings thus ranged from $200 to $250 per annum from 1833 to 1861. However, between 1800 and 1861, the annual average cost of employing free common laborers remained at about $310, not including supervision. By comparing these figures, it can be seen that slave hirelings remained between 25 and 40 per cent cheaper to employ than wage laborers.[38] Therefore, industrial slaves—whether hired or owned—were apparently more efficient and economical than the free labor available in the Old South.

Specific Competitive Advantages of Industrial Slavery

It is well known that southern industrialization lagged behind that of the North and of Great Britain. At least by the 1830's, northern and British industrialists had longer experience, more efficient management, larger markets, superior technology, and the ability to ship directly to the South. Northern products were of a better quality; Pennsylvania's iron and coal ores, for example, were superior to Virginia's and Kentucky's.[39] The earlier development of internal improvements in the North reduced transportation costs, which in turn reduced the prices of northern products generally. The availability of cheap labor—native and immigrant—in the North lowered prices further; the immigration of skilled Europeans increased the quality of northern products even more. The abundance of commercial capital for industrial investment enabled northern manufacturers to expand production, absorb business losses, withstand depressions, and, most important, to engage in cutthroat competition with southern producers. Thus, whatever the long-range causes and consequences of southern industrial backwardness,[40] the immediate question facing southern businessmen—especially manufacturers—was how best to compete with outside producers.

Southerners attempted to overcome their competitive disadvantages in various ways. They tried to foster direct trade with consumers of cotton, to promote internal improvements, and to recapture western markets.[41] But the most interesting means by which Southerners attempted to raise the quality and reduce the cost of their products was the use of industrial slave labor in several specific ways. First, southern businessmen extensively exploited slave women and children (and

Stemming Tobacco

sometimes superannuates). Second, they trained a Negro slave managerial group to complement white overseers. Finally, they "coupled" inexpensive slave workers with highly skilled white technicians—northern and foreign. In short, Southerners attempted to take advantage of the efficiency and inexpensiveness of slave labor to improve their competitive position in national market places.

Slave women and children comprised large proportions of the work forces in most slave-employing textile, hemp, and tobacco factories. Florida's Arcadia Manufacturing Company was but one example of a textile mill run entirely by 35 bondswomen, ranging in age from fifteen to twenty years, and by 6 or 7 young slave males.[42] Young slaves also operated many Kentucky and Missouri hemp factories. One visitor entered a ropewalk's "long apartment, where there were 18 or 20 boys, of from 8 to 15 years old, spinning the 'filling.'" As early as 1820, Fayette County, Kentucky, hemp factories alone employed 135 slave children to work with 199 slave men. Four decades later, Missouri hemp factories employed 100 slave children to help 125 bondsmen. Slave women and children also worked at "light" tasks in most tobacco factories; one prominent tobacco manufacturer, who employed twenty slave women "stemmers," six boys, and a few girls, used for the arduous task of "pressing" the tobacco only ten mature slave males in the entire factory.[43]

Slave women and children sometimes worked at "heavy" industries such as sugar refining and rice milling. "All along the endless carrier [the conveyor belt connecting the outside yard with the inside sugar milling machinery]," wrote one observer, "are ranged slave children, whose business it is to place the cane upon it, when it is conveyed through the shed into the main building, where it falls between the rollers, [and] is crushed." At another sugar mill several slave girls placed the cane in the small trams discharging loads at the foot of the roller mill. Twelve other slave girls fed cars, three boys potted, four boys carted trash, four women boiled scum or washed, ten boys boiled juice, while adult slaves attended to heavier jobs.[44] Another sugar miller who included twenty-five females and ten "supernumings" on his "Sugar Making Roll" for 1851 followed a typical arrangement.[45] During the height of the rice milling season, one large steam rice mill added fifty bondswomen to the normal work force of forty-eight bondsmen, while another steam rice mill supplemented twelve slave men with ten boys and girls.[46]

Other heavy industries such as transportation and lumbering used slave women and children to a considerable extent. In 1800, slave women composed one-half of the work force at South Carolina's Santee Canal. Later, women often helped build Louisiana levees. Many lower South railroads owned female slaves, who worked alongside the male slaves. Two slave women, Maria and Amelia, corded wood at Governor John A. Quitman's Mississippi woodyard. The Gulf Coast lumber industry employed thousands of bondswomen.[47]

Iron works and mines also directed slave women and children to lug trams and to push lumps of ore into crushers and furnaces. The Nesbitt Manufacturing Company in South Carolina and the Yeatman Iron Works in Tennessee, for example, owned scores of slave women and children. In Virginia the Oxford Iron Works owned twenty Negro boys, twenty-nine women, and six girls, who assisted its sixty-two males. These slave women and children worked mainly either at Oxford's coaling grounds and ore banks or at its furnaces and forges, where ten women, one boy, and one girl joined nineteen prime male slaves.[48]

Slaveowners used women and children in industries in several ways in order to increase the competitiveness of southern products. First, slave women and children cost less to capitalize and to maintain than prime males. John Ewing Colhoun, a South Carolina textile manufacturer, estimated that slave children cost two-thirds as much to maintain as adult slave cotton millers. Another Carolinian estimated that the difference in cost between female and male slave labor was even greater than that between slave and free labor.[49] Evidence from businesses using slave women and children supports the conclusion that they could reduce labor costs substantially.[50]

Second, in certain light industries, such as manufacturing, slave women and children could be as productive as prime males, and sometimes they could perform certain industrial tasks even more efficiently. This was especially true in tobacco, hemp, and cotton manufacturing, where efficiency depended more upon sprightliness and nimbleness than upon strength and endurance. The smaller hands and agile fingers of women and children could splice cotton or hempen threads more easily than the clumsy fingers of males. Delicate palms and dexterous digits processed tobacco more carefully. "Indeed it is well known that children are better adapted to some branches of manufacturing labor than a grown person," editorialized the Jackson *Mississippian*.[51] Similarly, another promoter observed that slave children, women, and superannuates could spin and gin cotton more efficiently than males:

> The great feature of success is the number and sort of hands we shall use the machinery with. These we have already selected out, and have them training; they run thus: one old man sixty five years old at the "gin and lap;" one man (maimed, forefinger off) at "cards;" one old man sixty years old at "drawing;" one boy ten, and one girl twelve years old at "speeders;" three boys seven to nine, and three girls and boys, ten years old, "spinning;" six women and girls to the reels; but one good field hand, and she a girl but fourteen years old—17 all told.[52]

In addition, some industrialists believed that slave women could do as much work in some heavy occupations as males. "In ditching, particularly in canals . . . a woman can do nearly as much work as a man," concluded a Carolinian. *De Bow's Review* also advocated the use of women ditchers. Fugitive slave Solomon Northrup recalled that bondswomen could chop and pile lumber as capably as bondsmen. One year a rice mill overseer even proposed to use female labor exclusively to thresh the rice.[53]

Third, industrialists used slave women and children in order to utilize surplus slaves fully. "Negro children from ten to fourteen years of age are now a heavy tax upon the rest of the planter's force," editorialized the Jackson *Mississippian*. "Slaves not sufficiently strong to work in the cotton fields can attend to the looms and spindles in the cotton mills," concluded a visitor to a cotton mill where 30 of 128 slaves were children, "and most of the girls in this establishment would not be suited for plantation work." Placing Negroes in cotton mills "render[s] many of our slaves who are generally idle in youth profitable at an early age," observed a textile promoter. "Feeble hands and children can perform this work," concluded a rice miller, "leaving the effective force for improvements or to prepare for another crop." [54]

The intention of industrialists to utilize slave capital fully by employing women and children extensively is confirmed by an analysis of the manuscript census schedules. This study reveals that almost one-half of the slave population was in the labor force—a figure which is close to, if not at, the maximum possible participation rate. Since 44 per cent of the slaves were under fourteen years of age and 4 per cent were adults over sixty, then most slave women, most teen-age slaves, many slave children, as well as most adult males seemed to be at work. Moreover, the slave participation rate in the labor force was 60 per cent greater than the white participation rate.[55] This suggests that slaves of all age groups were forced to labor more extensively than whites.

It has already been seen that one of the greatest costs and problems at southern industries was supervision. Since the cost of management contributed to the price of industrial products, Southerners sought to reduce its expensiveness and to increase its competence. Each of the types of free white management available—personal supervision, native white technicians, and imported directors—had serious limitations. When more than thirty slaves were employed, personal supervision was difficult, since sales, supplies, and bookkeeping occupied the owner's time. Native white managers were scarce, and they were often technically incompetent. Imported directors—northern and foreign—commanded high salaries for their superior abilities and to compensate for the rigors of the southern climate. No matter what the source, therefore, free white industrial management was expensive, ranging from $200 to $3000 per annum and averaging about $800.[56] Given these circumstances, industrial enterprises often trained their own Negro slave managers.

Black slave managers were used by many southern industries. Simon Gray and Jim Matthews, slave hirelings of the Andrew Brown Lumber Company of Natchez, were responsible for rafting lumber and sand down the Mississippi River to customers along the way and to a New Orleans depot. Simon Gray directed as many as twenty raftsmen—both free whites and slaves—either owned or hired by the company. He disciplined the crewmen, distributed the wages—about $20 monthly—of the white workers and the overtime payments to the slaves, and he paid the expenses of both. After each trip to New Orleans, Gray returned to Natchez by steamboat with his crew.

Simon Gray was an exceptionally capable bondsman. Guiding hundred-foot rafts of lumber down the twisting river required great skill; bargaining with planters and sawmillers along the way demanded considerable business acumen. Simon Gray knew reading, writing, and arithmetic, kept accurate accounts, and collected and disbursed large sums of money. He once delivered $800 to a creditor; on another occasion he escorted a newly purchased bondsman from a slave market to the industrial site—a responsibility ordinarily entrusted only to white men. He had his own pass, and he could charge goods to his personal account at the company store.[57]

Simon Gray had many counterparts in southern industry. As early as the 1790's, Andrew, a slave, rafted lumber down Georgia rivers, directed other slave raftsmen, and responsibly delivered bills of lading as well as valuable lumber for sawmiller Alexander Telfair. A Savannah factor paid each crewman $1 per trip, but they once received $3 to $5 each. Andrew served Telfair until the early 1800's; other slave managers shouldered similar responsibilities for Telfair until the Civil War. In the 1840's, before he fled, Solomon Northrup rafted lumber from Louisiana camps to river towns for his master.[58]

Other slave managers handled large sums of money with fidelity. One slave ferryboat operator faithfully collected company tolls, controlled disbursements, and seemed to manage the entire business without difficulty. One railroad company hired Phocian, a slave, who served as a business agent, delivered company correspondence, faithfully handled sums of money ranging up to $200, and received many privileges, including a pass to visit his wife. Harry, a slave, delivered iron and procured supplies for an iron works during the 1830's and 1840's.[59]

Other industrial slave managers were also trained as business agents. From as early as 1857 until 1862, Nathan, a fifty-seven-year-old bondsman, responsibly transacted much of the affairs of a North Carolina tannery. Without much supervision, Nathan made week-long business trips to sell leather at markets within a fifty-mile radius of the company. He bargained with buyers over prices, tracked fluctuations in the leather market, knew arithmetic, kept accounts, and, after selling the leather, returned to the tannery with valuable hides and large sums of money. From ten business trips in 1858, for example, Nathan brought back over $560 in cash as well as hundreds of dollars' worth of hides.[60]

Many slave engineers skillfully operated complicated industrial machinery. Two slave rice millers, Frank the "headman" and Ned the engineer (whose tragic personal lives were poignantly depicted by Fanny Kemble), capably ran the steam engine and the milling machinery at one establishment.

Sandy Maybank was the slave head carpenter at another Georgia rice mill. A "full-blooded" black man superintended a Carolina cotton mill; a slave machinist attended the machine shop of a Virginia railroad; and Emanuel, a locomotive engineer owned by a Louisiana line, had an admirable record during ten years' service. One master's coal pits were, according to Edmund Ruffin, "superintended and directed entirely by a confidential slave of his own (whom he afterwards emancipated, and then paid $200 a year wages), and the laborers were also slaves; and they only knew anything of the condition of the coal." [61] The best description, however, of the duties of a slave rice mill engineer comes from Frederick Law Olmsted, who wrote:

> We drove to the "mill" . . . with more extensive and better machinery for threshing and storing rice, driven by a steam-engine, than I have ever seen . . . before. . . . We are attended through the millhouse by a respectable-looking, orderly, and gentlemanly-mannered mulatto, who was called by his master, "the watchman." His duties, however, . . . were those of a steward, or intendant. He carried, by a strap at his waist, a very large number of keys, and had charge of all the stores of provisions, tools, and materials of the plantation, as well as of all their produce before it was shipped to market. He weighed and measured out all of the rations of the slaves and the cattle; superintended the mechanics, and himself made and repaired, as was necessary, all the machinery, including the steam-engine.
>
> In all of these departments, his authority was superior to that of the [white] overseer. . . . His responsibility was much greater than that of the overseer; and Mr. X. said, he would trust him with much more than he would any overseer he had ever known.[62]

Some slave managers were quite talented. Horace, a slave architect and civil engineer, and Napoleon, his slave assistant, designed and executed Black Belt bridges for Robert Jemison, Jr., a wealthy Alabama planter-industrialist. Horace's most notable achievement for the year 1845 was the erection of a bridge in Columbus, Mississippi, for which he served as "chief architect." This project won Horace his employer's praise as "the most extensive and successful Bridge Builder in the South." Upon the completion of Horace's next project, a bridge in Lowndes County, Mississippi, Jemison wrote: "I am pleased to add another testimony to the style and despatch with which he [Horace] has done his work as well as the manner in which he has conducted himself." [63]

There can be little doubt that industrial slave managers were less expensive to employ than white managers, and that by reducing the costs of supervision they increased the competitiveness of southern industries. Simon Gray, the riverman, clearly reduced the management costs for the Andrew Brown lumber company. As a head raftsman Gray at first received twelve dollars monthly; this was about one-fourth the wages of a white head raftsman. Even when Gray's incentive was raised to twenty dollars monthly, the same wages as ordinary white raftsmen, it was still only *half* that of white head raftsmen. A white manager with Gray's skills and responsibilities would have cost the lumber company annually almost as much as Gray's total market value.

Similarly, Nathan, the tannery business agent, cost much less than a comparable white manager. Nathan received for his services only a dollar or two per trip, for about ten trips per year. He incurred in addition only his maintenance, which amounted to several cents per day. A white business agent with Nathan's responsibilities would have cost at least $2.50 daily in wages alone and might have been less trustworthy than the slave. Sandy Maybank, the slave head carpenter at the Georgia rice mill, was as skillful as, yet less expensive than, a comparable white manager. Moreover, his master reaped extra financial benefits from Maybank's ability to hire himself out in the slack season. Horace and Napoleon, the slave bridge builders, cost only five dollars daily plus board; two comparable white managers probably would have cost twice as much. Even at these rates, Jemison considered Horace's services so indispensable and profitable that he continued to engage Horace for many years. Olmsted concluded that the slave rice mill engineer he observed was "extremely valuable to his owner." [64]

While some industries employed slave managers, others used highly skilled white technicians—imported from the North or Europe—to improve the quality and the competitiveness of industrial products. Of course, imported managers were more expensive than native ones—free or slave; but businessmen discovered that the use of inexpensive slave common laborers made possible the employment of expensive skilled foreign technicians. By "coupling" common slaves with these skilled white managers industries could raise the quality of products without increasing overall labor and management costs. By engaging the best foreign technicians available Southerners thus attempted to compete with northern and British manufacturers. [65]

Among the many southern industries which coupled cheap slaves with expensive white engineers was textile manufacturing, where competitiveness depended greatly on quality. As early as 1815, cotton millers realized the advantages of skilled management, when one Carolinian who hired three northern superintendents "thought it best so to do—for to depend upon our hands to learn would take a considerable time before we could cleverly get underway." Similarly, a Tennessee textile mill employed a Providence, Rhode Island, foreman; John

Ewing Colhoun, whose products were so widely praised, also employed a northern superintendent; and an experienced "Loweller" managed a Mississippi mill.[66]

Combining inexpensive slaves with skilled technicians was also common in extractive industries. Mining companies often hired experienced Welsh, English, Cornish, and other foreign supervisors to direct the blasting, tunneling, seam tracking, and other work performed by common slave miners.[67] Lumbering enterprises often engaged skilled sawyers from Maine or northwest forests to supervise unskilled slave lumbermen. "Those who would engage in a scheme of this kind," advised an early shipbuilding promoter, "would however find it their interest to instruct negroes in the art of working on ships under two or three master-builders." [68]

Experienced foreign civil engineers likewise executed many heavy construction projects, since native southern technicians were scarce. Architect B. H. Latrobe designed the New Orleans Water Works, Loammi Baldwin administered the Gosport Navy Yard, while his brother, James, executed the Brunswick and Altamaha Canal. After 1819, Hamilton Fulton, an Englishman, supervised North Carolina and then Georgia's river improvement programs. European-trained J. Edgar Thompson planned the Georgia and the Southern Pacific railroads. Charles Crozet, a French engineer, served the Virginia Board of Internal Improvements.[69]

The coupling of inexpensive bondsmen with skilled white artisans was also important to the iron industry which attempted to compete with northern and foreign producers. South Carolina's Nesbitt Manufacturing Company imported several New York founders. Four experienced Connecticut Yankees managed the Hecla Iron Works in Virginia. Another iron company employed a "Jersey founder"; William Weaver's hiring agent tried to engage one of Virginia's most famous colliers, while another iron monger sought the services of James Obrian, Weaver's skilled hammerer.[70]

Many southern businessmen clearly understood the competitive advantages of combining skilled white technicians with inexpensive slaves. Textile manufacturers and promoters, such as E. Steadman, who advocated paying cotton mill superintendents well enough to attract the "best talent and skill" to the South, seemed especially aware of these advantages. If the Saluda cotton mill had only hired "a carder, spinner, dresser, weaver, and an active and skillful young man as overseer, taking the best talents that Massachusetts could afford . . . and offered inducements that would have commanded the very best," editorialized the Columbia *South Carolinian* in 1844, the company would have been more successful. "If it is desirable to establish cotton factories in the South," agreed a "practical" English manufacturer who visited South Carolina, "let the proprietors select the proper man to make out the plans, select the machinery, manage the manufacturing details, and let them pay such men sufficient remuneration for their services, and I venture to affirm that there will be no difficulty in building up a manufacturing business, equally as successful, and much more profitable, than the majority of Northern factories." [71]

Other manufacturers were also aware of the advantages of coupling slaves with skilled managers. Manufacturing was less expensive in the South, according to one promoter, mainly because "the manual labor, costing even now as little as northern labor, may be and will be, under a . . . skilful and eminently practical management, made, by the judicious intermingling of slave male and female labor with that of native whites, and their imported tutors, cheaper than it can possibly be had for in any northern locality. Here then, with all the elements of cost at the lowest rate," he concluded, "the wares

Dipping Tobacco

of this factory would contend successfully, even for a foreign market, with the keenest Yankee competition." [72]

Transportation companies also comprehended the advantages of skilled management. As early as 1822, the Upper Appomattox Company of Virginia reported,

> . . . we have reason to believe the capital employed would have fallen very far short of executing the work, nor would it have been so well executed, had we not adopted the custom of the country in obtaining and directing labor. We began our operations by purchasing what we judged a requisite number of laborers, including a blacksmith; employed a good stone mason, under whom, we placed a number of such as we judged best qualified to learn the trade. The labor of the rest of the

hands was directed by as industrious and enterprising an overseer as we could obtain. . . . The same laborers being continued, they became expert, and were qualified to execute the most difficult parts of the work, in the best manner.[73]

This company's experiment was successful, and during the 1830's and 1840's, other transportation projects also engaged skilled engineers. By the 1850's, as railroad construction forged ahead, the advantages of "coupling" had become widely known.[74] When the directors of the Southern Pacific Railroad pondered the merits of various labor forces, for example, promoter Thomas Jefferson Green proposed to combine common bondsmen with skilled engineers. "It may not be out of place to remark," advised Green, "that the experience of the entire South is in favor of building roads with negro Labor, as the *cheapest*, the most reliable in all works of road building, the best, and not liable to strikes & riots & the consequent of tearing up rail & burning depots & bridges, the best Labor too to operate a road when built and as ordinary help in the machine shops." Citing the "wonderful" facts that southern railroad mileage cost one-third that of northern mileage and made better profits, Green concluded: "It may be safely estimated that the natural increase of negroes upon the healthy line of our road together with the increased value of turning field labour into railroad mechanicks will eaqual 15 pr. cent per annum, whilst the interest upon their cost would be 6 pr. cent—leaving a difference of 9 pr. ct. in favor of the company which would go far toward covering Engineering expenses & head mechanics—and other incidental charges." [75] Green thus understood that the use of slaves would save the company enough money to permit the employment of high-salaried civil engineers.

It remained, however, for Joseph Reid Anderson of the Tredegar Iron Works of Richmond, Virginia, consciously to systematize the coupling of common slaves with expensive technicians in order to increase competitiveness. In 1842, Anderson contracted skilled white "puddlers" to train common slave apprentices. Then, in 1847, some of these bondsmen, now more skillful, were promoted to the position of puddler. The next year Anderson explained the theory behind this practice:

> . . . I am employing in this establishment [Tredegar] as well as at the Armory works, adjoining, of which I am President, almost exclusively slave labor except as to Boss men. This enables me, of course, to compete with other manufacturers and at the same time to put it in the power of my men to do better for themselves. With this view, I am now giving my men, who are steady and respectable as are to be found, each to furnaces at puddling, and furnish them three of my own hands who are blacks—one of them capable of acting as Foreman of the Furnaces. . . . I am getting on very satisfactorily and will eventually have enough of Puddlers here. . . .[76]

Throughout the 1850's, Anderson continued these arrangements, and he was soon able to reduce his labor cost per ton of rolled iron by 12 per cent.[77]

The Character of Industrial-Slave Capitalization

It is possible that the capitalization of the slave labor force crippled the finances of industries, even though industrial slavery was both profitable to investors and an efficient labor system. In this respect, industrial slavery may have been unviable in the long run because it reduced the flexibility of capital and the mobility of labor. Slave capital was so frozen, according to some scholars, that it could not easily be converted into cash. To transfer slaves from one place to another or to use them in different kinds of employment was allegedly difficult. "Negro slave labor was expensive," argued one historian, "because it was overcapitalized and inelastic. . . . Circulating capital was at once converted into fixed capital. . . . The capitalization of labor lessened its elasticity and its versatility; it tended to fix labor rigidly in one line of employment" —namely, in agriculture.[78]

Contrary to this view, the available evidence suggests that slave ownership did not seriously lessen the mobility of labor nor did slavery inhibit investment in industrial enterprises. Indeed, the funding of slave-based industries was primarily an internal process, intimately linked to slave-based agriculture.[79] Many industries were actually capitalized by transferring bondsmen from farming or planting to manufacturing, milling, mining, and transportation. And slaveowners themselves, not merchants or bankers, were the chief source of capital for industrial investment.

Slaveowning planters capitalized many manufacturing enterprises, such as cotton mills and hemp factories, by shifting some less-than-prime field hands or house servants to weaving and spinning. In such cases slave labor itself contributed to capitalization, while profits from planting or slavetrading provided additional funds. "The staples of the lower country require moderate labour, and that at particular seasons of the year," reported a Virginian to Alexander Hamilton, as early as 1791. "The consequence is, that they have much leisure and can apply their hands to Manufacturing so far as to supply, not only the cloathing of the Whites, but of the Blacks also." A visitor to Kentucky calculated: "The surplus [farm] labor is chiefly absorbed by the rope and bagging factories, which employ a vast number of slaves." [80]

To finance larger textile factories slaveowning planters often pooled their slaves and cash and sold stock to neighboring agriculturists. David Rogerson Williams's South Carolina Union Factory was but one example of a textile mill where close financial relationships developed between investors and the company. James Chesnut, the prominent planter, bought company stock and arranged to rent to Williams's factory several of his surplus slaves. The company credited Chesnut for the amount of the hirelings' rent, against which he drew cotton and woolen goods manufactured at the mill. The factory purchased Chesnut's raw cotton, paying him in cash or credits which he used to buy finished textile goods for his plantation hands. Of course, Chesnut also received a share of the company's earnings.[81] To the company, Chesnut was a welcome source not only of capital, but of labor and raw material at comparatively low prices, while Chesnut's plantation served as a market for its manufactured goods. To Chesnut, the mill absorbed surplus slaves, cash, and cotton, while the company provided comparatively cheap manufactured goods and yielded profitable returns on his investment. Such financial relationships were mutually beneficial to planters and manufacturers alike.

Slaveowning planters also financed many iron works—the Nesbitt Manufacturing Company, a large South Carolina concern, being an interesting case. Like other Nesbitt investors, its president, Franklin Harper Elmore, a leading slaveholding and landowning banker, had strong personal, political, and financial ties in South Carolina and neighboring states. To raise capital, the company's founders agreed to permit investors to purchase stock with an equivalent value of blacks. Financial records reveal that several planters, including Wade Hampton, Pierce Mason Butler, and the Elmore Brothers, each invested thousands of dollars' worth of bondsmen in return for company certificates. The iron works thereby accumulated about 140 Negroes, worth about $75,000. Though two nearby banks loaned cash, a large portion of the company's capital consisted of slave labor.[82]

Similarly, slaveowning planters capitalized many extractive

enterprises. As early as 1804, Moses Austin observed Missouri farmers sending or accompanying their slaves to the lead diggings after harvest, to supplement their incomes. In the 1840's, John C. Calhoun periodically worked some of his cotton plantation slaves at his Dahlonega, Georgia, gold mines. In 1849, the *American Farmer* reported that Alabama cotton planters were shifting their bondsmen into turpentine extraction and distillation.[83]

Slaveowning planters and farmers also financed the majority of southern railroads, canals, and turnpikes. Some planters bought company stock with cash; others purchased or received shares for the labor of their slaves. "The cleaning, grubbing, grading, and bridging of the road," reported the Mississippi Central Railroad, "have been undertaken by planters residing near the line, who, almost without exception, are shareholders in the company. They execute the work with their own laborers, whose services they can at all times command." [84] Some slave-employing railroad contractors were paid company stock instead of cash, while some planters exchanged their slaves' labor for the privilege of having a railroad pass nearby their plantation.[85] The advantages of such financial relationships were clearly understood by many southern railroad officials, including the president of the Charlotte and South Carolina line, who reported in 1849:

> The practice of allowing stockholders to pay up their subscriptions in labor, is one of recent origin; is admirably calculated to increase the amount of stock subscribed, to facilitate its payment; and gives to the slave States great advantages over the free in the construction of railroads. . . . Although this road was not, in the first instance, let in this manner, yet it has virtually resulted in it. The contractors, in many instances, hiring the hands of other stockholders, and purchasing their supplies of them, have contributed largely to the payment of stock in labor.[86]

While private investment by slaveowners predominated, public investment in industries and internal improvements by state and local authorities comprised only a small portion of the total capitalization of southern industries. Such public funds went almost entirely into slave-employing transportation projects rather than into other types of industry.[87] Moreover, federal [88] and foreign [89] funding of southern industries was also negligible. This situation contrasted with the process of capitalization in the North and West, where more industrial capital came from commercial surpluses, rather than agricultural, and where state, federal, and foreign funding of industries played an important role.[90] Indeed, the ratio of public to private investment, especially in transportation, seemed lower in the South than in the North. Thus, Southerners derived industrial capital from their own internal, private sources, specifically from the earnings of plantation agriculture. Southerners seemed to be developing industries in their region almost exclusively by their own efforts.

Regarding the flexibility of industrial slave capital, the records of several southern enterprises reveal that slave ownership did not cripple industrial finance. It is, of course, possible that larger industrial enterprises and wealthier businessmen were able to manipulate their slave investments more easily than smaller operators and less secure investors. But it is also true that industrial slavery reduced neither the flexibility of capital nor the mobility of labor to the extent that financial problems could not be solved. At the Nesbitt Manufacturing Company, a large South Carolina iron works, for example, finance remained quite flexible. In 1840, a planter-investor proposed to rent twelve blacks to the company rather than to invest them. The annual rate of hire would be $120 for each slave, the duration of hire four years, and the rent paid in company stock at the end of each year. The company accepted this proposal. The same year Pierce Mason Butler decided to withdraw some of his slave capital. Having transferred $12,315 worth of slaves to the company in 1837, Butler now withdrew eight bondsmen worth $4,850, including four whose skill and value had increased. Even when the company terminated operations and settled its obligations, the original stockholders were reimbursed merely by returning their slaves, whose offspring counted as a bonus.[91]

The Nesbitt Company's slave capital was sufficiently flexible so that in the first case the investor obtained shares by renting his slaves, utilized some of his surplus bondsmen, received company earnings, and withdrew his slaves when they had become more skillful and valuable. In the second and third instances, investors suffered little financial embarrassment and they retained appreciated slave capital when the enterprise was terminated. In each case, slave capital seemed sufficiently mobile to meet the company's needs.

Slave labor supposedly was less flexible than wage labor during commodity market fluctuations and business depressions when income dropped and labor costs had to be reduced. However, many slaveowning industries found that during such periods slave labor was as flexible as wage labor, even though whites could be dismissed and slaves could not. "The certainty of a regular and adequate supply of mining labor at reasonable prices is the surest avenue of success in coal mining," privately confided the slaveowning coal miner William Phineas Browne in 1847. "In this respect slave labor owned by the mining proprietors is greatly superior to free labor even if the latter were as abundant as it is in Europe or in the mining districts of the North." To Browne, the purchase of slave coal miners was less expensive than paying wages to free laborers. To retain large stocks of coal during dull periods the capital required to sustain free-labor mining operations economically would amount to nearly enough to purchase

Negroes, he argued. If enterprises owned slaves, on the other hand, sufficient funds could be realized from current sales to maintain full mining operations without financial embarrassments during periods of depressed market conditions. Browne also argued that slave ownership enabled enterprises to capitalize on market fluctuations. Mining companies should therefore depend mainly upon slave labor; free labor should be worked only as a "subordinate adjunct" to the regular slave force. "The employment of slave labor besides being more in harmoney with our institutions," concluded Browne after much experience, "ensures a successful business against all contingencies and will enable proprietors to pass through all disturbing crises without being sensibly affected by them." [92]

Browne's confidence in the flexibility of slave capital was confirmed by the experiences of many southern transportation enterprises. The Upper Appomattox Company of Virginia, which owned its black diggers, was able, in 1816 and again in 1835, to rent out twenty bondsmen to obtain funds to complete the work. The Roanoke Navigation Company of Virginia, which also owned Negroes, was able, in 1823, to obtain capital by either selling or renting out several slaves. During the panic of 1837, this company rented out some bondsmen for five months for $3,167; within a few months the company thereby recouped 23 per cent of its original $14,025 investment in thirty-three slaves. Of course, the company still operated the canal and owned its slaves. In 1839, the company sold half its blacks for $7,044, rented some of the remaining bondsmen to a nearby railroad, and thereafter earned additional income by hiring out slaves each winter and spring, while using them for repairs during summers. [93] Similarly, after 1827, the Slate River Company of Virginia, which owned five Negroes worth $1,900, rented out four of them at $235 per annum each. One Alabama railroad, which owned $9,575 worth of slaves, realized $2,503 annually (a 26 per cent

return) by hiring them out in the 1830's. Upon the completion of the slaveowning Bayou Boeuf Navigation Works in
Louisiana, the company totally reimbursed its original investors and continued to pay them dividends.[94]

Confidence in the flexibility of slave capital was also evident in the financial schemes of A. C. Caruthers, a Tennessee
turnpike promoter. "We have a Charter for a Road to Trous-
dale's Ferry," confided Caruthers to a friend in 1838. "We
will build our Road—the State takes half. The plan is de-
vised—a few men—8 or 10—will take the stock—pay it all in
at once—get the State Bonds—& with the fund build the Road.
. . . If you have any means of ascertaining the prices of
negroes . . . I should be glad to receive the information—
I mean all sorts—and especially such little & big [Negroes] as
would suit to work on a Turnpike—pound rock & c. Perhaps
you could also learn whether three or four hundred might not
be got of some three or four large slave holders in North
Carolina—Virginia & Maryland.· . . ." Proposing a clever plan
of finance, the promoter concluded:

> With this fund, they can buy say 300 negroes, who will
> do the work in one year. The interest of the $70,000 bor-
> rowed—the tools—support of hands, mechanicks & all cant
> cost more than $40,000. When the Road is done the
> $140,000 is theirs—the bond to the Directors is cancelled.
> The 300 Negroes are theirs—They can sell them for an
> advance of at least of $100 each = $30,000. The whole
> sale would be $140,000 original cost & $30,000 proffit =
> in all $170,000. Out of this they must repay the $70,000
> borrowed, & the $40,000 expenses in all $110,000—leav-
> ing a clear profit of $60,000 & their road stock, which is
> $6,000 each partner & $10,000 in road stock. . . .[95]

The experiences of slaveowning industries regarding the
flexibility of slave capital have been confirmed by some recent
studies. In South Carolina there seemed to be adequate sources

of capital for industrial investment, while Texas masters converted slave capital into liquid capital, according to one historian, by selling, mortgaging, or renting out their Negroes. "At the same time that slave labor was being used as an instrument of production, that labor was also creating capital," he concludes. "It is difficult to understand how the notion became current that the slave became a frozen asset and a drain upon the capital resources of a region." [96] Of course, slave hiring was an even more flexible use of capital than slave ownership, and since demand for slaves remained high, slave capital tended to remain liquid.

Even if these findings—that slave labor in southern industries was profitable, efficient, and economically viable—are valid, it still should be explained why southern industry did not develop more rapidly. While the reasons for this are, of course, complex, an explanation seems to rest in the limitations of southern markets, the South's difficulty competing with northern and foreign producers, unfavorable balances of southern trade, and, perhaps most important, in the ability of southern agriculture to outbid industry for investment capital.

The slow development of southern industries stemmed partly from various restrictions on consumer demand. Slaveowners usually maintained their slaves at subsistence living standards, and some of the largest plantations were almost entirely self-sufficient. The poor whites lacked purchasing power because they did not produce for regional markets. Isolated from transportation facilities, yeoman farmers produced only for limited markets and had difficulty competing with more efficient planters. Moreover, the South lacked urban markets, since by 1860 only about 10 per cent of its population lived in cities, compared to the Northwest's 14 per cent and the Northeast's 36 per cent. Except for New Orleans and Baltimore, the South had only a handful of cities with populations over fifteen thousand,[97] and many urban dwellers were slaves or free blacks whose purchasing power was minimal. Relatively few foreigners emigrated to the South, where economic opportunity was poorer and the climate sicklier than in the North. In addition, as late as 1861, the southern transportation network still primarily tied plantation districts to ports, rather than providing a well-knit system which might have increased internal consumption. Finally, the distribution of wealth, which helps determine consumption propensities, was less even in the South than in the North,[98] although the rate of growth and the level of southern income compared favorably with other sections.[99]

Southern industries also lagged because southern manufacturers had difficulty competing in national market places. Compared to northern and foreign producers, Southerners had less experience, less efficient management, smaller markets, inferior technology, poorer transportation, indirect trade routes, and, perhaps most important, smaller capital resources. Credit arrangements and unfavorable balances of trade drained plantation profits northward and permitted northern merchants increasingly to dominate the commerce in cotton, the leading export both of the South and of the nation. Imports came first through New York, rather than directly to the South, because ships were assured of more cargo on the westward passage from Europe to northern ports than to southern ones.[100] The South would have had to pay for loans and services obtained from the North in any event, but capital accumulated by northern merchants, bankers, and insurance brokers tended to be reinvested in northern industries and transportation enterprises rather than in southern ones.

Southern backwardness was not inevitable; rather, it was the result of human decisions which could have led in a different direction. After all, from the 1780's to about 1815, southern planters had been investing much of their surplus capital in industries and transportation projects. During these years, when the South sustained one-third of the nation's textile mills, southern industrial growth seemed to be paralleling that of the North.[101] After 1815, however, southern industries waned as the rapidly developing textile industry of Britain and New England demanded cotton, the invention of the cotton gin stimulated short-staple cotton cultivation, and fertile southwestern plantations yielded quick profits to investors. Southerners now began to invest more in new lands and in slave labor than in industry and internal improvements. This decision stemmed not only from the agrarian tradition and the prestige of owning real property, but also because the production of staples seemed to promise the easiest financial success. In the competition for capital, agriculture thus outbid industry.[102]

As a result of this process, by the 1830's key slave-state industries were already a generation behind those of the free states, and they were having great difficulty competing against outsiders. By 1860, the South had only one-fifth of the nation's manufacturing establishments, and the capitalization of southern factories was well below the national average. Thus, as Eugene Genovese has pointed out, Southerners could provide a market for goods manufactured by Northerners and foreigners, but that same market was too small to sustain southern industries on a scale large enough to be competitive.[103]

Though these factors helped inhibit southern industries, it is hard to demonstrate that slavery was the *sole* cause of industrial backwardness. Slavery was only partly to blame for the South's difficulty competing with outside manufacturers, for unfavorable patterns of trade, and for restricted consumer demand. Other factors, such as geography, topography, and climate, were at least as important as slavery in retarding southern industry. Can slavery be blamed, for example, for the natural attractiveness of farming in a fertile region? Was slavery responsible for the South's natural waterway system, which delayed railroad development? It therefore seems doubtful that slavery alone decisively retarded the industrialization of the South.[104]

However, it must also be understood that, in the long run, extensive industrialization would have been difficult, if not impossible, under a rigid slave system. To develop according to the British or northern pattern, the rural population of the South would have had to be released from the land to create a supply of factory workers and urban consumers. Greater investment in education for skills and greater steps toward a more flexible wage labor system would have been necessary than were possible in a slaveholding society. Changes in the southern political structure permitting industrialists, mechanics, and free workers greater participation in decision-making processes affecting economic development were prerequisite to any far-reaching program of modernization.

On the other hand, even if slavery is theoretically and practically incompatible in the long run with full industrialization, the point at which this inconsistency would manifest itself had, apparently, not yet been reached between 1790 and 1861. Tensions were present in southern society, to be sure, but Southerners were not yet foundering upon their domestic contradictions. The time when slavery would be absolutely detrimental to southern industries remained quite far off. Moreover, the development of slave-based industries was still necessary and desirable, given the imperatives of the proslavery ideology and the political realities of the period.

CHAPTER SIX

The Politics of Industrial Slavery

No people on earth have the means of building railroads so economically, so speedily, and with such certainty of success, as we of the South and West . . . [partly because of our] . . . available cheap negro labor. . . .

J. D. B. De Bow, addressing railroad conventions in New Orleans, Louisiana, and in Jackson, Mississippi. *De Bow's Review,* 12 (1852), 557–559.

Between the American Revolution and the Civil War, industrial slavery was often a significant political issue in the South. During these years, Southerners attempted to develop their own industries and periodically debated whether slaves were the best industrial labor force. Important on both local and regional levels, there were three more or less distinct political campaigns for slave-based industries. The first campaign ran roughly from 1790 to 1815; the second occurred in the late 1820's; the third lasted from about 1845 to 1861. The first two campaigns for slave-based industries were stymied by changes in southern society. The final political thrust was intimately related to the sectional strife of the 1850's, and contributed in part to the secession of the slave states in 1861.[1] Industrial slavery thus assumed an important role in the politics of antebellum America.

The Early Campaigns for Slave-Based Industries

At the turn of the nineteenth century, leading Southerners began a campaign to complement their plantation agriculture with industrial enterprises worked by slave labor. As a result of this effort a host of slave-operated industries was begun. Thomas Jefferson experimented with a slave-run nail factory and produced plantation tools. George Washington promoted the Potomac Company to furnish transportation facilities for the upper South. South Carolinians founded several textile mills operated by slave labor to turn out cheap clothing in their region. Even Alexander Hamilton encouraged Southerners to manufacture certain articles with slave labor to supplement northern industrial production.[2]

After 1815, this early campaign for southern industrialization was subsumed by new pressures on the southern economy. The availability of fertile western lands, the impact of the invention of the cotton gin, and the demand for cotton and other southern staples by northern and foreign manufactures all combined to stimulate expansion of agriculture into the Piedmont, Black Belt, and transmontane regions. New York cotton prices, to use one index, climbed from ten cents per pound in 1811 to thirty-four cents in 1817.[3] As a result most Southerners were now more inclined to invest in agriculture than in industry or internal improvements. In effect, King Cotton defeated the first campaign for southern industrialization.

In the 1820's, changes in the economic situation again made conditions more favorable for the renewal of the campaign for slave-based industries. Over-expansion of agriculture and diminishing demand for cotton had joined to create a serious depression. Cotton prices tumbled to twelve cents per pound in 1822 and to nine cents—an all-time low—in 1830. Almost simultaneously, trading patterns were shifting, as eastern merchants, cities, and states financed transportation projects to tap western raw materials and to serve western consumers. Proportionally more western trade began flowing eastward than southward, even though the volume of the South's commerce with the Northwest increased.[4] Southerners came to believe that eastern merchants were dominating national and international commerce to deprive them of their rightful share of profits.

Political problems were also very upsetting. During the debates over the admission of Missouri in 1819–20, some Northerners sharply criticized the institution of slavery; even worse, slavery was prohibited north of the line 36°30′, denying Southerners access to most of the Louisiana Purchase. In 1822, a slave insurrection plot led by Denmark Vesey, a free black who had heard of the Missouri debates, was uncovered in Charleston. Two years later, John Quincy Adams, a New Englander, won the Presidency by defeating three southern candidates, all of whom were slaveowning planters. Then, in 1828, a high protective tariff was passed which many Southerners felt directly threatened them.

Southerners attempted to deal with these crises in various ways. Some planters increased cotton production, which only aggravated the problem of cotton surpluses. Some politicians raged hysterically against the "Tariff of Abominations" and threatened to nullify federal law. Carolinians claimed that import duties depressed foreign trade, raised the cost of imported manufactures, and diminished the South's share of western trade, since tariff revenues went mainly for northern public works. Other Southerners almost instinctively began to strengthen the proslavery argument in response to moral criticism by the Abolitionists and internal slave unrest. However, the solution to southern sorrows which was most interesting was the idea of economic self-sufficiency—a proposal which implied the use of slave labor to develop southern industries and internal improvements in order to liberate the slave states.

Emerging out of the crises of the 1820's, the second phase of the debate and the campaign for the use of slave labor to industrialized the South was especially evident in southern periodicals. In 1827, the widely read Baltimore *American Farmer*, for example, posed a series of questions. "Here is a new subject for the consideration of our southern friends," editorialized the *Farmer*. "The increase in the growth of their great staple has so far exceeded the demand, that those engaged in it must now abandon it for something else (heaven knows what), or some new source of demand must be created to keep pace with the augmented and augmenting production." To conclude, the *Farmer* requested information on whether manufacturing cotton bagging instead of hempen baling would increase the consumption of the cotton crop.[5] By asking whether slaves should be used in southern factories the *Farmer's* editorial caused considerable controversy.

Though many problems (such as cotton overproduction, the availability of power sites, and economic and political unity) were aired by respondents to the *Farmer's* appeal, most contributors dwelled on whether free labor or slave labor should be used in manufacturing industries. This question raised several corollaries, such as the usefulness of slave women, children, and superannuates; the problem of slave control; the uses of slave capital; and the profitability and efficiency of slave labor compared to free labor. Moreover, this debate also became tangled with the tariff controversy, a leading political issue of the late 1820's and early 1830's. Industrial slavery's relationship to the politics of this period and to key issues in southern society is therefore clear.[6]

Many contributors to the *American Farmer* held the opinion that slave women and children could be profitably employed in textile mills. "A Tennessean" described at length a

Sugar Mill

young bondswoman productively working ginning, carding, and spinning machines. This testimony supported the conclusion of another slaveholder, ironically signing himself "A Slave to Them," who suggested that if slave "women and children be furnished with good machinery . . . they will more than quadruple the value of [southern] labour." A Pennsylvanian, who reminded the *Farmer* of northern practices, advocated the extensive use of slave women and children in southern textile mills. He stimulated William Fitzhugh to inquire whether slaves younger than ten years old could be used profitably in cotton factories.

Other contributors to the *Farmer* were convinced that slaves would be less troublesome than white workers in textile factories, since bondsmen were easier to control than freemen.

Not only were slaves more economical than whites, testified "Mississippi" who had long experience, but with blacks "there would be no turning out for higher wages in the South, and the consequent loss and delay—no abandonment of the factory by any of the hands, no fluctuation in the labour. The water power will scarcely be more steady than the slave power. . . ."

Some respondents seemed anxious to utilize their surplus slave capital to the fullest extent by developing southern industries. One writer claimed that manufacturing with slaves would "diminish the number of cultivators of the soil; of course diminish the gluts of the market—and, further, increase the home market for their edible products, by the conversion of producers into consumers." He concluded that "among its [cotton-bag manufacturing] beneficial results will be, to render the slaves more valuable; to secure them more indulgent treatment; to improve their faculties; and accelerate their fitness for final emancipation."

Much of the disagreement among the *Farmer's* readers soon reduced to a narrow dispute over whether slave labor was cheaper than free labor in manufacturing enterprises. Though most contributors believed that bondsmen were more economical than freemen in factories, this debate often involved wild estimates of costs and untested economic theories. These analyses remained confused, therefore, until the anonymous contributor "B." wisely suggested that "If any doubt remains of the capacity and fitness of slaves to conduct the operations of a factory, let the experiment be fairly made by selecting an equal number of slaves and *free white* persons, and place them in rival factories."

Despite the paucity of theory and data at the time, the advantages of slave labor compared to free labor were best explained by Dr. Thomas P. Jones, whose speech before Philadelphia's Franklin Institute was published by the *American Farmer* in the winter of 1827–28. "The negro possesses, in general, a degree of emulation, equal, at least to that of the white labourers . . . but, in my estimation superior," stated Jones flatly, after presenting a remarkably sophisticated analysis of the inexpensiveness of slave labor. "I am thoroughly convinced, not only that they [Negroes] may be profitably employed as manufacturers, but that they are peculiarly suited to this purpose," he continued. "Only a small degree of intelligence is necessary to the acquisition of the utmost skill in the performance of an individual operation, however delicate it may be."

Other Southerners defined the relationship between the proposal to manufacture with slave labor and the current tariff controversy. In 1827, upon the occasion of the Harrisburg, Pennsylvania, woolen bill convention, one contributor to the *American Farmer*—"A Natchez, Mississippi, Gentleman"— seemed especially upset by protective tariffs. ". . . Why then should we not manufacture our *coarse goods* in the slave states, where cotton is *lower* than in any part of the world, the goods *higher*, the water power as *efficient*, and the slave labour the *best* and the *cheapest?*" he asked. "Let capitalists attend to these hasty suggestions; let us convert one-tenth of our field labourers into operatives, and we shall soon be independent." In 1828, "Agricola" reported that "a patriotic" Georgia farmer was manufacturing all of the coarser clothing, bagging, and bale rope for his plantation, "to cheat the *Tariff*, as he calls it." Similarly, in 1829, the anti-tariff Columbia, South Carolina, *Telescope* commented on David Rogerson Williams's cotton mill as follows:

> The large capital and the great intelligence and energy of Gen. Williams will make this a thorough experiment in the capacity of slave labor for manufacturing. If it shall be successful, and large capital be invested in this way, we may expect an immediate repeal of the tariff. Our Northern brethren will no more consent to the competi-

tion of our manufactures than to that of Europe. We are
well satisfied that whatever direction may be given to
the capital and labor of the South, if it is successful, will
be legislated upon for the advantage of the North, without the slightest compunction for the injury it may bring
us. . . .[7]

"If Withers [the editor] of the Telescope had as good a ba-
rometer of the anti-tariff excitement as we have, in this little
manner of the Factory," answered Williams, "I verily believe
he would go mad outright, or rave less . . . . We may preach,
till the cows come home, about *staple* and tariff imposers, etc.
etc.; if we do not sell cheaper [than northern and foreign man-
ufacturers] we shall have no preference [for our products]."

By the nullification winter of 1832–33, even the most na-
tionalist-minded Southerners had begun to understand the relationship between slave-based industries and the tariff issue.
"May there not be a more important alleviation [of the tariff
problem] in embryo—an assimilation of the employment of
labor in the South to its employment in the North?" confided
James Madison to Henry Clay, in prophetic terms. "A difference, and even a contrast, in that respect, is at the bottom
of the discords which have prevailed. . . . unless agriculture
can find new markets for its products, or new products for
its markets," concluded Madison, "the rapid increase of slave
labor . . . must divert a large portion of it from the plow
and the hoe to the loom and the workshop."[8]

Paralleling the debate in periodicals, southern politicians also
considered whether to use slaves in manufacturing enterprises,
and the campaign for industrial slavery thus became a political
issue on the legislative level. On January 1, 1828, Charles
Fisher of Rowan, North Carolina, presented a lengthy "Report on the Establishment of Cotton and Woollen Manufactures" to his state assembly. "We have been growing poorer,
the manufacturers have been growing richer," proclaimed

Fisher, who also accounted for the overproduction of cotton, the surplus of slaves, and the unfavorable balances of southern trade. After computing that slave labor was cheaper than free labor in textile mills, Fisher asked rhetorically: "What branch of mechanics have we in our country, in which we do not find negroes often distinguished for their skill and ingenuity?" Fisher unhesitatingly answered: "In every place we see them equalling the best white mechanics." Within one month, Fisher's report had been reprinted in full by the Baltimore *American Farmer* and was being circulated throughout the South.[9]

By the same year, Governor John Murphy of Alabama had reached conclusions similar to Fisher's. Representing the manufacturing interests of Black Belt planters, Murphy urged his legislature to help Southerners avoid the North's "double monopoly" in the purchase and sale of goods. "The most obvious, and indeed the only remedy which depends on us, is to commence manufacturing ourselves. . . . It will be found in experience," he continued, "that slave labour will prove extremely well adapted to manufactures. It can be perfectly commanded, and reliance upon it will be subject to fewer disappointments, than usually happen in the voluntary labour. There must be less embarrassing collision between the proprietors and the workmen," concluded Murphy, "and several causes will combine to render the entire cost of the labour comparatively less. . . ."[10]

At the same time, support for slave-based manufacturing came from the federal level. Joseph Marshall, an experienced British textile manufacturer, testified before a committee of Congress that cotton bagging was cheaper than, but as durable as, hempen baling. Seizing upon Marshall's testimony, the advocates of industrial slavery used it in the disputes still raging in southern statehouses and periodicals.[11]

The campaign for manufactures stimulated a parallel discussion over whether free labor or slave labor should be used in southern transportation enterprises. In this debate virtually no one advocated employing white workers—native or immigrant —exclusively on internal improvements. Most participants assumed that whites would be an untractable work force or unable to survive sickly summers. For these reasons, the discussions dwelled on whether state governments should prosecute public works with slaveowning contractors, slave hirelings, or with bondsmen owned directly by the state.

The campaign for slave-based transportation facilities followed different courses in each southern state. In Georgia, as early as 1816, the Oconee River commissioners resolved to purchase slaves to improve their waterway. In 1821, the *Georgia Journal* asserted that bondsmen were less expensive than contractors for river improvement. In 1825, Governor George Troup recommended investing state funds in a "description of labor" capable of building canals and roads. Then, in 1827, Hamilton Fulton, the State Engineer, made an extensive report to the legislature's Committee on Internal Improvements in which he advocated that the state acquire slaves. "I feel satisfied from the experience I have had in the Southern States that it will be impossible to go on with such operations [as river improvement and the construction of canals, turnpikes, or railroads] in an expeditious and satisfactory manner, unless there are a number of negroes purchased by the State," reported Fulton. "It appears to me it would be the most economical plan for the State to purchase as many slaves as the nature and extent of the proposed improvements will require." The legislature responded at first by appropriating money to purchase thirty slaves to improve the Altamaha River, and by 1830, the state had acquired 207 bondsmen, worth about $100,000. In 1833, after the completion of some major projects and the election of an administration favorable to private enterprise, however, the legislature directed these slaves to be sold.[12]

The Alabama assembly also considered state slave ownership, after Governor John Murphy proposed to construct with slave labor a canal at the Muscle Shoals of the Tennessee River. Acknowledging that this canal could be built either by contractors, slave hirelings, or by state-owned bondsmen, Murphy concluded with an analysis worth quoting at length:

> . . . The first [plan, contractors] would be liable to loss from the imperfection of estimates, as no prudent man . . . would be inclined to make a closed contract where many uncertainties prevailed . . . and it is scarcely possible in such cases to be so vigilant to defeat the multiform subterfuges and expedients which self-interest will devise. . . .
>
> The second method [hired slaves] would indeed be favorable to the proper accomplishment of the work, but unfavorable in point of expense and of time. There would always be uncertainty in procuring hands, and those who had hands to hire, might take occasion from the public necessity, to hold back and combine so as to enhance the price. . . .
>
> In our peculiar situation the third method [purchasing slaves] seems to combine the three essential advantages. Hands it is presumed may readily be purchased at a reasonable price, and from time to time, to the full extent of our disposable means, and sufficient to accomplish the work within the time prescribed in the donation. In this way the work would only cost the interest on the money invested; the loss sustained on the property by death or casualty, the subsistence of the hands, and the charges of superintendence.—The work would be accomplished without any difficulty in its details, and with just reference to its durability and usefulness. With the effective

hands, it might be convenient to purchase a suitable number of women to cook, wash, and perhaps perform the lighter parts of the work, and this would be perfectly consistent with the humanity of purchasing men with their wives, whenever such opportunities of purchase might offer. . . . At suitable places along the canal, the hands might cultivate . . . the vegetables which would be proper to promote their comfort, and the preservation of their health. It might be so arranged that they could work on the canal during the sickly season, at points least exposed to sickness or fatality. . . . This corps of pioneers . . . might afterwards be employed on Railroads, Turnpike roads, improving the navigation of our rivers, and opening other canals where the public good might require. . . .[13]

The North Carolina legislature instructed a special committee to investigate the expediency of the state purchasing its own slave force, after Governor John Owen delivered his 1830 message. "No reason can be conceived," asserted Owen, "why that course which an individual pursues with the best results in the management of his private concerns, should not also be the best for the State in the prosecution of a similar enterprise. Individuals who hire slaves soon become embarrassed. If *they* cannot succeed in the management of this kind of labour," concluded Owen, "it is but reasonable to suppose the State cannot. . . . [Purchased] slaves constitute the only effective force. To employ white labourers to drain our swamps cannot succeed. They have not the physical ability."[14]

Louisiana and Mississippi confronted the state slave ownership issue later than most other states, since they already had navigable river systems. However, as the Erie Canal and other east-west transportation routes increasingly diverted western trade from the lower South, these states began to undertake extensive public works of their own, thus raising the state slave ownership question. To the 1834 legislature Louisiana

Governor A. B. Roman explained that contractors were wasteful, free day-laborers unreliable, and that hirelings—slave or immigrants—were unobtainable. Indeed, two private companies (the Bayou Boeuf, and the Barataria and Lafourche) had, according to Roman, already completed their canals with purchased slaves, who were being resold at their original cost. Public ownership of slaves was "not only the cheapest, but the only means of succeeding in a regular and permanent system of Internal Improvements," concluded Roman. Louisiana soon acquired four hundred bondsmen who worked for the state until shortly before the Civil War.[15]

In Mississippi the conflict over state slave ownership was more protracted than elsewhere. In 1830, the House Committee on Internal Improvements expressed a "decided preference to slave labor, the property of the State, as being decidedly the most economical, [and] more expeditious." A majority of the river commissioners preferred to employ slaveowning contractors, however, and the legislature took no action. Then, in 1834, General F. Huston argued before a group of Natchez promoters: "Nearly the whole labor of a railroad is so simple and plain, that it can be executed by slaves, which is cheaper than the white labor in the Northern States or Europe." Despite such pressure, in 1836 the Committee on the Judiciary held that "it should never be the policy of the State to become the holder of that species of property, as the delicate relations that subsist between master and slave could not exist through a State agency."[16] In 1838, Governor A. G. McNutt again requested legislation to provide for state slave ownership, on the following grounds: "Experience has fully demonstrated that the contract system will not answer for the improvement of the navigation of rivers. Contracts are sought for with avidity by individuals, in order to obtain the usual advance," concluded McNutt. "The funds of the State are often perverted to private purposes, and contracts rarely executed according to stipulation." Not until the following year, however,

was the Board of Internal Improvements authorized to purchase slaves for public works.[17] The Board was so hesitant
about buying bondsmen for a proposed state-financed railroad,
however, that it stalled several years and then solicited advice
from two private Georgia railroad companies. In response to
these queries the president of the Central of Georgia line described his disastrous experiment with white workers: "In the
course of two or three months, it was manifest that the plan
adopted would soon bring the company to ruin. The waste
of fuel, the turbulence and general confusion were fearful."
As a result, he concluded, slaveowning contractors were employed instead. After slaveholding contractors had graded the
right of way, explained the president of the Georgia Railroad,
the company purchased $40,000 worth of Negroes for shop
and road work. Finding "much advantage in their [slaves']
greater expertness and efficiency, from long experience, and
from the ability at all times to control their services," he concluded that slave ownership was the best labor system for railroads. Apparently impressed by this testimony, the state of
Mississippi invested heavily in the slaveowning Southern Railroad.[18]

Despite such victories, the second campaign for slave-based
industries was, for various reasons, clearly subsiding by the
mid-1830's. Returning prosperity once again increased demand for agricultural staples and for slaves. Expansion onto
southwestern lands renewed, the Piedmont gold rush pumped
millions of dollars into the southern economy, and cotton
prices rose from the nadir of 9 cents in 1830 to 17 cents in
1834 and to 15 cents per pound in 1838.[19] By 1828, the political
outlook for the South also seemed more encouraging. With
considerable southern support the Jacksonian Democrats defeated the commercial and manufacturing interests of New
England, represented by President Adams. Then, in 1833, the
Compromise Tariff, which guaranteed to lower duties gradually over the next decade, replaced the hated Tariff of 1828.

Canal Barge

Southerners once again seemed secure in the national "political saddle." Preoccupied with economic pursuits and expanding their influence into Texas, Southerners became less interested than before in the question of self-sufficiency and terminated the second phase of the campaign for industrial slavery.

Slave-Based Industries and the Politics of Sectionalism

During the last two antebellum decades, a number of frustrating problems once again beset the slave states. After 1839, economic stagnation struck southern agriculture anew, as overspeculation and lagging demand caused cotton prices to drop to as low as 6 cents per pound. Cotton would never sell for more than 12 cents per pound thereafter.[20] Western trade increasingly flowed eastward over northern canals and railroads rather than southward, while northern merchants tightened their control of southern overseas trade.

To make matters worse, the political picture again darkened considerably. The Abolitionists continued to expose the sinfulness of slavery and the seaminess of the southern way of life. Southern expansionism soon gave rise to new political parties dedicated to the principle of free soil, if not to the destruction of slavery altogether. Free-state politicians began to obstruct southern expansionism successfully and to shatter southern dreams of an empire for slavery in California and the Caribbean. Southern congressional power waned as the northern population grew, and, after 1850, as more free states than slave states entered the Union. Despite "doughface" support, control of the Supreme Court, and domination of the Washington bureaucracy, the South's political power seemed jeopardized and its ultimate security seemed threatened.

Conscious of losing their economic and political hegemony, many Southerners again felt constrained within national and international economies to which they heavily contributed but over which they had little control. Under moral attack by the Abolitionists, many Southerners felt bound to defend slavery as a "positive good" by strengthening the proslavery argument. Fearful that political power and moral leadership might be turned against them, some Southerners began again to dream of economic self-sufficiency and to scheme for separate southern nationhood to insure their future security. The old question of slave-based industries thus arose once again and the previous debate resumed.

Though all of the old economic issues, such as the tariff,[21] appeared in the new campaign for industries, they were now subordinate to the leading political problems of the heightening sectional conflict of the 1840's and 1850's. Such issues as the role of the poor whites and the yeomanry in southern society, the territorial expansion of the slave states, the economic growth of the region, the reopening of the African slave trade, and southern secessionism were all now entwined with the movement for slave-based industries. The relationship between industrial slavery and these political issues of the 1840's and 1850's was therefore manifest.

The campaign for southern industry and the debate over the best labor force to use in it both resumed, for all practical purposes, on November 25, 1851, when James Henry Hammond delivered the "Anniversary Oration" before South Carolina's State Agricultural Society. A leading planter, politician, and proslavery ideologist, Hammond devoted most of his speech to southern economic problems and to his principal panacea of agricultural diversification. But Hammond also advocated shifting some slaves into iron manufacturing, mining, and quarrying industries. "Experience has proved," he concluded, "that our slaves can be made as expert as any other class in all, or nearly all, the operations of a cotton factory. . . ." [22]

Hammond's proposal to use slave labor in industries was soon criticized by his friend William Gregg. Under the pseudonym "South Carolina," Gregg wrote a series of widely reprinted essays on "Domestic Industry" for the Charleston *Courier* in the winter of 1844–45. Assuming the necessity of manufactures for southern economic development, Gregg grappled with the problem of supplying such factories with inexpensive labor. "I may safely assert that southern labor is the cheapest in the world," stated Gregg. "Which of the two is the cheaper, free or slave labor, is a question not yet decided by manufacturers at the South. All concur that there is no difference as to capability; the only question is," he concluded, "whether hired white labor is not cheaper than free black, or slave labor?" [23] Though Gregg theorized that slaves could manufacture textiles as capably as whites, he soon founded a cotton mill at Graniteville, South Carolina, which employed poor white laborers exclusively. This left no doubt where Gregg stood in practice.

Gregg's decision to manufacture textiles with free labor was supported by his associate James H. Taylor, a Charleston merchant, agent of the Charleston Cotton Mills, and treasurer of the Graniteville Manufacturing Company from 1848 to 1849. "Crowd from these employments [textile factories] the fast increasing white population of the South, and fill our factories and workshops with our slaves," warned Taylor in *De Bow's Review* for January, 1850, "and we have in our midst those whose very existence is in hostile array to our institutions." Slaves should be confined to agriculture, argued Taylor, because they would become prone to revolt in factories. Rather than excluding them from the fruits of a slave society, poor whites should be employed in textile factories so that they would be able to purchase slaves, and "from the deepest principle of self-interest become . . . firm and uncompromising supporters of our institutions." [24] To Gregg and Taylor, therefore, providing economic opportunity for poor whites would eliminate class conflict from southern society.

This position soon received support from James H. Hammond in his 1849 address to the South Carolina Institute, which signified a shift from his 1841 oration. "There is no question but that our slaves might, under competent overseers, become efficient and profitable operatives in our factories," granted Hammond. "It may be of much consequence to us, that this fact has been fully tested, and is well known and acknowledged, as it would give us, under all circumstances, a reliable [labor] source." The removal of large numbers of slaves from cotton cultivation, reasoned Hammond, would increase the cost of labor and goods and would reduce the power of the "agricultural class." Purchasing slaves would greatly increase the capitalization of factories; hiring poor whites would therefore be cheaper in the long run. Moreover, Hammond "seriously doubted whether . . . extensive employment [of slaves] in manufactures and mechanic arts, is consistent with safe and sound policy. Whenever a slave is made a mechanic," he feared, "he is more than half freed, and soon becomes, as we too well know, and all history attests . . . the most corrupt and turbulent of his class." Thus exhuming the ghost of Denmark Vesey and raising the specter of the collapse of the planter class, Hammond concluded with this astute analysis:

> . . . it has been suggested, that white factory operatives in the South would constitute a body hostile to our domestic institutions. If any such sentiments could take root among the poorer classes of our native citizens, more danger may be apprehended from them, in the present state of things . . . than if they were brought together in factories, with constant employment and adequate remuneration. . . . But all apprehensions from this source are entirely imaginary. The poorest and humblest freeman of the South feels as sensibly, perhaps more sensibly than the wealthiest planter, the barrier which nature, as well as law, has erected between the white and black races, and would scorn as much to submit to the universal degradation which must follow, whenever it is broken down.
>
> Besides this, the [white] factory operative could not fail to see here . . . that the whole fabric of his fortunes was based on our slave system, since it is only by slave labor that cotton ever has been, or ever can be, cheaply or extensively produced. Thus, not only from natural sentiment and training, but from convictions of self interest . . . this class of our citizens might be relied on to

sustain, as firmly and faithfully as any other, the social institutions of the South. . . .[25]

Hammond's reasoning was carried to its logical conclusion by the Virginia intellectual, George Fitzhugh, in 1854. "The poor . . . constitute our militia and our police. . . . They secure men in possession of a kind of property [slaves] which they could not hold for a day but for the supervision and protection of the poor," warned Fitzhugh in his *Sociology for the South*. "Educate all Southern whites, employ them not as lackeys, ploughmen, and menials, but as independent freemen should be employed, and let negroes be strictly tied down to such callings as are unbecoming to white men, and peace would be established between blacks and whites." [26] To Hammond and Fitzhugh, therefore, white solidarity would resolve class and caste conflicts in the South. Racial antagonisms between poor whites and Negro slaves would always subsume class antagonisms between Labor and Capital.

The Gregg-Hammond-Fitzhugh position did not go unchallenged for long, however. C. G. Memminger, the brilliant Charlestonian who would become the Confederacy's Secretary of the Treasury, saw to that. With great prophecy, Memminger warned Hammond against excluding slaves from industry and against creating a free white working class:

> . . . in this State and City . . . I find an opinion gaining ground that slaves ought to be excluded from mechanical pursuits, and everything but agriculture, so as to have their places filled with whites; and ere long we will have a formidable party on this subject. The planters generally do not perceive how it affects their interest, and very frequently chime in with this cry. I think our friend Gregg of Graniteville, with those who are agog about manufactures, without knowing it, are lending aid to this party, which is in truth, the only party from which dan-

ger to our Institutions is to be apprehended among us. Drive out negro mechanics and all sorts of operatives from our Cities, and who must take their place. The same men who make the cry in the Northern Cities against the tyranny of Capital—and there as here would drive all before them all who interfere with them—and would soon raise hue and cry against the Negro, and be hot Abolitionists—and every one of those men would have a vote. In our Cities, we see the operation of these elements —and if the eyes of the planting community are opened, the danger may be averted. Fill Barnwell District with some hundred Lowellers, and how do you think they will vote at elections. The scheme by which "Brutus" has expected to foment division among us is based on this element of Discord. For you know that even in our lower Country, there are many that could be Marshalled against the Planter, upon the idea that they were fighting against the aristocracy. These things I have no doubt you will keep in a view. But I think you would do much good by giving a timely warning to our agricultural community. . . .[27]

Memminger's fears were shared by many other leading Southerners. Chancellor William Harper, the famous proslavery ideologist from South Carolina, openly advocated the use of slaves in industry in order to guard society from the white working classes. Slaves "may be commanded and combined with more facility than any other sort of labor," warned Harper in his *Memoir on Slavery*; "and the laborer, kept in stricter subordination, will be less dangerous to the security of society than in any other country, which is crowded and overstocked with a class of what are called free laborers." Slaves are not only cheaper than whites to employ in factories, added "A Mississippi Planter," but "there is no haggling or striking for wages, no contention about hours. Uniformity, obedience, and wholesome discipline, mark the [black] labor of the South."

Planters and their friends at the several commercial conventions of the 1840's and 1850's usually supported these views.[28]

The foregoing controversy was related in part to current political activity by white artisans in several southern states and cities. Free craftsmen had long been attempting to exclude blacks from certain skilled trades and to replace them with all-white working forces. White journeymen, for example, sometimes refused to employ slave artisans on public works. "From my experience with coloured workmen," wrote one contractor to the commissioners for the new capitol at Raleigh, North Carolina, in 1839, "I must state that with them, I do not think I could perform to your satisfaction what the state requires in the execution of the building." [29] "I wish to bring out and introduce upon the works *white laborers* from the North," implored the Lieutenant of Engineers constructing Fort Marion, Florida, to the Army's Chief of Engineers the same year, "as the laborers I have at present (slaves) are of the most worthless kind . . . as no others can be obtained in the vicinity, and the owners of slaves are very unwilling to have them at a distance from themselves. I believe," concluded the Lieutenant, "that the plan above proposed would obviate such difficulties in future." [30] Such suggestions were rarely followed, however, since white laborers were generally less reliable and more expensive than slaves and since planters insisted on employing bondsmen.[31]

As white craftsmen began to organize so-called "mechanics associations," they increasingly protested against the employment of slaves in skilled trades. They also fought against privileges extended to slave artisans, such as "board-money" payments, which allowed blacks to live away from their work places, and "self-hire," which permitted slaves to "hire out their own time." To abolish these practices white artisans resorted to a variety of tactics, which sometimes included violence. In 1857, in Wilmington, North Carolina, for example, free carpenters burned a structure recently built by slaves and posted a warning that all buildings erected by slaves in the future would receive similar treatment.[32] More often, white mechanics lobbied for local legislation to exclude slaves from certain crafts.[33] However, only in a few areas, such as Georgia, did white artisans obtain significant legislation, as when in 1833 the Assembly forbade printers to employ slave compositors and, in 1845 black craftsmen—free or slave—were prohibited from erecting or repairing buildings.[34] In Richmond, in 1858, "board-money" payments to slave tobacco workers were finally regulated after a long campaign by the *Dispatch*.[35] In almost every other region white mechanics failed to make legislative headway against slave craftsmen. For instance, in 1859, a South Carolina legislative committee rejected a petition from white artisans, with the proclamation: "We are, as a slaveholding people, habituated to slave labor. Slave labor constitutes, and ought to constitute, the bulk of the agricultural and domestic labor of our State."[36] By 1861, Georgia's white mechanics had failed to strengthen the law of 1845.[37]

Though some historians have suggested that these protests by white craftsmen implied opposition to slavery, such implications have been exaggerated.[38] Objectively, such attitudes may have been anti-slavery, but they were not difficult to assimilate into a slaveholding society. White artisans did not object to the use of slaves in *all* industrial occupations, only to their use in certain skilled crafts. White artisans did not seek to abolish slavery altogether, only to exclude Negroes from certain trades and to curtail such pernicious practices as board-money payments and self-hire privileges. Indeed, such protests were often led by prominent proslavery newspapers which desired neither to abolish slavery nor to use free labor in industries. Such forces really wanted to strengthen slavery by curbing specific abuses. The net effect of most protests by white artisans was thus not to weaken slavery but to entrench it more firmly in southern society.

These effects and implications were clearly understood by slave employers and white artisans alike. Richmond's tobacco manufacturers willingly acceded to the regulation of board-money payments to their slaves because they understood that such reforms did not threaten slave ownership. The Jackson, Mississippi, Mechanical Association—an organization of white artisans—resolved in December 1858:

> . . . our fidelity to the institution of slavery is unques-tionable. . . . We believe that there is not by reason of the institution and should not be any antagonism between free and slave labor in the South, but that they can and should harmonize and assist each other. And for the furtherance of this state of affairs, we express it as our opinion that the suppression of the practice of making public mechanics of negroes would operate advanta-geously not only to the white mechanics, but would tend to strengthen the institution of slavery itself. . . .[39]

Leaders of southern industry thus faced difficult dilemmas and had to make far-reaching decisions. If either slaves or poor whites were transferred from agricultural to industrial work, then the existing southern political and social structures might be subverted. However, if both slaves and whites were main-tained in agricultural pursuits, then industries would not de-velop at all. Yet, if poor whites were continually denied access to landownership and slaveholding, they might become op-posed to the institution of slavery. And if white craftsmen were forced continually to compete against skilled Negroes, they might, as Memminger warned, organize a formidable anti-slavery party. In theory, therefore, Southerners seemed damned if they did create industries and damned if they did not.

In practice, southern industrial leaders managed to reach several compromises concerning occupational patterns of black and white workers. Similar to the arrangements of the so-called New South Period, these understandings provided that poor whites would be employed mainly in upcountry textile factories; slaves would be employed in most other industries—light and heavy—exclusively, as well as in most low country cotton mills. Blacks would be confined to menial, dirty, and hazardous industrial occupations—"nigger work," as it was called, while whites in textile mills would enjoy the "benefits" of capitalist benevolence. White artisans would be granted exclusive work privileges to some, but not all, building trades; slave artisans would be prohibited from competing with skilled whites in certain crafts. By thus bringing some poor whites and white craftsmen into the mainstream of economic life, Southerners believed that politics would remain stable, slavery would remain intact, and industry could develop.

Industrial leaders also grappled with the knottiest issue of the 1840's and 1850's—territorial and economic expansionism. Southern expansionism stemmed from many causes—specifically, soil exhaustion in the seaboard slave states, the waning of southern political power, the desire to establish "buffer zones" against hostile political and economic concentrations in the free states and elsewhere, and the need to provide land for restless, pushy, and grasping slaveowners and yeoman farmers. But some Southerners also assumed—as Eugene Genovese has pointed out—that expansion would enable them to use slave labor in mining and sugar milling in Mexico and the Caribbean.[40] Other businessmen were more interested in using slave labor in mining, lumbering, and transportation enterprises in the American West. A direct relationship therefore existed between the industrial uses of slave labor and southern expansionism.

Southerners had long desired to use slaves in western mining ventures. In the early 1810's, Southerners pressured the Illinois Territory into permitting the use of slaves in the salt mines at Shawneetown. Illinois residents and Southerners alike reasoned that Negroes were better suited than white men to withstand salt mine labor. Thus, slaves were eventually allowed, with their masters' consent, to enter Illinois and "to hire themselves out" at the salines on an annual basis. Upon the bondsmen's return home, the masters received most of the "wages." Illinois also adopted "indenture" laws permitting slaveowners to bring their slaves into the territory under lifetime contracts. Largely the work of former Southerners, these laws and practices met little objection from a federal government directed by southern Presidents.[41]

In the 1820's, when gold was discovered in the southern Piedmont, slaveowning Carolinians and Georgians attempted time and again to abrogate federal treaties protecting Indian lands to the west. Despite federal prohibitions, slaveowners illegally entered the Cherokee Territory and began digging gold. ". . . My worthy friend," begged one miner to President Andrew Jackson, "the object of this letter is to crave your friendly permission for myself to dig for Gold in the Cherokee Country. I have three sons and as many son in laws living not far distant from me," the slaveowner stated, "and we can spare among us forty strong and active [black] hands and still retain a force sufficient to make our bread, and that is all we can do in a country like ours where we cannot grow Cotton or Tobacco. . . ." By 1835, slaveowning miners had occupied Indian lands, while the Cherokees were being prodded along the "Trail of Tears." [42]

By the late 1840's, Southerners were anxious to work mines

in Mexican territories and to keep the gold, silver, copper, and rock mines of California, New Mexico, and Utah within slave territories or states. Along with other "forty-niners" slave-owners came to California seeking wealth, and, by 1850, several hundred slaves were already at work in the gold mining districts. Since many whites considered slave labor unfair competition, especially after some bondsmen helped their masters strike it rich, slavery became an important issue in early California politics. The slavery expansion issue surfaced at the California constitutional convention of 1849, where it was, along with the related issue of Negro exclusion, the chief topic of debate. Several delegates said they had received letters from slaveowners inquiring about the attitude toward bondage in California and declaring their intention of emigrating if their property could be assured of protection. Others argued against slavery because it could out-compete free labor and would eventually leave a residue of free blacks in the state. In the end, the convention unanimously prohibited slavery and barely defeated Negro exclusion.[43]

The relationship between southern expansionism and slave-based mining was also manifest during the congressional debates of 1849–50 over the status of California. "I hold that the pursuit of gold-washing and mining is better adapted to slave labor than to any other species of labor recognized among us," declared Jefferson Davis. Another Mississippi representative feared that California's gold mines would be seized by Free Soilers and lost to the South; Representative Albert Gallatin Brown reiterated to his Mississippi constituents that slave labor was so admirably suited to mining that California should be made a slave state.[44] In spite of such rhetoric, California entered the Union in 1850 as a free state.

The exclusion of slavery from California did not prevent its continued existence in the state after 1850, however. White settlers did not demand the strict enforcement of prohibition and many slaves were unaware that they could claim their freedom. More important, Southerners made further attempts to introduce slavery as late as 1851, when over twelve hundred citizens of South Carolina and Florida petitioned the California Legislature for permission to settle in the state with their slaves. Similarly, James Gadsden, the former president of the slaveowning South Carolina Railroad and the soon-to-be minister to Mexico, attempted to found a slaveowning colony in California. "I was much disappointed at not having recd the result of my Memorial to Your Legislature," Gadsden confided to Thomas Jefferson Green, a Southerner who had earlier mined gold in California with his slaves and then become a state legislator. "But if it is responded to favourably You may rest assured it will be the stimulating basis for the Organization of a Colony under my lead, . . . a colony which is to be the basis and stimulating influences to the permanent & future prosperity of California—Negro Slavery under Educated & Intelligent Masters can alone accomplish this," Gadsden continued. "They have been the Pioneers & basis of the civilization of Savage Countries—Without an enduring & well regulated labor the agricultural resources of the Pacific will never be developed—and a profitable agriculture is the foundation of a nations prosperity, happiness & wealth— The Mines may & will prove powerful auxiliaries: & combined with the Cultivation of the Soil must make California all that the Most Sanguine & Even Romantic have pictured. . . . So I am in Earnest if you only make the grants. . . ." Though such ambitions came to naught, slavery expansion still remained a political issue in California until the late 1850's.[45]

Free-soil congressmen were aware of southern schemes to capture western mines for slavery. "As to California, I am equally clear," responded Oregon's well-traveled congressional delegate to a query by Horace Mann of Massachusetts. "California will always be a mining country, and wages will range high. At present slave labor in California would be . . . profitable. . . . And I have always been of the opinion, that wherever there is a mining country, if not in a climate uncongenial to slave labor, that species of labor would be profitable. That it would be in California mines, is evident. That these whole regions are filled with rich mines, is little less than certain, and that they can be run with slave labor is sure. Hence, were I a southern man and my property invested in slaves," he concluded, "I should consider the markets of New Mexico, Utah, and California, for slave labor, worthy of an honorable contest to secure." Mann himself surmised that "mines are the favorite sphere for slavery, as the ocean is for commerce." [46]

The loss of the gold mines when California became a free state severely shocked many Southerners. At the Nashville disunion convention of 1850, for example, it was resolved that "California is peculiarly adapted for slave labor." Mississippi's Governor John A. Quitman, the slaveowning woodyard operator, cried to a special legislative session in 1850:

> . . . The value of slaves depends upon the demand for their labor. The history of the cultivation of our great staples shows that this value is permanently enhanced by the opening of new fields of labor. The immense profits which have and still continue to reward well directed industry in the gold mines of California, exceed those which have ever flowed from mere labor, inexhaustible in extent and indefinite in duration. Had this wide field for investment been open to the slave labor of the Southern States, wages would have risen, and consequently the value of slaves at home would have been greatly enhanced. Many hundreds of millions of dollars would have been added to the capital of the Southern States. . .

> These estimates of pecuniary interest . . . are founded
> upon the fixed opinion of almost every well informed
> person among us. . . .

If free-soil agitators had not interfered, complained a North
Carolina congressman in 1850, Southerners would have been
able to work the gold mines of California with their slaves and
they would soon have secured it as a slave state.[47]

Throughout the last antebellum decade, Southerners
mourned the loss of western mines. "We said, three years ago,
in a public journal," wailed the Richmond *Dispatch* in 1852,
"that California would be sure to remove every restriction
that could be placed upon her by the general government;
and that she would be the largest slaveholder of all the States.
The thing seemed to us so palpable that we could not see how
any man could doubt it. What makes Louisiana and Texas
such large slaveholders?" asked the *Dispatch*. "—Why, the remuneration received for slave labor. What makes any country
a slaveholding country? The prospect of gain. And where can
slave labor be so profitably employed as in the gold mines of
California? . . . The only way to develop the resources of
a piece of gold property belonging to an individual," concluded the editor, "is to employ slaves." [48] "I want Cuba, I
want Tamaulipas, Potosi, and one or two other Mexican
[mining] states," raged Mississippi's Albert Gallatin Brown
in 1858, "and I want them all for the same reason—for the
planting or spreading of slavery." If slaves were excluded
from territorial mines, moaned a Mobile citizen, as late as
1860, "it would present a case of monstrous injustice." Pointing
to the mineral wealth in New Mexico, Arizona, and even,
potentially, Kansas, the Charleston *Mercury* concluded: "The
right to have property protected in the territory is not a mere
abstraction without application or practical value. . . . When
gold mines were discovered, slaveholders at the South saw
that, with their command of labor, it would be easy at a

The Gold Hill Mine

moderate outlay to make fortunes digging gold. . . . There is no vocation in the world in which slavery can be more useful and profitable than in mining." [49]

Southerners also promoted expansionism to be able to use slave labor in western lumbering and in Caribbean sugar milling enterprises. ". . . There are many more places [besides western Florida and southern Alabama] where [saw] mills may be erected very advantageously—" confided one Carolinian to another in 1854. "You have the facts as they have been told me and you can judge of the results. I have no doubt . . . that more money can be made in this business [cypress and juniper lumbering and sawmilling] than any other when [slave] manual labor is used in the S. West." [50] Southern sugar millers frequently advocated the annexation of Cuba, despite fears of glutted markets. In the 1850's, some Louisiana planters even moved to Cuba to invest in sugar milling; they also realized that Cuban sugar production would complement that of the slave states and that Cuban blacks could be brought to the mainland to work. In any event, seizing Cuba and the Southwest would strengthen the political power of the slave states.[51]

For much the same ends southern expansionists also proposed to construct transcontinental railroads with slave labor. Southwestern lines would tap the Pacific Coast and Oriental trade for southern merchants and cities, and, according to one Texan, a "Mississippi and Pacific" railroad would turn the western territories into slave states by making mining districts accessible to slave labor. "Now as to the route," wrote James Gadsden in 1851 concerning a railroad to a California slave colony, "I shall go by land & endeavor to be the pioneer on the Route I indicated for a Railroad. . . . I should like to know . . . whether Vehicles can descent the valley of the Gehela. . . . We will . . . make our Road as we go by an organized Corps of Pioneers & Axe men & reach California with both Negroes and animals in full vigor to go to work. . . . The neighbourhood of San Diego has presented attractions—& the Mouth of the Colorado with the Gila: an imposing Point," concluded Gadsden. "That Point if accessible would control the Gulf of California." [52]

By the mid-1850's, the United States had acquired the Gila River valley with Gadsden's Purchase, Secretary of War Jefferson Davis had surveyed a southerly transcontinental route, and southern expansionists had begun to construct this railroad through Texas with slave labor. "A considerable amount of the companies Lands along the line of the road may be settled with the old [,] the youth &/ females [slaves belong to the company]," wrote Thomas Jefferson Green to the Southern Pacific Railroad's executive committee, of which he was a member, in 1856. "A considerable number of hands (negroes) are at work on this road [The Southern Pacific]," a prominent Texas physician reminded his legislature the same year. "The importance of pushing forward the construction of this road cannot be overestimated for the South. Being built by slave labor it insures a tier of slaveholding States along its line to the Pacific Ocean." [53]

While some Southerners promoted expansionism, others attempted to reopen the African slave trade to provide labor for slave-based industries, to increase southern political power, and as a panacea for southern sorrows. As early as 1853, South Carolina slave trade advocates claimed that African emigration would lower slave prices so that slaveless yeomen would be able to become masters. Reviving the slave trade would thereby strengthen slavery, broaden slave ownership, and reduce tensions between slaveowners and non-slaveowners. If Negro bondage was a "positive good," reasoned the slave traders from the proslavery argument, then the constitutional prohibition against African slave trading should be rescinded or circumvented.[54] The slave traders also proposed to use slaves—native or imported—to industrialize the South. Reopening the African slave trade—one of the most reactionary proposals of the 1850's—was thus related to the campaign for industrial slavery.

This relationship was evident in the propaganda of the movement to revive slave trade. In his legislative message of November 24, 1856, South Carolina's Governor James H. Adams, for example, held that African slaves were "necessary to the full development of our whole round of agricultural and mechanical resources. . . . It is much better that our drays should be driven by slaves—that our factories should be worked by slaves—that our hotels should be served by slaves—that our locomotives should be manned by slaves," concluded Adams, "than that we should be exposed to the introduction, from any quarter, of a population alien to us by birth, training, and education, and which, in the process of time, must lead to . . . conflict between capital and labor." [55]

Executing transportation projects with African slaves was proposed by other slave-trade advocates. "A Countryman" urged Virginia to import fifty thousand Africans under a one-hundred-year "apprenticeship" program to complete public works without further public funding. "As to the trouble of taming the young [slave] barbarians," editorialized the Richmond *Whig*, which supported the same proposal, "we have a great number of public works, which would be just the places for breaking to harness some million or two of these wild colts." [56] Meanwhile, a Louisiana legislative committee reported:

> . . . The demand for an increased amount of labor is not asserted alone in the cultivation of cotton and sugar in the soil of Louisiana. It is . . . in various channels of industrial enterprise . . . pressing and imperative. . . . It must be apparent to all that no species of labor can possibly be better adapted to various works of internal improvement in our State, or for constructing and building up the railroads of the Southern states. [57]

The favorite scheme of some slave-trade advocates was to use Africans in southern and western mining enterprises. "I have an interest in a gold mine whose work requires no very great intelligence, and which yields from two to four dollars a day to the hand," confided one Carolinian. "I am now purchasing negroes at from eight hundred to eleven hundred dollars each. If I could have an opportunity of purchasing some one or two thousand at about two hundred dollars each, I . . . could even find it in my heart to take them with a knowledge that they had come from Africa. We want labor, and only labor," he concluded, "to a most rapid and astonishing de-

velopment of wealth." Valuable mineral deposits exist in the
Piedmont and in Arkansas, Missouri, and Arizona, claimed a
Georgia State University professor. "All I ask or contemplate
is to take a million of men and women, now worthless in
Africa, and make their labor so productive in working the
now unproductive gold, copper, iron, coal, and other mines
in the Southern states, as to cause these mines to pay a good
interest on a thousand million dollars at their just valuation. . . ." [58]

Most proponents of reopening the African slave trade were
conscious of the connection between developing southern industry and achieving southern independence. Some slave traders thus advocated shifting American slaves into industry and
replenishing the plantations with African bondsmen. Imported
blacks should build levees and railroads, advised the Jackson
Mississippian, while "seasoned" slaves were shunted from the
fields to the factories. Others, like the chairman of the South
Carolina legislature's Committee on the Slave Trade, favored
confining Africans to agriculture so that yeoman farmers
could obtain industrial work. In either case, most slavetraders
probably believed, along with C. W. Miller of South Carolina,
that "labor is needed for . . . making railroads, for manufactures, and the mechanic arts. It is a proposition too well
proved, that no nation can attain the highest degree of liberty,
independence and power without the trinity of agriculture,
manufactures and commerce. Agriculture alone will not make
us entirely independent," concluded Miller, "and slave labor
may well be employed in manufactures and the preparatory
departments of commerce . . . and if slave labor should become redundant in agriculture, it might and would be made
a great blessing to our country when a portion of it should be
diverted into numerous other occupations in aid of our national protection and independence." [59]

Gaining considerable support, the movement to revive the

slave trade reached its height in the deep South states in 1858 and 1859. The Louisiana legislature narrowly defeated an African Apprenticeship Bill at this time, while the Southern Commercial Conventions at Montgomery and Vicksburg vigorously debated whether the slave trade should be reopened. At Montgomery the leading advocate of reopening the African slave trade, Leonidas W. Spratt, editor of the Charleston *Standard*, held that "intelligence is necessary to the construction of the machine, and to its operation; and the negro, in his common absence from reflection, is perhaps the best manupalatist in the world." [60] If the slave trade were revived, wrote a Mississippian to the Vicksburg delegates, "We would build our own vessels and steamboats, railroads and dirt roads, erect manufactories, and foundries, build our levees and dikes, beautify and make comfortable our dwelling houses and negro cabins, and fling over the whole face of our country a smiling cheerfulness which is always evidence of prosperity and happiness." After much discussion the Vicksburg meeting finally supported the proposal to revive the African slave trade. [61]

Vicksburg marked a Pyrrhic victory, however, for by 1860 leading secessionists had realized that the African slave trade issue was becoming a political liability. Reopening the slave trade could create intense political feelings, and it promised that every Southerner would be able to afford to own a slave. But it also threatened drastically to devalue existing slave property and thus further to divide the upper South, dependent upon the domestic slave trade, from the lower South, demanding more slaves. Increasingly preoccupied with exploiting the fears raised by John Brown's Raid and the rise of Black Republicanism, such fire-eaters as Robert Barnwell Rhett, whose Charleston *Mercury* had once embraced the proposal to revive the slave trade, now deserted this issue and permitted it to fall by the wayside of the road to secession. [62]

Though the process of disunion in 1860–61 has received much attention, the relationships between secessionism, slave-based industries, and the campaign for southern self-sufficiency have received little study. If it was hardly coincidental that the concepts of slave-based industry and disunion partly entwined during the Nullification Controversy of 1832–33, it should not be surprising that many industrial slaveowners became disunionists during the 1850's and actively supported a war for southern independence in the 1860's. Indeed, the idea of slave-based industries became especially evident during the disunion crises of 1849–50 and that of 1860–61.

By the time of the Compromise of 1850, one of the central themes of southern nationalism had become economic self-sufficiency [63]—a theme which implied, directly or indirectly, developing local industry by means of slave labor. "Your intention of placing the subject of manufacturing fairly before the people of the State," wrote a reader of the Jackson *Mississippian* in 1849, "cannot be too highly appreciated, as they have been too long . . . making themselves tributary to the North. . . ." "The Effects of Secession," responded the editor a year later, would enable slave craftsmen to fabricate products—boots, shoes, carriages, iron goods—previously produced in the North. Southern independence would also stimulate manufactures, allow full utilization of slave capital, and prevent funds from leaving the South.[64] Similarly, it was reported to the Mississippi Legislature in 1850 that the slave-owning Southern Railroad served to unite the South commercially and to prevent domestic insurrection and external invasion. Concerning "Slavery and Manufacturing"—"a subject fraught with the most important consequences to the people of slaveholding states"—a Tennessee industrial promoter wrote,

> . . . the true policy of the South is distinct and clearly marked. She must resort to the same means by which

power has been accumulated at the North, to secure it for herself. She must embark in that system of manufacturing which has been so successfully employed at the North. We hold the raw material, and if we will but go into its manufacture, we can control the world. . . . It will place us in a condition to dictate our own terms. The manufactories will increase our population; increased population and wealth will enable us to chain the Southern states proudly and indissolubly together by railroads and other internal improvements, and these works by affording speedy communication from point to point, will prove our surest defence either against foreign aggression or domestic revolt. . . . And above all it will enable us to defend successfully, those rights guaranteed to us by the constitution; and if the evil day should ever come, when the South shall be satisfied that she cannot remain in the Union upon equal terms, or with safety to her institutions, it will place her in a condition to maintain her separate nationality.[65]

After the Compromise of 1850, *De Bow's Review* continued to publish articles analyzing the political and economic options facing the South and stressing the theme of self-sufficiency. In one especially thoughtful piece the author acknowledged that while the slave population was increasing so rapidly that it might become "excessive," Southerners did not have equal access to the territory won from Mexico so that the further expansion of slavery had become impossible. Since "slavery is confined within its present limits, the rapid increase in the number of slaves will compel the southern people to employ their slaves in the manufacture of such articles as are now made almost exclusively in the northern states," he reasoned. "In this way the slave labor of the South will . . . become the successful competitor of northern white labor . . . [and] we will be compelled to use the surplus black population in cotton and woolen factories [and] in iron furnaces. . . . [But] we will have for our market place the whole habitable globe, and all the people of the earth will be our customers. . . . The remedies then which we propose," the nationalist concluded, "are the employment of slave labor in the construction of rail-roads throughout the southern states, and the use of negroes in our factories and in our work-shops." [66]

In the late 1850's, as southern nationalism intensified, seces-sionists increasingly championed the employment of slave labor to help create southern industries. "Slave labor is certain to enable the South to manufacture so as to undersell the rest of the world," editorialized the New Orleans *Picayune* in 1858. A year later, another secessionist painted this picture of southern independence for a group of Georgians interested in reviving the slave trade:

> If the South would but . . . shake off those restrictions that cramp her energies, a bright future awaits her. Her rich valleys will be cultivated, her streams bridged and her rivers levied, her plains traversed by Railroads, and dotted with villages. . . . Her forests will be disturbed by the sound of the woodman's axe, accompanied by the hum of the factory and the shrill snort of the locomotive. In short, she would be what she ought to be, a progres-sive, prosperous and powerful country, able to command respect in the Union, or if need be, defend herself out of it.

"We think it rigidly demonstrable," wrote "Washington City" to *De Bow's Review* in May, 1860, "that the ultimate result of disunion would be to give increased activity and impetus to every branch of Southern industry." [67]

The relationships between disunion and slave-based indus-try were also expressed by many slaveowning manufacturers who became secessionists in the 1850's and supporters of the Confederacy in the 1860's. Georgia's Governor Charles J.

McDonald, a slaveowning textile manufacturer, joined the pro-secession faction of the Nashville disunion convention as early as 1850. Duff Green, the famous industrial promoter, was devoted first to John C. Calhoun and later to southern nationhood. Henry W. Collier, a leading Alabama cotton miller, preached moderation as Governor from 1849 to 1853, but he joined William Lowndes Yancey's secessionist faction by the end of the 1850's. Robert L. Caruthers, a prominent Tennessee textile manufacturer, likewise shifted from early unionism in time to be chosen a confederate governor in 1861.[68]

Similarly, William W. Harlee, president of the slave-employing Wilmington and Manchester Railroad, voted for immediate secession at the South Carolina disunion convention in December, 1860. Mark A. Cooper, a leading Georgia iron manufacturer, became an ardent advocate of southern economic independence. Joseph Reid Anderson, president of the slaveowning Tredegar Iron Works of Richmond, Virginia, eagerly became the "Ironmaker to the Confederacy." And Barrington King, a slaveowning Georgia textile miller, privately confided during the height of the secession crisis that "unless that abolition spirit is put down in the north, our only safety is to form a Southern Confederacy. . . . Water and oil cannot be united." [69]

Most southern industrialists may have been cautious about disunion or politically inactive, but many of them were in the forefront of southern nationalism. For the evidence indicates that those industrialists present at the secession conventions of 1860–61 were usually secessionists, either of the "immediatist" or "co-operationist" variety. Moreover, other industrialists, including William Gregg, Rufus L. Patterson, and Robert Jemison, Jr., to name but a few, signed their states' ordinances of secession and thereby lent their tacit support to the designs of the disunionists.[70]

After secession, many slaveowning manufacturers who had only reluctantly acceded to disunion became active supporters of the Confederacy—indicating further the link between industrial slavery and southern nationalism. Rufus Barringer, the prominent North Carolina manufacturer became a famous rebel army general. The Bell-Yeatman family, which controlled one of the largest slaveowning iron works in middle Tennessee, became a staunch backer of southern nationhood. More than a score of other industrialists served in the Confederate Congress.[71] Governor Francis W. Pickens, however, perhaps best summed up the sentiments of the secessionists in his November, 1861, message to the South Carolina Assembly. "True war is a great calamity," he wrote, "but if this war shall end, as there is every prospect that it will do, by making us not only independent of our most deadly enemies, but commercially independent also, and at the same time, shall develop our own artisan skill and mechanical labor, so as to place us entirely beyond their subsidy hereafter, then, indeed, will it prove, in the end, a public blessing." [72]

By the time of secession in 1861, the use of slave labor to industrialize the South had become accepted in theory and practice. This movement—to "bring the cotton mills to the cotton fields," so to speak—did not begin suddenly in the 1840's or even in the 1880's, as some historians have suggested. Industries emerged at least as early as the 1790's, and the campaigns for industry became most intense when Southerners felt least secure within the Union. The greatest interest in slave-based industries thus occurred from the late 1820's to the early 1830's, when southern agriculture was in difficulty, the tariff controversy raged, and when the South was coming under intense moral criticism. Interest also developed during the late 1840's and 1850's, when anti-slavery parties emerged and the sectional conflict was most bitter.

By the time of the Civil War, the struggle for southern self-sufficiency had reached a climax. Slaveowning agriculturists were now vigorously campaigning for slave-based industrialization and they were investing some of their surplus capital in southern industries. Such men, who included many influential Southerners, had overcome their traditional agrarianism and whatever backward-looking tendencies they may have had. They were seeking to create a balanced economy in which the South's great natural potential for agriculture would be complemented by its opportunities for extracting, processing, manufacturing, and transporting its resources and staples. Indeed, one reason why they wanted to expand slavery into the territories, and if possible to reopen the African slave trade, was to accelerate the development of southern industries.

Slaveowners were determined to industrialize the South under their own auspices exclusively, however, so that existing class and caste relationships would remain unchanged. They therefore opposed the creation not only of a slaveless industrial bourgeoisie independent of planter control, but also of a free industrial labor force. Had either of these two groups come into being, it might have challenged the slaveowners' domination of southern society. Unless slaveowners directed industries themselves, their ultimate security as a class was in jeopardy.

To maintain their hegemony, slaveowners insisted that slaves continue to be the chief labor force in southern industries. Long experience had demonstrated that bondsmen were more tractable, efficient, and profitable than alternative labor forces. The proslavery ideology also dictated that slaves were less troublesome than whites and better suited to work in tropical climates. Slaveowners also stymied the challenges of poor whites and free artisans by permitting the former to work in some textile mills and the latter to compete with some slave craftsmen. Finally, slaveowning agriculturists insisted that they themselves, or their allies, should continue to control southern industries, in order to prevent the emergence of independent entrepreneurial groups. Industrialists hoped that by these arrangements caste conflicts would continue to subsume class conflicts and that slaveowners would remain the dominant class.[73]

Industrially minded Southerners also came into conflict with their northern counterparts for various reasons. Since southern industries lagged behind those of the North and trading patterns seemed unfair, slave employers had great difficulty competing in market places. The use of slave labor in industries helped reduce these disadvantages, but it could not overcome lost time entirely. The political power of slaveowners within the Union also seemed threatened by outsiders, as the North's population increased, as the Abolitionist attack became more shrill, as more and more free states entered the Union, and especially as the Republican Party—dedicated at least to the containment of slavery in the states—gained ground.

As a result, by the 1850's, many Southerners felt frustrated so long as they remained within a hostile Union. They believed that economic self-sufficiency, territorial expansion, the continuance of slavery, and their political survival depended on southern independence and could only be achieved by disunion. Slave-based industrialization and slave-state nationalism had, by 1861, entwined in a bloody struggle for southern sovereignty. Industrial slavery had, in this sense, directly contributed to the coming of the Civil War.

Notes

Key to Abbreviations in the Notes

JOURNALS

AH . . . Agricultural History

AHA . . . American Historical Association

AHQ . . . Alabama Historical Quarterly

BHS Bulletin . . . Business Historical Society Bulletin

CHR . . . Cotton History Review

DH . . . Delaware History

EEH . . . Explorations in Entrepreneurial History

FHQ . . . Florida Historical Quarterly

FCHQ . . . Filson Club History Quarterly

GHQ . . . Georgia Historical Quarterly

JEH . . . Journal of Economic History

JMH . . . Journal of Mississippi History

JNH . . . Journal of Negro History

JPE . . . Journal of Political Economy

JSH . . . Journal of Southern History

KHSR . . . Kentucky Historical Society Register

LHQ . . . Louisiana Historical Quarterly

MdHM . . . Maryland Historical Magazine

MVHR . . . Mississippi Valley Historical Review

NCHR . . . North Carolina Historical Review

PSQ . . . Political Science Quarterly

R&LHS Bulletin . . . Railway and Locomotive Historical Society Bulletin

SAQ . . . South Atlantic Quarterly

SCHA Proceedings . . . South Carolina Historical Association Proceedings

SCHM . . . South Carolina Historical Magazine

THQ . . . Tennessee Historical Quarterly
THR . . . Textile History Review
VMH . . . Virginia Magazine of History and Biography
WMQ . . . William and Mary Quarterly

MANUSCRIPTS

AA . . . Alabama Department of Archives and History, Montgomery
Baker . . . Baker Library, Harvard University, Cambridge, Mass.
CLS . . . Charleston Library Society, Charleston, S.C.
Clemson . . . Clemson University Library, Clemson, S.C.
Columbia . . . Columbia University Library, New York City
Duke . . . Duke University Library, Durham, N.C.
Emory . . . Emory University Library, Atlanta, Georgia
Filson . . . The Filson Club, Louisville, Ky.
GA . . . Georgia Department of Archives and History, Atlanta
GHS . . . Georgia Historical Society, Savannah
Houghton . . . Houghton Library, Harvard University, Cambridge, Mass.
HPL . . . Huntsville Public Library, Huntsville, Ala.
Huntington . . . Huntington Library, San Marino, Calif.
LC . . . Library of Congress, Washington, D.C.
LSU . . . Louisiana State University Library, Baton Rouge
MA . . . Mississippi Department of Archives and History, Jackson
MCH . . . Mobile City Hall, Mobile, Ala.
MdHS . . . Maryland Historical Society, Baltimore
MoHS . . . Missouri Historical Society, St. Louis
NA . . . National Archives, Washington, D.C.
NCA . . . North Carolina Department of Archives and History, Raleigh
NOPL . . . New Orleans Public Library, New Orleans, La.
NYPL . . . New York Public Library, New York City
SCA . . . South Carolina Archives, Columbia
SCHS . . . South Carolina Historical Society, Charleston
TSL . . . Tennessee State Library, Nashville
Tulane . . . Tulane University Library, New Orleans, La.
UA . . . University of Alabama Library, Tuscaloosa
UG . . . University of Georgia Library, Athens
UK . . . University of Kentucky Library, Lexington
UMo . . . Western Historical Collection, University of Missouri

Library, Columbia

UNC . . . Southern Historical Collection, University of North
Carolina Library, Chapel Hill

USC . . . South Caroliniana Library, University of South Carolina,
Columbia

UT . . . University of Tennessee Library, Knoxville

UV . . . Alderman Library, University of Virginia, Charlottesville

VHS . . . Virginia Historical Society, Richmond

VSL . . . Virginia State Library, Richmond

WSHS . . . State Historical Society of Wisconsin, Madison

Chapter One: Slavery and Industry in the Old South

1. D. North, *The Economic Growth of the United States* (Englewood Cliffs, N.J., 1961), tables; S. Bruchey, ed., *Cotton and the Growth of the American Economy: 1790–1860* (New York, 1967), tables.

2. *Ibid.*

3. F. L. Owsley, *Plain Folk of the Old South* (Chicago, 1965).

4. K. M. Stampp, *The Peculiar Institution* (New York, 1956), ch. 1.

5. *Ibid.*, ch. 1 and 2; C. Eaton, *The Growth of Southern Civilization* (New York, 1961), 156.

6. A. H. Conrad and J. R. Meyer, *The Economics of Slavery* (Chicago, 1964), ch. 3.

7. W. J. Cash, *The Mind of the South* (New York, 1941), books 1 and 2.

8. Stampp, *Peculiar Institution*, ch. 1.

9. *Ibid.*, ch. 5.

10. *Ibid.*, ch. 2, 4, 6, 7, and 8.

11. R. Wade, *Slavery in the Cities* (New York, 1964), appendix.

12. Stampp, *Peculiar Institution*, 29.

13. Wade, *Slavery in the Cities*, 5.

14. *Ibid.*, appendix.

15. Eaton, *Southern Civilization*, ch. 11.

16. Wade, *Slavery in the Cities*, appendix and p. 244 on interior towns like Montgomery, Alabama.

17. *Ibid.*, 30.

18. *Ibid.*, ch. 5 and 6; P. Randolph, *Sketches of Slave Life* (Boston, 1855), 58–59.

19. For the rural locale of northern industry in the 1860's, see D. Montgomery, *Beyond Equality: Labor and the Radical Republicans* (New York, 1967), 27–29.

20. See R. Starobin, Industrial Slavery in the Old South, 1790–1861 (Ph.D. dissertation, University of California, Berkeley, 1968), chapter 1, note 20 and appendixes.

21. This figure has been computed from tables on urban slave population in 1850 in Wade, *Slavery in the Cities*, appendix. J. D. B. De Bow, *Statistical View of the United States . . . Being a Compendium of the Seventh Census* (Washington, 1850), 94, estimated that about 400,000 slaves lived in southern cities and towns in 1850, while Stampp, *Peculiar Institution*, 60, estimates that the *total* city, town, and non-agricultural slave population was about 500,000 in 1860. If two-thirds of the *male* population of towns *and* cities was engaged in industrial enterprises and occupations, then the 160,000 to 200,000, or 5 per cent, figure seems approximately correct for the years 1850 to 1860. See tables in my dissertation for some large slaveholdings by deep-South industries. For further estimates, see J. C. Sitterson, *Sugar Country* (Lexington, 1953); J. F. Hopkins, *A History of the Hemp Industry in Kentucky* (Lexington, 1951); J. C. Robert, *Tobacco Kingdom* (Durham, 1938); Eaton, *Southern Civilization*, 64–65, 134–135, 99–101, and ch. 10; K. Bruce, *Virginia Iron Manufacture in the Slave Era* (New York, 1930); and S. Lebergott, "Labor Force and Employment, 1800–1960," National Bureau of Economic Research, *Output, Employment, and Productivity in the United States After 1800* (New York, 1966), vol. 30, pp. 117-210. Slaves comprised the bulk of the southern industrial workforce.

22. Wade, *Slavery in the Cities*, 30 and appendix.

23. Eaton, *Southern Civilization*, 64–65.

24. See pioneering studies by Richard Griffin, E. M. Lander, and J. G. Van Deusen, *Economic Bases of Disunion in South Carolina* (New York, 1928), 264–303.

25. Eaton, *Southern Civilization*, ch. 10; Gray, *Southern Agriculture*, II, 935; and above, footnote 24.

26. *Ibid.*; cf. below, ch. 4.

27. McGehee Papers (LSU). See *Hunt's Merchants' Magazine*, 15 (1846), 417 and 17 (1847), 323; *Niles' Weekly Register*, 40 (1831), 281; Richmond *Dispatch*, Jan. 5, 1860; Colhoun Notebook (Clemson); J. K. Menn, The Large Slaveholders of the Deep South, 1860 (Ph.D., University of Texas, 1964), 408; Bell Cotton Mill Letter-

book (HPL); F. L. Fries Diary (NCA); Woolley Papers (UK); Graham Papers (UK); and King Papers (GA) for information on other slave-employing textile mills.

28. This figure and those below for total numbers of slaves in various industries are estimates only; they are not based on precise statistical data. Census schedules have been consulted, but the returns for 1790, 1800, and 1830 contain little of value for manufactures, while those for 1810 and 1820 are of partial usefulness. The schedules for 1840, 1850, and 1860, even if completely analyzed, cannot yield precise information, since the population tables list names of masters and the size of their slaveholdings without indicating their occupations, while the industrial tables list the names of entrepreneurs without indicating the size of their slaveholdings. Moreover, many planters were also engaged with their slaves in industrial pursuits, and the extent of slave hiring is also almost impossible to determine. Though sometimes less complete than census schedules, the local tax lists which have been consulted reveal the actual size of slaveholdings in industries far more accurately.

29. *De Bow's Review*, 9 (1850), 432–433, and *Hunt's Magazine*, 23 (1850), 575–576. Cf. *Niles' Register*, 75 (1849), 344; *De Bow's Review*, 11 (1851), 319–320; and Charleston *Courier*, June 29, 1840, for the operation of the Saluda Cotton Mill with slave labor.

30. Eaton, *Southern Civilization*, ch. 10.

31. *Ibid.*; Bolling Papers (Duke); Ross Letterbook (VHS); Polk-Yeatman Papers (UNC); Edmundson Papers (VHS); *Hunt's Magazine*, 28 (1853), 644; Tredegar Papers (VSL); C. Dew, *Ironmaker to the Confederacy* (New Haven, 1966), *passim;* Weaver Papers (UV and Duke); Graham Papers (UV); Davis Papers (UV); and Jordan and Irvine, and Jordan and Davis Papers (WSHS).

32. Elmore Papers (USC and LC); U. B. Phillips, ed., *Plantation and Frontier Documents* (Cleveland, 1909), II, 304–305; Brevard Papers (NCA and UNC); Shelby Iron Works Papers (UA); Browne Papers (AA); and James Collection (UMo); Northampton Furnace account and time books, Ridgely Collection (MdHS). The experiences of two slave blacksmiths are recounted in R. W. Logan, ed., *Memoirs of a Monticello Slave* (Charlottesville, 1951) and J. W. C. Pennington, *The Fugitive Blacksmith* (London, 1850), 1–8.

33. Eaton, *Southern Civilization*, ch. 10; Robert, *Tobacco Kingdom*,

tables; Gray, *Southern Agriculture*, II, 754.

34. Robert, *Tobacco Kingdom*, tables; C. R. Weld, *A Vacation Tour in the United States* (London, 1855), 313–314.

35. Leslie Papers (Duke); Wade, *Slavery in the Cities*, 22, 33–35; cf. City of Richmond Personal Property Tax Book, 1861 (VSL).

36. Thomas Papers (Duke); Eaton, *Southern Civilization*, ch. 10. The personal experiences of slave tobacco factory workers are recorded in Henry Box Brown, *Narrative* (Boston, 1849), 36–47; H. C. Bruce, *The New Man* (York, Pa., 1895), 17, 21, 65–71; K. Pickard, ed., *The Kidnapped and the Ransomed* (Syracuse, 1856), 43–55; and Burrell W. Mann's letters in C. Woodson, ed., *The Mind of the Negro* (Washington, 1926), 16–47.

37. Eaton, *Southern Civilization*, ch. 10; Hopkins, *Hemp Industry*, *passim*.

38. B. Moore, *The Hemp Industry in Kentucky* (Lexington, 1905), appendix V.

39. N. P. Poor, comp., *Haldeman's Picture of Louisville* (Louisville, 1844), 88–90; Hunt Papers (Filson); Hunt-Morgan Papers (UK); *Niles' Register*, 67 (1844), 128; Wade, *Slavery in the Cities*, 23.

40. [A New England Traveller], "Original Correspondence," Lexington, Ky., Oct. 16, [1830], reprinted in Louisville *Journal*, Nov. 29, 1830, typescript, misc. papers H (Filson); for the recollections of a slave ropewalk worker, see W. Hayden, *Narrative* (Cincinnati, 1846), 24–52.

41. J. Bancroft, *Census of Savannah, 1848*, 16; *American Cotton Planter*, n.s., I (1857), 156; D. Dodd, "The Manufacture of Cotton in Florida," *FHQ*, 13 (1934), 7 note 16; Hawkins Papers (UNC); Yuille Papers (UA); Mobile Tax Book, 1860 (MCH). J. L. Smith, *Autobiography* (Norwich, 1881), 24–37, recounts the experiences of a slave shoemaker.

42. F. Dugan and J. Bull, eds., *Bluegrass Craftsman: Being the Reminiscences of E. H. Stedman* (Lexington, 1959), 101–102; E. M. Lander, "Paper Manufacturing in South Carolina," *NCHR*, 29 (1952), 221–222; Gales Reminiscences, 139–142, 162–167 (UNC); Frankfort, Ky., *Argus*, Jan. 21, 1829; M. L. Fullerton to ———, Aug. 25, 1830, American Colonization Society Papers (LC); Charleston *Courier*, Dec. 11, 1844.

43. N. Hickman, *Mississippi Harvest* (Oxford, 1962), 32; *Hunt's Magazine*, 26 (1852), 514–515; B. H. Wall, Ebenezer Pettigrew

(Ph.D., University of North Carolina, 1946), 313–315; Howe Papers, May 20, 1836 (Duke); letters of April and Sept., 1829, McDonogh Papers (Tulane); in 1849, Charleston's John Horlbeck made four million bricks with eighty-five hands, most of whom were slaves, according to E. M. Lander, "Charleston," *JSH*, 26 (1960), 344.

44. J. H. Ingraham, *The South-West* (New York, 1835), II, 249.

45. Eaton, *Southern Civilization*, 99–101, 134–135, ch. 10; Sitterson, *Sugar Country*, 155–156; *De Bow's Review*, 2 (1846), 331.

46. Eaton, *Southern Civilization*, 134–135; Sitterson, *Sugar Country*, 155–156; *American Farmer*, series 4, vol. 12 (1856), 131–132; V. Clark, *History of Manufactures* (New York, 1929), 491; *Harper's Monthly*, 7 (1853), 746–767.

47. *Southern Agriculturist*, 6 (1833), 518–529, 576–577.

48. Eaton, *Southern Civilization*, 99–101.

49. *De Bow's Review*, 14 (1853), 611; Wade, *Slavery in the Cities*, 23; *Charleston List of Taxpayers, 1859*, and *1860*; Savannah Tax Digest, 1860 (GA); Menn, Large Slaveholders, 217; F. A. Kemble, *Journal of a Residence on a Georgia Plantation* (New York, 1961), 54–55; Manigault Papers (UNC, Duke, and SCHS); A. B. Flagg rice plantation journal, Plimton Collection (Columbia); F. M. Weston Laurel Hill Rice Mill Account Book, 1845–64 (SCHS); items on rice mill, 1858, 1859, and 1860, Jordan Papers (Duke).

50. Walton Account Books (UNC); Hill Carter Papers (LC and VHS); Richmond *Dispatch*, Dec. 21, 1852; City of Richmond Personal Property Tax Book, 1861 (VSL); Eaton, *Southern Civilization*, 197, 238.

51. Wade, *Slavery in the Cities*, 23, 36; J. S. Buckingham, *The Slave States of America*, I, 338; *List of Taxpayers of the City of Charleston for 1860*; Augusta *Southern Cultivator*, 16 (1858), 337; Savannah Tax Digest, 1860 (GA); New Orleans's Fireproof Cotton Press Company, Charleston's Union Cotton Press, and Savannah's Hydraulic Cotton Press also used slave labor.

52. Couper-Fraser Papers (GHS); Couper Papers (UNC); C. Eaton, "Slave-Hiring in the Upper South," *MVHR*, 46 (1960), 675; the Louisville *Democrat*, Jan. 4, 1854, advertised two black packing-house workers for sale; J. Bancroft, *Census of Savannah, 1848*, 16, listed five slave butchers.

53. Eaton, *Southern Civilization*, ch. 10; the experiences of slave coal miners are recorded in L. Black, *Life and Sufferings* (New Bed-

ford, 1847), 6–11, and A. Mott, ed., *Narratives of Colored Americans* (New York, 1877), 97–99.

54. Bruce, *Virginia Iron Manufacture*, 102, 101; H. T. Catterall, ed., *Judicial Cases Concerning American Slavery* (Washington, 1926–37), I, 246; Richmond *Dispatch*, Dec. 30, 1854 and Jan. 5, 1861; Heth Papers (UV); W. P. Browne to A. Saltmarsh, Sept. 24, 1859, Browne Papers (AA).

55. Eaton, *Southern Civilization*, ch. 10.

56. Calhoun Papers (USC and Clemson); Clemson Papers (Clemson); J. B. Smith to —— Woodruff, April 3, 1854, Smith Letterbook and Papers (Duke). Cf. Fisher Papers (UNC); Silver Hill Mining Company Ledger, 1859–62 (UNC); High Shoal Gold Mine Records, Hoke Papers (UNC); Hart Gold Mine accounts, Latimer Plantation Book (UG); *Mining Magazine*, 4 (1855), 285. Buckingham, *Slave States*, II, 222; B. C. Steiner, ed., "The South Atlantic States in 1833, as Seen by a New Englander," *MdHM*, 12 (1918), 347; and E. W. Phifer, "Champagne at Brindletown," *NCHR*, 40 (1963), 491–493.

57. E. C. Barker, ed., *The Austin Papers* (Austin, 1926), I, 60; H. R. Schoolcraft, *A View of the Lead Mines* (New York, 1819), 126–128; H. M. Brackenridge, *Views of Louisiana* (Pittsburgh, 1814), 154; T. M. Marshall, ed., *The Life and Papers of Frederick Bates* (St. Louis, 1926), II, facing 168; *Niles' Register*, 31 (1826), 278.

58. E. S. Abdy, *Journal of a Residence and Tour* (London, 1835), II, 326; T. Guthrie, Report on Salt Manufacture, *House Exec. Doc.* #36, 33 C., 1 s., Jan. 26, 1854, 4–5; S. D. Ingham, Report on Salt Works, *House Doc.* #55, 21 C., 2 s., Feb. 8, 1830, 4–9, 36–37, 66; G. W. Erwin Account Book, 1846–50 (Filson); Palfrey Papers (LSU and Houghton); A. Royall, *Sketches of Life in the United States* (New Haven, 1826), 44, 46–47; Eaton, *Southern Civilization*, ch. 10; *Harper's Monthly*, 15 (1857), 435–451.

59. Eaton, *Southern Civilization*, ch. 10; Charleston *Courier*, Sept. 23, 1845. According to Lander, "Charleston," 338, citing the census of 1850, the sawmilling industry "continued to grow until mid-century, by which time Charleston had become an important lumber manufacturing and shipping center. . . . Located along the city's waterfront were four mills with a capital value in 1850 ranging from $36,000 to $50,000 each and labor forces, mainly slaves, between twenty-four and sixty workers each."

60. Hickman, *Mississippi Harvest*, 23, *passim*, and, especially, tables of slaveholding lumbermen; inventory and deed, 1862, Criglar Papers (UNC); W. H. Stephenson, *Isaac Franklin, Slave Trader* (Baton Rouge, 1938), 105–107, 109, 177–180; Zachary Taylor Papers (LC); Savannah Tax Digest, 1860 (GA); Wall, Ebenezer Pettigrew, 301–312; Trouard Lumber Yard Account Book, 1854–68, Kuntz Collection (Tulane); Asa Hursey Papers (LSU); Calvin Taylor Papers (LSU); Telfair Papers (GHS); Dismal Swamp Land Company Papers (Duke); Florida *House Journal*, sixth session, 1852–53, appendix, p. 15; John Carter sawmill daybook (UG); J. H. Moore, *Andrew Brown and Cypress Lumbering in the Old Southwest* (Baton Rouge, 1967); S. Northrup, *Twelve Years a Slave* (Auburn, N.Y., 1853), 89–99, and M. Grandy, *Narrative* (Boston, 1844), 5–25, for material on other slave-employing lumbering, sawmilling, and shingling enterprises.

61. Eaton, *Southern Civilization*, ch. 10; Charleston *Courier*, Sept. 23, 1845.

62. Grist Papers (Duke); Jordan Papers (Duke); F. L. Olmsted, *A Journey in the Seaboard Slave States* (New York, 1861), 338–350; H. A. Kellar, ed., *Solon Robinson* (Indianapolis, 1936), II, 219–223; *De Bow's Review*, 4 (1847), 407, reported 150 stills in operation in North Carolina; and Eaton, *Southern Civilization*, ch. 10.

63. J. Martin, ed., *A New Gazetteer of Virginia* (Charlottesville, 1835), 480–481; J. D. B. De Bow, ed., *Industrial Resources of the Southern States* (New Orleans, 1852), II, 182; Olmsted, *Seaboard Slave States*, 351–352; Greenfield Fishery Account Books, 1848–1861, Hayes Collection, vols. 2, 3, 4, 6 (UNC).

64. W. D. Valentine Diary, 1840 (UNC). Charles Ball, *Fifty Years in Chains* (New York, 1860), 204–241, also describes the working routine of slave fishermen.

65. G. R. Taylor, *The Transportation Revolution* (New York, 1951), 79; J. G. Randall and D. Donald, *Civil War and Reconstruction* (Boston, 1961), 8. In 1850, the *slave states* had 2372 of 8588 miles of national railroad; in 1860, they had 10,842 of 30,592.

66. This information has been compiled from printed railroad reports, from reports of railroads to state boards of internal improvements, and from the following manuscript sources: McRae Letterbooks (WSHS); Buford Papers (Duke); Pontchartrain Railroad Minutebook (Tulane); New Orleans and Carrollton Railroad Papers

(Tulane); Marston Papers (LSU); Clinton and Port Hudson R.R. Papers, in East Feliciana Parish Archives Collection (LSU); Clinton and Port Hudson R.R. journal, 1841–42, Palfrey Papers (LSU); Fisher Papers (UNC); Hawkins Papers (UNC); Western and Atlantic R.R. Papers (GA); Western, and North Carolina R.R. Papers (NCA); Richardson Papers (Duke); J. D. Frost Account Book, 1850–54 (USC).

67. Virginia *Board of Public Works Reports;* reports to various state legislatures, especially Louisiana; Phillips, ed., *Plantation and Frontier Documents,* II, 348; A. Gallatin, Report on Roads and Canals (1808), *American State Papers, Misc.,* I, 763, 819; Kemble, *Journal,* 104, 122–125, 129; Buckingham, *Slave States,* 136–137; *Harper's Monthly,* 13 (1856), 443.

68. James River and Kanawha Canal Report, Virginia *Board of Public Works Report,* 1854, 388–389; see also London Papers (UNC); Cape Fear and Deep River Navigation Company Papers (UNC); Cape Fear and Deep River Navigation Works Papers, in Treasurers' Papers: Internal Improvements (NCA); M. L. Webber, ed., "Colonel John C. Senf's Account of the Santee Canal," *SCHM,* 28 (1927), 114–120; and Wall, Ebenezer Pettigrew, 251–262.

69. Rose Bay and Swan Quarter Turnpike Company minutes and accounts, 1837–40 (NCA); Nolensville Turnpike Company minutebook, 1829–65, and turnpike company collection (TSL); Allegany Turnpike Papers, in Edmundson Papers (VHS); Junction Valley, Swift Run Gap, Rockymount, Martinsburg and Potomac, and Sinking Creek and Craig's Creek turnpike company reports in Virginia *Board of Public Works Reports;* Hardinsburg and Cloverport Turnpike Road Company Accounts, 1860 (Filson).

70. Other slave-hiring companies were the Fredericksburg and Valley Plank Road, reported in the Virginia *Board of Public Works Reports,* 1851, 1854, and 1855; and the Fayetteville and Western Plank Road Company of North Carolina, cited in R. B. Starling, "The Plank Road Movement in North Carolina," *NCHR,* 16 (1939), 16–17.

71. Obed, a slave, operated the Potomac Bridge Company's ferry, while another bondsman captained the Blue Ridge Ferry of the James River and Kanawha Canal, according to the Virginia *Board of Public Works Reports,* 1858, 1854. For other slave ferrymen, see Springfield plantation account book, 1841–53, Quitman Papers (MA); M. Grandy, *Narrative,* 5–25; Olmsted, *Seaboard Slave*

States, 307. For slave pilots, see Report of Committee on Pilotage System, Louisiana *Journal of the House of Representatives,* 2 L., 1 s., Feb. 28, 1854, 88 and appendix; Report on Pilots' Association, Louisiana *Senate Journal,* 5 L., 1 s., March 3, 1860, 91–92.

72. Ebenezer Clark Shipyard Account Books, 1838–56 (MA); Frederick Douglass, *Narrative* (Boston, 1845), 93–98, 101–105; shipyard account books, 1840–44 and 1841–51, Matthew Marine Collection (MdHS); J. J. Williamson Account Book, 1831–38 (MdHS); according to the *Charleston Census, 1848,* 31–35 and Lander, "Charleston," 341, five Charleston shipyards engaged about 160 white and Negro mechanics in 1848.

73. N. P. Willis, *Health Trip to the Tropics* (New York, 1853), 381; Menn, Large Slaveholders, 1860, 217; T. Flint, *Recollections of the Last Ten Years* (Boston, 1826), 106–107.

74. W. W. Brown, *Narrative* (Boston, 1847), 23, 31, 76–97; L. C. Hunter, *Steamboats on the Western Rivers* (Cambridge, 1959), 654, 443; J. Hall, *Notes on Western States* (Philadelphia, 1838), 247; Olmsted, *Seaboard Slave States,* 369–370; U. B. Phillips, *A History of Transportation in the Eastern Cotton Belt to 1860* (New York, 1908), 75; receipts, 1860, 1861, Hunt-Morgan Papers (UK); Steamboat *Vesuvius* Account Book, 1821–23 (MA); Steamer *Savage* Account Book, 1843 (LSU); Receipt Book, 1853–58, for steamers *Heroine, Empress, Eliza, Battle, Jeanette, Selma,* and *Duke* (Duke); Dunn steamer payroll book, 1855–59 (Duke); Buckingham, *Slave States,* I, 471–472; F. Bremer, *Homes of the New World* (New York, 1853), II, 174.

75. Memorandum of the work on Tar River Bridge, n.d., and vol. 17, Hawkins Papers (UNC); Jemison Papers (UA). Cf. H. Fulkerson, *Random Recollections of Early Days in Mississippi* (Baton Rouge, 1937), 130–131; Anderson Account Books, 1833–53 (VHS); List of Carpenters Hired to Rebuild Waverly [Rice] Mill, 1837, in J. H. Easterby, ed., *The South Carolina Rice Plantation as Revealed in the Papers of Robert F. W. Allston* (Chicago, 1945), 341; T. R. Borden to R. W. Withers, June 30, 1851, Withers Papers (UNC); B. L. C. Wailes Diary #5, Nov. 26, 1852 (Duke); and Memoranda of Artesian Well in New Orleans, 1854 (Tulane), for slave bridge builders, carpenters, and well-drillers.

76. Eaton, "Slave Hiring," 675; *Report of the Mayor of Savannah, 1861,* 16, 31; B. H. Latrobe Papers (Tulane); Wade, *Slavery in the Cities,* 292; H. Sinclair, *The Port of New Orleans* (Garden City,

1942), 190–191; *List of Taxpayers of the City of Charleston for 1859; Report of Mayor of Savannah, 1857,* 29–30.

77. T. P. Abernethy, *From Frontier to Plantation in Tennessee* (Chapel Hill, 1932), 278; *Report of the Mayor of Savannah, 1856–61;* Mobile Aldermen Committee Reports, p. 39, Feb. 20, 1834, Minutes of Aldermen, Mobile, May 2, 1844, Feb. 28, 1845, and Mobile Ordinances, Jan. 26, 1855 (MCH); Latrobe Papers (Tulane); mandates of payment, 1814–22, Kuntz Collection (Tulane); New Orleans Police Reports, 1833, Slavery Manuscripts (Columbia); New Orleans Police Records, 1823, 1836–40, Commissioner of Public Roads and Streets Records, 1839–43, and Journal of Council of 1st Municipality, 1841–45 (NOPL); J. Stuart, *Three Years in North America* (Edinburgh, 1833), II, 201; and W. R. Hogan and E. A. Davis, eds., *William Johnson's Natchez* (Baton Rouge, 1951), 192 note.

78. For road work, see J. B. Grimball Diary, Aug. 26, 1840 (UNC); Road List, 1833, John Ball Papers (SCHS); A. B. Flagg rice plantation book, Plimton Collection (Columbia); List of Hands, Ste. Genevieve Archives Misc. Mss.: Roads (MoHS); list of slaves, 1819, Corbin Papers (NYPL); report of road work, April 21, 1834, Liddell Papers (LSU); D. J. Wilkinson to J. B. Grimball, Dec. 15, 1856, Grimball Papers (Duke); Road Calendar, 1861, Harper Diary, vol. 3 (UNC); Knox County, Tenn., Road Commissioners Minutebook, 1808–19 (TSL); Lancaster County, S.C., Board of County Commissioners Minute Book, 1849–68 (USC); and the minute books of the commissioners of high roads, St. Stephen's and Berkeley Parishes, S.C., 4 vols., 1769–1853 (SCHS). For river improvement and levee work, see McDonogh Papers (Tulane); *De Bow's Review,* 12 (1852), 455; the journals of the legislatures of Louisiana, Mississippi, and Arkansas; W. R. Bivins Journal, 1836 (GA); and South Carolina Legislative Papers: Slavery Petitions and Public Improvements (SCA).

79. Message of Governor John Owen, North Carolina *Journal of House of Commons,* Nov. 17, 1829, 146. For state ownership of slaves, see reports of boards of public works and journals of the various state legislatures, especially Louisiana, Mississippi, Alabama, Georgia, Virginia and Kentucky; for Georgia after 1827, see Milledgeville *Federal Union;* London Papers (UNC); Cape Fear and Deep River Navigation Papers, Treasurers' Papers: Internal Im-

provements (NCA and UNC); and comment by F. Oliver, March 3, 1855, Liddell Papers (LSU).

80. B. H. Latrobe, Report on Public Buildings, *American State Papers, Misc.*, II, #271 (1809), 18; Leckie Papers (Duke); Commissioner of Public Buildings of the District of Columbia Letterbook, vol. 7, 1815–33 (NA, RG 42); C. E. Carter, ed., *The Territorial Papers, Florida* (Washington, 1962), vol. 23, 439.

81. Records of Quartermaster General: consolidated correspondence file: slaves (NA, RG 92); Report on Harper's Ferry Armory, *House Exec. Doc.* #111, 17 C., 2 s. (1822), statements 98, 88, 103, 107; Records of the Office of the Chief of Ordnance, for Augusta, Bellona, Fort Monroe arsenals (NA, RG 156). Mackay-Stiles Papers, vol. 34 (UNC); E. Hayward, Report on Levees, *American State Papers, Public Lands*, 8, #1349 (1835), p. 305.

82. A. Pairpont, *Uncle Sam and His Country* (London, 1857), 244–245; E. Stuart-Wortley, *Travels in the United States* (London, 1851), I, 154; C. Ball, *Fifty Years in Chains*, 19; Records of the Bureau of Yards and Docks and Naval Records Collection of the Office of Naval Records (NA, RG 71 and 45), for the Gosport, Washington, D.C., Pensacola, Savannah, New Orleans, and Memphis navy yards; T. D. Weld, ed., *American Slavery As It Is* (New York, 1839), 136; Baldwin Papers (Baker); Bernhard, *Travels through North America* (Philadelphia, 1828), I, 204; and records for Forts Morgan, Calhoun, and Monroe, Records of the Office of the Chief of Engineers (NA, RG 77).

83. *House Doc.* #201, 26 C., 1 s. (1840); various letters and affidavits consolidated correspondence file: slaves, Records of the Office of the Quartermaster General (NA, RG 92).

84. J. C. Spencer, Colored Persons in the Army, *House Doc.* #286, 27 C., 2 s., 1842.

85. A. P. Upshur, Colored Persons in the Navy, *House Doc.* #282, 27 C., 2 s., 1842; J. G. deR. Hamilton, ed., *The Papers of William A. Graham* (Raleigh, 1961), vol. 4, 61–64, 138–199.

Chapter Two: Working and Living Conditions

1. Stampp, *Peculiar Institution*, ch. 2 and 7.
2. Slave List of unidentified railroad, 1854–1855 (Tulane); Report of the Secretary of the Treasury, *House Exec. Doc.* #6, 29 C.,

1 s. (1845), 676, 647–648; Commissioner to J. McComb, May 25, 1818, Commissioner of Public Buildings of the District of Columbia, Letterbook, vol. 7, pp. 269–270 (NA, RG 42).

3. W. Thomson, *A Tradesman's Travels* (Edinburgh, 1842), 116; G. Lewis, *Impressions of America* (Edinburgh, 1845), 304; Time Books, 1833–39, 1837–52, 1860–65, Graham Papers (UV).

4. J. McDonogh to J. Pitot, July 12, 1814, McDonogh Papers (Tulane); W. R. Bivins Journal, 1837 (GA); V. Tixier, *Travels on the Osage Prairie* (Norman, 1940), 70.

5. Ball, *Fifty Years in Chains*, 215; *Harper's Monthly*, 14 (1857), 440, 441; Valentine Diary, 1840 (UNC).

6. W. Turnbull, Report on Potomac Aqueduct, *House Doc.* #459, 25 C., 2 s. (1838), 39, 75; and *Senate Doc.* #178, 26 C., 2 s. (1841), 12, 24; W. Hollister to W. A. Graham, Feb. 11, 1847, Treasurers' Papers: Internal Improvements: Raleigh and Gaston R.R. (NCA); F. L. Fries Woollen Mill Diary, 1840–42 (NCA); D. Battle to R. H. Battle, Sept. 19, 1844, Battle Papers (UNC).

7. J. Habermehl, *Life on Western Rivers* (Pittsburgh, 1901), 8; Hunter, *Steamboats*, 455.

8. B. Broomhead to B. Smith, Sept. 7, 1857, J. B. Smith to G. Moore, July 26, 1853, Smith Papers and Letterbook (Duke); Martin, *Gazetteer of Virginia*, 152; Time Book, 1850–53, Gold Hill Mining Company Papers (UNC); D. W. Lord, Journal of a Trip, May 20, 1824 (LC); Olmsted, *Seaboard Slave States*, 48; *American Railroad Journal*, 24 (1851), 650; *De Bow's Review*, 9 (1850), 555; *Journal of the Franklin Institute*, 27 (1839), 25; contract between John Buford and James River and Kanawha Canal Company, Aug. 4, 1855, Buford Papers (Duke).

9. Tift Diary, Jan. 18, 1850 (UNC); articles of agreement, Jan. 1, 1839, Stonebraker-McCartney Papers (UNC); Kemble, *Journal*, 191; Catterall, *Cases*, II, 405; Z. Taylor to R. Taylor, June 11 and 12, 1850, Taylor Papers (LC); New Orleans *Bulletin*, July 10, 1842.

10. J. Squire to W. P. Browne, May 18, 1861, Browne Papers (AA).

11. Various sugar-mill records at UNC and LSU; *Southern Agriculturist*, 3 (1830), 140. Cf. Olmsted's conversation with a "merry" slave (quoted in *Cotton Kingdom*, I, 337–388) which is often cited by historians to "prove" that sugar millers were "happy," despite their long working hours.

12. Sugar Making Roll, Oct. 31, 1851, Liddell Papers (LSU); Residence Journal of R. R. Barrow, Thursday, Dec. 3, 1857 (UNC);

Distribution of Hands in Sugar Rolling, 1857, Randolph Papers (LSU); T. Spalding, *Observations on the Sugar Cane* (Charleston, 1816), 236–238, 248.

13. *Farmers' Register*, 4 (1837), 519–520; Tixier, *Travels*, 82; S. H. Williams to parents, Oct. 22, 1853, and Jan. 16, 1858, Williams Papers (UNC).

14. E. A. Davis, ed., *Plantation Life in Louisiana as Reflected in the Diary of Bennet H. Barrow* (New York, 1943), 310–311; Charleston *Mercury*, Oct. 20, 1856.

15. *De Bow's Review*, 22 (1857), 389–391; Milledgeville *Federal Union*, Oct. 19, 1858.

16. Diary #16, p. 96, Oct. 14, 1856, Wailes Papers (Duke); Columbus *Soil of the South*, 5 (1855), 332; J. Myers vs. J. S. T. Redding, Jan. 6, 1837, Sparrow Papers (UNC).

17. W. H. Fox to J. Fox, April 25, 1852, Fox Papers (Duke); Charleston *Mercury*, March 5 and Aug. 27, 1859; Woods, Lewis & Co. to Woods, Yeatman & Co., July 26, 1856, Polk-Yeatman Papers (UNC).

18. C. A. Wycliffe, Report on Steamboat Explosions, *House Reports* #478, 22 C., 1 s. (1832); J. P. Van Tyne, Statements of Steamboat Accidents, Loss of Life, & c., *House Doc.* #21, 26 C., 2 s. (1840); Report on Steam Marine, *Senate Exec. Doc.* #42, 32 C., 1 s. (1852), 108, 80–86; Steamboats on the Mississippi, *House Doc.* #170, 27 C., 3 s. (1843), 2, 6; *De Bow's Review*, 8 (1850), 91–92 and 377; Report on Steamboat Explosions, *Senate Exec. Doc.* #18, 30 C., 2 s. (1848); Documents Relating to Steamboat Accidents, *Senate Doc.* #4, 31 C., special session (1849), p. 10, 67; W. M. Gouge, Report on the Steamboat Act, *Senate Exec. Doc.* #2, 34 C., 2 s. (1856), 462–471; J. T. Lloyd, comp., *Lloyd's Steamboat Directory and Disasters on Western Waters* (Cincinnati, 1856), *passim;* and R. Starobin, Industrial Slavery, ch. 2, note 18, for other sources, statistics, and accounts of steamboat disasters involving slave crewmen.

19. *American Railroad Journal*, 2 (1833), 322–325; S. M. Derrick, *The South Carolina Railroad* (Columbia, 1930), 83; *House Doc.* #21, 26 C., 2 s. (1840).

20. New Orleans *Picayune*, Nov. 27, 1845; G. B. Mason to P. Brown, Sept. 7, 1834, Browne Papers (AA); Olmsted, *Seaboard Slave States*, 550–551; C. Lyell, *A Second Visit to the United States* (New York, 1849), II, 47; *De Bow's Review*, 4 (1847), 287; P. O.

Hebert, Report of the State Engineer, Louisiana *Senate Journal*, 1 L., 1 s., 1846, p. 16 and 1 L., 2 s., 1847, p. 50; Catterall, *Cases*, I, 427–428; Virginia and Tennessee R.R. Report, Virginia *Board of Public Works Report, 1855;* Richmond *Enquirer,* Aug. 12, 1853; New Orleans *Picayune,* June 30, 1841; Charleston *Mercury,* Jan. 1, 1856; W. G. Thomas to R. H. Battle, March 17, 1856, Battle Papers (UNC).

21. Documents in relation to the Claim of James Johnson, *House Exec. Doc.* #110, 16 C., 2 s. (1821), testimony of W. W. Snell and T. F. Riddick.

22. H. Laurens, Jr., to J. Lucas, Nov. 27, 1796, Misc. Mss. (SCHS); Davis, ed., *Diary of Bennet Barrow,* 296; N. Tift Diary, 1838 (UNC); South Carolina Legislative Papers: Slavery Petitions, 1807, Nov. 19, 1811, 1816, 1817, 1835–47, 1840, and n.d. (SCA); New Orleans *Picayune,* Sept. 20, 1845.

23. J. Buford to ———, Feb. 1, 1854, Buford Papers (Duke); Tixier, *Travels,* 52–53; Slave Time Books, 1829–32, 1833–39, Graham Papers (UV); Richmond *Dispatch,* Jan. 14, 1858.

24. J. H. Howard to F. Carter, June 28, 1845, J. B. Baird to F. Carter, April 13, 1846, J. H. Howard to F. Carter, April 15 and 26, 1846, and J. F. Carter to F. Carter, April 30, 1846, Carter Papers (UNC); Catterall, *Cases,* I, 253–254, II, 207, 535.

25. Virginia *Board of Public Works Report, 1855,* 1062–1064.

26. *American Journal of Science,* 43 (1842), 2; *Mining Magazine,* 4 (1855), 316–317.

27. Richmond *Dispatch,* Dec. 15 and 16, 1856; *Farmers' Register,* 5 (1837), 317; B. Randolph and D. Street to H. Heth, Aug. 24 and 25, 1810, Heth Papers (UV); A. D. Richardson, *Beyond the Mississippi* (Hartford, 1867), 212–214.

28. *Farmers' Register,* 5 (1837), 317; Richardson, *Beyond the Mississippi,* 212–214; H. Eavenson, *The American Coal Industry* (Pittsburgh, 1942), 102–103, 135; *Hunt's Magazine,* 34 (1856), 537; *American Journal of Science,* 1 (1818), 127–129.

29. Lyell, *Second Visit,* I, 214–215; G. W. Featherstonhaugh, *Excursion Through the Slave States* (London, 1844), 354–355.

30. Richardson, *Beyond the Mississippi,* 212–214; *Farmers' Register,* 5 (1837), 317; Eavenson, *Coal,* 102–103.

31. Slave hire agreement, Jan. 2, 1832, Hawkins Papers (UNC); Richmond *Dispatch,* Jan. 29, 1858 and Dec. 31, 1859.

32. Lewis, *Impressions*, 304; Bremer, *Homes*, II, 490, 509–510; Marshall, ed., *Bates Papers*, I, 244; Brackenridge, *Views of Louisiana*, 150; Richardson, *Beyond the Mississippi*, 212–214; Richmond *Enquirer*, Jan. 8, 1858; cf. Featherstonhaugh, *Excursion*, 362; W. H. Russell, *My Diary North and South* (New York, 1863), 41.

33. W. H. Fox to J. Fox, April 25, 1852, Fox Papers (Duke); M. White to Stillman, Allan & Co., Dec. 1, 1845, White Letterbook (UNC); J. H. Grant to D. Jordan [ca. 1855], Jordan Papers (Duke); W. Rex to W. Weaver, Aug. 27, 1860, Weaver Papers (Duke); J. G. Taylor, *Negro Slavery in Louisiana* (Baton Rouge, 1963), 76.

34. Wade, *Slavery in the Cities*, ch. 3, 5, and especially p. 134, claims that "Better housing, clothes and food meant better health for urban slaves . . . [compared] to slaves in the corn, cane, and rice country."

35. These conclusions are based on the business records of various southern industries; see, for but one interesting example, account sheet, July 25–Aug. 7, n.d., Western North Carolina R.R., Section 60, Fisher Papers (UNC).

36. Bills and receipts, 1859–60, Treasurers' Papers: Internal Improvements: Cape Fear and Deep River Navigation Works (NCA); J. Ball Back River Plantation Account Book, 1812–34 (SCHS); Ball, *Fifty Years in Chains*, 223–224; A. Grist to J. Grist, March 22, 1853, Grist Papers (Duke); A. B. Flagg, Oaklawn plantation book, Plimton Collection (Columbia); Spalding, *Observations on the Sugar Cane*, 262.

37. Savannah River Improvement, provisions for 3rd and 4th quarters, 1835, Mackay-Stiles Papers (UNC); vegetables, chickens, butter, eggs, and potatoes were purchased by the Richmond Mining Company, Accounts, 1836–1838, Brock Collection (Huntington); eggs, greens, sugar, flour, fish, whiskey, coffee, and beef were bought by the Raleigh and Gaston Railroad, vols. 30 and 41, Hawkins Papers (UNC).

38. M. Austin, Memorandum, Feb. 22, 1815, Barker, ed., *Austin Papers*, I, 247–248, 250, furnished his Missouri lead miners over five pounds of pork weekly. New Orleans *Picayune*, Feb. 20, 1853.

39. *Farmers' Register*, 10 (1842), 411–413; Weaver Papers (Duke and UV); Report of the Southern Railroad, Sept. 23, 1852, Mississippi *Journal of the House of Representatives*, called session, 1852, 26; B. King Ledgers and Letterbooks (GA).

40. R. Leckie to S. Lane, May 16, 1817, Commissioner of Public Buildings of the District of Columbia, Letterbook, vol. 7 (NA, RG 42).

41. J. Doyle to A. W. Davis, Dec. 31, 1828, Weaver Papers (UV);
W. W. Davis to W. Weaver, Dec. 4, 1829; W. W. Davis to
A. H. Davis, Dec. 7, 1829; Jordan, Davis & Co. to A. W. Davis,
Aug. 11, Oct. 13, and Oct. 27, 1830; S. F. Jordan to W. Weaver,
Dec. 7, 1830, Weaver Papers (Duke).

42. C. Gorgas to W. Weaver, March 29, April 6, 11, May 6, 1859;
W. W. Rex to D. Brady, July 26, 1859, Weaver Papers (UV);
C. K. Gorgas to D. Brady, April 2, 1860; C. K. Gorgas to W. W.
Weaver, April 2, 1860; W. W. Rex to D. Brady, May 29, June 29,
July 6, July 25, Sept. 10, and Aug. 7, 1860, Weaver Papers (Duke).

43. J. Mackay to G. L. Cope, July 13, 1835, Mackay-Stiles Papers
(UNC); M. White to M. White, Jr., March 17, 1852, White Papers
(UNC).

44. D. Ross to T. Hopkins, Aug. 25, 1813, Ross Letterbook (VHS);
J. H. Couper to F. P. Corbin, March 21, 1855, Corbin Papers
(NYPL).

45. Buckingham, *Slave States*, II, 427–428. Wade, *Slavery in the Cities*,
ch. 5, seems to assume that holiday and Sunday urban slave dress
was identical with workaday gear; Phillips, *American Negro
Slavery*, 416–417, assesses weekend dress more realistically.

46. C. Manigault to J. Haynes, Aug. 16, 1847, Manigault Letterbook
(SCHS); Ingraham, *The South-West*, I, 236–237; A. MacKay, *The
Western World* (London, 1850), II, 74; J. H. Couper to F. P.
Corbin, March 21, 1855, Corbin Papers (NYPL); *Maryland
Gazette*, Feb. 1, 1798; descriptions of the clothing of industrial
slave runaways in, for example, the Lexington *Reporter*, March
31, 1830; Richmond *Enquirer*, March 18, 1845; and Richmond
Police Guard Day Book, May 30, 1836 (UV) confirm these
generalizations.

47. Louisa Furnace Account Book, 1854–69, vol. 2 (UNC) indicates
that each slave received six pairs of shoes annually; the slave hire
records, 1847–54, in Harper Papers (Duke) suggest that contracts
often required two pairs of shoes per year for slaves working at
rough-on-the-feet industries like mining, iron working, and construction.

48. R. L. Allston memo, n.d., Allston Papers (SCHS); D. Ross to
R. Richardson, Jan. 1813, Ross Letterbook (VHS).

49. W. W. Rex to D. Brady, Feb. 25, 1859, Weaver Papers (UV); W. W. Rex to D. Brady, May 29, June 19, June 29, July 6, Sept. 6, Sept. 21, and Sept. 26, 1860; C. K. Gorgas to W. Weaver, April 2, 1860; C. K. Gorgas to D. Brady, April 2, 1860, Weaver Papers (Duke).

50. E. Patrick to D. W. Jordan, March 8, 1858, Jordan Papers (Duke); J. B. Carrington to J. M. Sutherlin, April 5, 1858, Sutherlin Papers (Duke); S. F. Jordan to W. Weaver, Dec. 7, 1830, Weaver Papers (Duke).

51. See Wade, *Slavery in the Cities*, ch. 3 and 5, for an excellent account of urban housing; Silver Hill Mining Company *Report* for 1860, 3, 9; *Niles' Register*, 75 (1849), 484; W. Blanding Journal, Aug. 5, 1828 (Duke); Steiner, "South Atlantic States, 1833," 347; Hurricane Iron and Mining Company Record Book, ca. 1840 (UT); Norris, *Frontier Iron*, 43–44; J. Palfrey to J. G. Palfrey, Feb. 15, 1837, Palfrey Papers (Houghton); A. B. Flagg, Oaklawn rice plantation book, Plimton Collection (Columbia); Green, "Gold Mining in Virginia," 358–361; *American Journal of Science*, 13 (1828), 208.

52. M. Liddell to J. Liddell, Nov. 29, Dec. 20, 1843, Liddell Papers (LSU); A. Giffen to J. G. Palfrey, Dec. 29, 1843, Palfrey Papers (Houghton); newspaper advertisement, n.d., Corbin Papers (NYPL); *Southern Agriculturist*, 6 (1833), 167; Charleston *Courier*, July 19, 1844; R. L. Allston, memo, n.d., Allston Papers (SCHS).

53. Kemble, *Journal*, 100–101.

54. Court of Claims Report in the Case of David Myerle vs. the United States, *Report of Court of Claims* #81, 34 C., 3 s., Feb. 23, 1857, pp. 59, 62; Notes in the Field #2, March 19, 1852, p. 17, Wailes Papers (MA); Charleston *Mercury*, Nov. 26, 1859; Sinclair, *Port of New Orleans*, 190–191; Richmond *Dispatch*, Nov. 12, 1853; Dew, *Ironmaker to the Confederacy*, 26; Patton, Donegan & Co. to Haddock, Haseltine & Co., Dec. 11, 1847, Patton, Donegan & Company Letterbook (HPL); Louisville *Journal*, Nov. 29, 1830, typescript, misc. papers H (Filson); report for 1838–39, Tredegar stockholders' minutebook (VSL).

55. *American Journal of Science*, 13 (1828), 208; *Farmers' Register*, 4 (1837), 518; W. Holburn to W. Greenlaw, March 22, 1809, Holburn Letterbook, Tayloe Papers (VHS); Lewis, *Impressions*, 122–123.

56. Habermehl, *Life on Western Rivers*, 55; Hunter, *Steamboats*, 451; J. C. Hawkins to C. C. Morgan, Dec. 28, 1860, Dr. L. P. Yanstell to C. Morgan, April 5, 1861, Hunt-Morgan Papers (UK); Report of James River and Kanawha Canal Company, Oct. 30, 1858, Virginia *Board of Public Works Report, 1858*.

57. Catterall, *Cases*, II, 243–244, 226.

58. *Farmers' Register*, 4 (1837), 518.

59. Olmsted, *Seaboard Slave States*, 346; Columbus *Soil of the South*, 5 (1855), 332; *Southern Agriculturist*, 6 (1833), 529; *Harper's Monthly*, 13 (1856), 450; J. Redpath, *The Roving Editor* (New York, 1859), 288–295.

60. Sitterson, *Sugar Country*, *passim* and P. Perry, The Naval Stores Industry in the Ante-Bellum South (Ph.D., Duke University, 1947), for example.

61. Reports of Feb. 1 and July 31, 1838 and various bills and receipts for medical care, 1830–50, Dismal Swamp Land Company Papers (Duke).

62. Overseer M. Jones Account Book, May–Oct., 1856; M. Jones to J. R. Grist, Aug. 22, Aug. 29, 1858, May 28, June 25, 1860, Grist Papers (Duke); cf. Gray and Pierce Account Book, 1847–49 (UNC); and Postell, *Health of Slaves*, 147–150, 159–163.

63. Entries from Dec., 1860 to Feb., 1861, vol. 6, White Papers (UNC); Mather plantation journal, Oct.–Dec., 1855 (LSU).

64. R. R. Barrow, Residence Plantation Journal, 1857–58 (UNC).

65. Catterall, *Cases*, II, 243–244, 226; S. Drewry to J. Buford, April 18, 1854, Buford Papers (Duke).

66. J. C. Hawkins to C. C. Morgan, Dec. 28, 1860; Dr. L. P. Yanstell to C. Morgan, April 5, 1861; J. C. Hawkins to C. C. Morgan, Dec. 22, 1860, Hunt-Morgan Papers (UK).

67. New Orleans *Picayune*, June 28 and June 9, 1853; Report of Tennessee Canal Commissioners, *House Exec. Doc.* #121, 24 C., 2 s. (1836), p. 1.

68. W. J. Minor plantation journal, fall 1855 and 1857 (LSU); G. Poindexter to ———, Aug. 15, 1810, Poindexter Papers (Duke); entries for August through November, 1860, vol. 6, White Papers (UNC); Buckingham, *Slave States*, I, 267; Van Buren, *Jottings*, 195–196; Tixier, *Travels*, 85.

69. Contract, January 21, 1836, Downey Papers (Duke).

70. J. T. Hicks to S. S. Downey, Feb. 27, 1836, Downey Papers (Duke).

71. Hicks to Downey, March 28 and May 14, 1836, Downey Papers (Duke).

72. Hicks to Downey, June 30 and July 14, 1836, Downey Papers (Duke).

73. Hicks to Downey, Aug. 25, 1836, Downey Papers (Duke).

74. —— Campbell to L. Baldwin, Aug. 5, 1832, Baldwin Papers, vol. 49 (Baker); Richmond *Enquirer*, Sept. 18, 1832; A. Henderson to Leslie & Brydon, Aug. 17, 21, and 30, 1832, Leslie Papers (Duke).

75. Gowrie record book, 1833–35, Manigault Papers (UNC); L. Manigault Prescription Book, 1852, and L. Manigault to father, Nov. 22, 1852, Manigault Papers (Duke).

76. J. T. Cooper to R. Habersham, June 20 and 30, 1848, Manigault Papers (SCHS); C. Manigault to J. T. Cooper, July 12, 1848, Manigault Letterbook (SCHS).

77. Holt Diary, Jan. 21, 22, 1848 (UNC); B. King Letterbook, June through Aug., 1847, Feb. through April, 1848 (GA).

78. Register of Births and Deaths, 1849–96, Ball Papers (USC); Deaths on Dirleton, 1854–59, 1860, vols. 6 and 8, J. R. Sparkman Papers (UNC); journal, 1844–47, W. E. Sparkman Papers (UNC); Record of Deaths, May 10, 1852, 1850–55, series E, vol. 4, Arnold-Screven Papers (UNC); A. Fries, ed., *Moravian Records,* Diary of Salem, Nov. 8, 1833, vol. 8, p. 4067; A. B. Flagg, Oaklawn plantation book, Plimton Collection (Columbia), D. B. McLaurin to W. H. B. Richardson, Aug. 3, 1855, Richardson Papers (Duke); Hamilton, ed., *Graham Papers,* IV, 315; time sheets, July 25–August 7, ca. 1850's, Western North Carolina R.R., section 60, Fisher Papers (UNC).

79. *American Railroad Journal,* 3 (1834), 114; Memorandum of Artesian Well in New Orleans, 1854 (Tulane); Slave List, 1854–55 (Tulane); Catterall, *Cases,*. I, 236; Board of Internal Improvement, Kentucky Legislature, *Reports,* Nov., 1851 session, p. 738; L. Baldwin to J. Baldwin, Dec. 25, 1831, Baldwin Papers, vol. 48 (Baker); *Western Journal and Civilian,* 15 (1855), 50; Nevitt Journal, Sept. 9, 1829 (UNC).

80. *Southern Agriculturist,* 6 (1833), 574; J. T. Cooper to R. Habersham, June 20, 1848, Manigault Papers (SCHS); Houmas plantation account book, July 12, 1842 (NYPL); S. Armistead to B. Nicholls, n.d., Nicholls Papers (NCA); medical account sheet, 1826–35, Jordan and Irvine Papers (WSHS); H. Clay to F. Brooke, Aug. 2, 1833, Colton, ed., *Correspondence of Henry Clay,* 368.

81. Medical accounts, Oct., 1830, Thruston Papers (Filson); R. J. Arnold's Orders to J. Baily for 1843, Arnold-Screven Papers (UNC); Dirleton plantation book, vol. 3, J. R. Sparkman Papers (UNC); C. C. Jones to T. J. Shepherd, Dec. 4, 1850 and T. J. Shepherd to C. C. Jones, Dec. 16, 1850, Jones Papers (Tulane); J. B. Carrington to J. M. Sutherlin, April 5, 1858, Sutherlin Papers (Duke).

82. Instructions for 1841 and Orders for 1843, Arnold-Screven Papers (UNC); Samuel Walker, Elia plantation journal (Tulane); *Southern Agriculturist*, 6 (1833), 574.

83. Richmond *Enquirer*, Dec. 25, 1845; J. Haynes to C. I. Manigault, Feb. 22, 1845 and March 27, 1846, Manigault Papers (SCHS); *Southern Agriculturist*, 6 (1833), 573–574; *American Farmer*, series 4, vol. 12 (1856), 132.

84. Such deficiencies were apparently remedied at other large sugar mills and coal mines, according to the Charleston *Courier*, July 19, 1844; *De Bow's Review*, 9 (1850), 202–203; *Harper's Monthly*, 7 (1853), 758–759; Richmond *Whig*, Jan. 2, 1846; and the Richmond *Dispatch*, Jan. 1, 1855.

85. Richmond *Enquirer*, Sept. 18, 1832.

86. Richmond *Enquirer*, March 20, 1860; Wade, *Slavery in the Cities*, ch. 5; W. Edmund to W. P. Browne, April 7, 1834, Browne Papers (AA); Pontchartrain Railroad Company Minutebook, May 6, 1834 (Tulane); receipt, Jan. 18, 1834, Thruston Papers (Filson); Phillips, *American Negro Slavery*, 404.

87. Phillips, *American Negro Slavery*, 363–364; Bancroft, *Slave Trading*, 157; Stampp, *Peculiar Institution*, 403.

88. Catterall, *Cases*, II, 289, 298, 300, 302–303, 306, and 368.

89. *Ibid.*, II, 22; Virginia *Journal of House of Delegates*, 1835, p. 267; 1836, p. 351; life insurance policies, 1855, Linn Papers (UNC); life insurance policies, 1855–57, London Papers (UNC); Richmond *Dispatch*, Jan. 1 and 2, 1855; Richmond *Enquirer*, Jan. 2, 1855 and Dec. 29, 1854; account book of Nautilus Life Insurance Co. of New York, 1847 (LSU); *Affleck's Southern Rural Almanac*, 1851, 47; Phillips, *American Negro Slavery*, 406–407, presents evidence for life insurance for hirelings as early as 1743.

90. This figure is a rough estimate of the total number of insurance policies issued for industrial slaves each year, based on the identification number for the surviving certificates. These policies were

issued on printed forms, suggesting further the frequency of the practice of insuring industrial slaves.

91. Insurance policy, June 8, 1854, Randolph Papers (LSU); various policies, 1855, Linn Papers (UNC); Rudd Account Book, 1856 (Filson); *De Bow's Review*, 4 (1847), 287.

92. Various life insurance policies, 1855–57; and H. A. London's accounts with the Cape Fear and Deep River Navigation Co., April and July, 1856, London Papers (UNC); Cape Fear and Deep River Navigation Company Account Books, vol. 14: treasurer's accounts, p. 34, Feb., 1856 (UNC); insurance policy, Jan. 18, 1856, Misc. Collections (NCA).

93. Richmond *Dispatch*, Jan. 1 and 2, 1855; Flanders, *Plantation Slavery in Georgia*, 198; Richmond *Whig*, Jan. 2, 1846; Richmond *Dispatch*, Jan. 1, 1855 and Dec. 22, 1856; E. G. Wilson, comp., *A Digest of All the Ordinances of the City of Savannah, 1858*, 538; S. Drewry to J. Buford, Dec. 13, 1853, Buford Papers (Duke); *De Bow's Review*, 17 (1854), 76–78, and 18 (1855), 404–405.

94. Richmond *Dispatch*, Dec. 20, 1854; Richmond *Enquirer*, Jan. 2, 1855.

Chapter Three: Patterns of Resistance and Repression

1. Wade, *Slavery in the Cities*, 34–35; J. C. Sitterson, "The William J. Minor Plantations," *JSH*, 9 (1943), 70; S. Elkins, *Slavery*, ch. 1–3; Robert, *Tobacco Kingdom*, 208; Taylor, *Slavery in Louisiana*, 77.

2. J. C. Fitzpatrick, ed., *The Writings of George Washington* (Washington, 1931), vol. 32, p. 365; Easterby, ed., *Allston Papers*, 366.

3. J. Squire to W. P. Browne, May 20, 1861, Browne Papers (AA); W. Staples to W. Weaver, Jan. 4, 1830, Weaver Papers (UV); S. Drewry to J. Buford, Dec. 30, 1854 and Jan. 16, 1855, Buford Papers (Duke).

4. F. Fedric, *Slave Life in Virginia and Kentucky* (London, 1863), 92; Etna Furnace Time Book, 1854–58, Weaver Papers (UV); Gold Hill Mining Company Time Book, 1850–53 (UNC); A. Grist to father, Nov. 4, 1855, Grist Papers (Duke); E. M. to H. A. London, Sept., 1859, London Papers (UNC).

5. J. Haynes to C. Manigault, Nov. 24, 1847, Manigault Papers (Duke); Mrs. Mackay to J. Mackay, Nov. 23, 1837, Mackay-Stiles Papers (UNC); *Southern Agriculturist*, 2 (1829), 507; V. McBee

to V. A. McBee, April 23, 1859, McBee Papers (UNC); W. T. Rackley to D. C. Barrow, March 16, 1859, Barrow Papers (UG); W. W. Rex to D. Brady, March 15, 1861, Weaver Papers (UV).

6. Richmond *Dispatch*, Jan. 27, 1853, Nov. 26, 1854, July 25, 1857; "One Who Knows," "Raleigh & Gaston R. Road as it is & as it might be," Treasurers' Papers: Internal Improvements (NCA); F. R. Bondervant to J. Buford, Jan. 30, 1856, Buford Papers (Duke); St. J. R. Liddell to M. Liddell, Aug. 7, 1842, Liddell Papers (LSU); runaway advertisement, Nov. 13, 1857, Pettigrew Papers (UNC).

7. Richmond *Dispatch*, Sept. 27, 1852, July 25, 1857; Charles City County petition, Dec. 27, 1831, Legislative Petitions (VSL); Wade, *Slavery in the Cities*, ch. 6.

8. Entry for Sept. 22, 1848, Anderson Account Book, vol. 2 (VHS); entry for Nov. 13, 1855, Harper Diary (UNC); Richmond *Dispatch*, Dec. 14, 1852, April 2 and Dec. 10, 1853; *Niles' Register*, 38 (1830), 419.

9. Olmsted, *Seaboard Slave States*, 104–105.

10. Robert, *Tobacco Kingdom*, 206; Nevitt Journal, Jan. 13, 1827, Feb. 8, 1831 (UNC); Charleston *Courier*, Aug. 18, 1845; L. Combs to J. L. Lawrence, Aug. 7, 1845 (UK).

11. Catterall, *Cases*, V, 293; Gavin Diary, 1855–56 (UNC); Richmond *Dispatch*, Jan. 31, 1854; C. Manigault to L. Manigault, Jan. 11, 1859, Manigault Papers (Duke); R. W. Taliaferro to J. G. Taliaferro, Dec. 9, 1860, Taliaferro Papers (LSU).

12. W. M. McKinley to D. C. Barrow, Aug. 4, 1851, Barrow Papers (UG).

13. Slave Time Books, 1830–31, 1837–52, Graham Papers (UV); W. W. Rex to D. Brady, May 10, 1859, Weaver Papers (UV); Manigault Papers, vol. 3 (UNC); Magnolia Journals, Warmoth Papers, vols. 2 and 3 (UNC).

14. Entries for July 11, 1823, and Oct. 5, 1837, Hill Carter Shirley Plantation Journals (LC); Magnolia Journals, vols. 2 and 3, Warmoth Papers (UNC).

15. B. H. Broomhead to Bel, July 9, 1857, Smith Papers (Duke); M. C. Monroe to J. R. Grist, Dec. 22, 1858, Grist Papers (Duke); W. R. Bivins Journal, 1837 (GA).

16. J. Squire to W. P. Browne, July 19, 1861, Browne Papers (AA).

17. This conclusion is based on a study of several southern newspapers, from 1820 to 1861, in which runaway advertisements appear as frequently for industrial slaves as for plantation hands and do-

mestic servants. Both plantation and industrial slave runaways gravitated toward the cities, which offered anonymity and escape routes. However, since industrial slaves were employed in cities as well as towns, and since industrial slaves were only a small fraction of the total slave population, which was overwhelmingly rural and agricultural, they seemed to abscond as frequently, proportional to their numbers, as did plantation slaves. This impression is confirmed by evidence from business records of industries, from plantation records, and from slave narratives, all of which suggest that slave disaffection was as great a problem at industries as on plantations.

18. Taylor, *Slavery in Louisiana*, 177; L. M. Child, *Isaac T. Hopper, A True Life* (New York, 1881), 139–140; New Orleans *Picayune*, March 2, 1839, Aug. 29, 1837, July 18, 1845; Catterall, *Cases*, IV, 169.

19. H. S. Clark to D. W. Jordan, Jan. 14, 1858; J. Joyner to D. W. Jordan, May 18 and 21, 1854, Jordan Papers (Duke).

20. Olmsted, *Seaboard Slave States*, 159–161; *Harper's Monthly*, 13 (1856), 451–453.

21. J. K. Watkins to W. W. Weaver, July 30, 1854; W. W. Rex to D. Brady, Oct. 26, 1860, Weaver Papers (Duke).

22. Richmond *Dispatch*, Feb. 27, 28, May 7, 12, and March 13, 1852.

23. New Orleans *Picayune*, Dec. 18, 1842; Magnolia Journal, Dec. 18, 19, 1860, Warmoth Papers (UNC); "Visit of 1867," Manigault Papers, vol. 4 (UNC); Charleston *Mercury*, Jan. 26, 1856.

24. Stampp, *Peculiar Institution*, ch. 3; H. Aptheker, *American Negro Slave Revolts* (New York, 1943).

25. *Ibid.*, 219–220, 268; Bernhard, *Travels*, II, 31; Wade, *Slavery in the Cities*, 238–239; Stampp, *Peculiar Institution*, 135; W. W. Freehling, *Prelude to Civil War* (New York, 1966), ch. 3; R. McColley, *Slavery and Jeffersonian Virginia* (Urbana, 1964), ch. 5; See also, R. Starobin, ed., *Denmark Vesey: The Slave Conspiracy of 1822* (Englewood Cliffs, N.J., Prentice-Hall, 1970).

26. H. Aptheker, *Nat Turner's Rebellion* (New York, 1966); R. E. Corlew, "Some Aspects of Slavery in Dickson County," *Tennessee Historical Quarterly*, 10 (1951), 360; Boston *Liberator*, Oct. 10, 1835; C. W. Turner, "Early Virginia Railroad Entrepreneurs and Personnel," *Virginia Magazine of History*, 58 (1950), 334; petition dated 1853 on Manassas Gap R.R. (VSL); W. S. Pettigrew to J. C. Johnston, Oct. 25, 1860, Pettigrew Papers (UNC).

27. Neither H. Wish, "The Slave Insurrection Panic of 1856," *JSH*, 5 (1939), 206–222, nor Corlew, "Slavery in Dickson County," fully explores the industrial nature of this revolt, while H. Aptheker, *Slave Revolts*, 345–350, ignores this aspect altogether.

28. Much of this information is based on the following newspapers for October, November, and December, 1856, and for January, 1857: Nashville *Union and American*, Nashville *Republican Banner*, St. Louis *Democrat*, Richmond *Dispatch*, New York *Tribune*, and Boston *Liberator*, all of which reprinted articles from other newspapers. See also, *Annual Report of the American Anti-Slavery Society* for 1857 and 1858; Catterall, *Cases*, II, 565–566; Phillips, *American Negro Slavery*, 485–486; J. H. Couper to F. P. Corbin, Dec. 26, 1856, Corbin Papers (NYPL).

29. Boston *Liberator*, Nov. 28, 1856.

30. R. C. Shinn to H. S. Harris, Jan. 17, 1857, Harris Papers (Duke); Richmond *Dispatch*, Dec. 12, 1856.

31. *Southern Agriculturist*, 6 (1833), 571–572.

32. Louisville *Journal*, Nov. 29, 1830, typescript, misc. papers H (Filson); P. Godwin, ed., *The Prose Writings of William Cullen Bryant* (New York, 1964); Bremer, *Homes*, II, 174.

33. Stampp, *Peculiar Institution*, 156–162; undated memo, R. L. Allston Papers (SCHS); *Niles' Register*, 65 (1843), 108–109.

34. Charleston *Courier*, July 19, 1844; receipt, June 1, 1846, Williams-Chesnut-Manning Papers (USC); Hudson Diaries, 1855 (UNC); Nov. 30 and Dec., 1856, vol. 2, Warmoth Papers (UNC); C. C. Jones Diaries, 1857–61 (Tulane); Holt Diary, Aug. 8 and Sept. 13, 1852, and April 24, 1853 (UNC); Richmond *Whig*, June 26, 1846; *Niles' Register*, 65 (1843), 108–109. For an excellent description of a religious service of slave turpentine and fishery workers, see W. D. Valentine Diary, Nov. 4, 1851 (UNC).

35. Moses Austin's memorandum, 1815, Barker, ed., *Austin Papers*, I, 247–249; Jordan, Davis & Co. to W. Weaver, Sept. 8, 1832, Weaver Papers (Duke); C. Manigault to J. F. Cooper, Jan. 10, 1848, Manigault Letterbook (SCHS); "Memo for 1857," Ledger, 1856, vol. 5, Walton Papers (UNC).

36. Sinclair, *Port of New Orleans*, 190–191; Dew, *Ironmaker to the Confederacy*, 26; Patton, Donegan & Co. to Haddock, Haseltine & Co., Dec. 11, 1847, Patton, Donegan & Co. Letterbook (HPL); Wade, *Slavery in the Cities*, ch. 3.

37. *Ibid.*, ch. 4; Olmsted, *Seaboard Slave States*, 153; J. Mackay to J. K. F. Mansfield, Oct. 27, 1835, Mackay-Stiles Papers, vol. 34 (UNC); blank printed pass of the New Orleans Gas Works, dated 186–, Slavery Papers (Emory).

38. J. Haynes to C. Manigault, Nov. 24, 1847, Manigault Papers (Duke); S. Armistead to B. Nicholls, Oct. 14, 1822, Nicholls Papers (NCA).

39. The Slave Time Books, 1833–39 and 1837–52, Graham Papers (UV), for example, reveal that Christmas was observed from Dec. 25 to Jan. 1, every year, without exception, at this iron works.

40. H. S. Clark to D. W. Jordan, Nov. 12, 1851, Jordan Papers (Duke); J. Chew to W. Weaver, Dec. 5, 1830, Weaver Papers (Duke).

41. J. Mackay to J. K. F. Mansfield, Dec. 1 and Dec. 30, 1835, Mackay-Stiles Papers, vol. 34 (UNC); Charleston *Mercury*, Dec. 15 and 24, 1859.

42. Burwell-Taylor Expense Book, 1832–39 (UNC); F. L. Fries Woollen Mill Diary, 1840–42 (NCA).

43. J. Liddell to M. Liddell, Dec. 28, 1851, Liddell Papers (LSU).

44. Bayside Plantation Journal, 1860 (UNC); Magnolia Journal, 1858–59, Warmoth Papers (UNC); Hudson Diaries (UNC).

45. Instructions to G. Swanston, May 26, 1838 and Instructions for Overseer for the Year 1841, Arnold-Screven Papers (UNC); B. Grist to J. Grist, Dec. 25, 1860, Grist Papers (Duke); Plantation diary in 1859 Almanac, Allston Papers (SCHS); Spalding, *Observations on the Sugar Cane*, 262.

46. F. Douglass, *My Bondage and My Freedom* (New York, 1855), 253–254.

47. McCollam Diary (LSU); McCutcheon Journal, 1838–42 (LSU); Sparkman Journal (UNC); Pré Aux Cleres plantation journals, 1852–54 (LSU); R. J. Arnold plantation journal, vol. 3, Arnold-Screven Papers (UNC); Comite journal, 1857, Kilbourne Papers (LSU); A. B. Flagg plantation journal, Plimton Collection (Columbia); *Harper's Monthly*, 7 (1853), 767; "Christmas Presents: 1842—Dc 25th," plantation book, 1841–44, Liddell Papers (LSU); "Memo of Money Paid or given to the Negroes in 1854," Stirling Papers (LSU).

48. Surviving business records suggest that about half of all industrial slaves—hired and owned—received incentive payments either in cash, kind, or credit.

49. C. Eaton, "Slave-Hiring in the Upper South: A Step toward Freedom," *MVHR*, 46 (1960), 663–678; R. B. Morris, "The Measure of Bondage in the Slave States," *MVHR*, 41 (1954), 219–240; J. H. Moore, "Simon Gray, Riverman: A Slave Who Was Almost Free," *MVHR*, 49 (1962), 472–484.

50. Paylists for 1827 and 1828, account book, 1850–52, Leslie Papers (Duke); account book, 1853–55, and receipts, ca. 1854 and 1858, Jordan Papers (Duke); "Mema of . . . Cash furnished the . . . Furnace & forge Hands," Dec., 1831, Jordan and Irvine Papers (WSHS); Tredegar payroll ledger, 1852 (VSL); reports for 1855, 1856, 1858, and 1859, Nolensville Turnpike Company Minutebook (TSL). Cf. Robert, *Tobacco Kingdom*, 203–206; Bruce, *Virginia Iron Manufacture*, 253–254; and Squire Gaines Account Book, 1843 (UK). For white wages, see below, ch. 5.

51. Weaver Papers (Duke and UV); *Farmers' Register*, 10 (1842), 411–413; "Negroes corn *1854*," Ledger, 1852–55, Liddell Papers (LSU); Bayside Plantation Journal, 1850, 1852 (UNC); J. Mackay to J. K. F. Mansfield, Nov. 21, 1835, Mackay-Stiles Papers, vol. 34 (UNC); Hawkins Papers, vol. 16, 1845 (UNC); Burwell-Taylor Expense Book, 1832–39 (UNC).

52. Account Books, vols. I and II, 1854–60, Louisa Furnace (UNC); vols. 25, 29, 41, Pettigrew Papers (UNC).

53. London Papers (UNC); bills and receipts in Treasurers' Papers: Internal Improvements: Cape Fear and Deep River Navigation Works (NCA); *Report of the Mayor of Savannah, 1857*, 29–30; *Digest of Ordinances, Savannah, 1858*, 157, 162; various receipts, account sheets, and letters, 1857, North Carolina Railroad Papers (NCA); James Hogg Account Book, 1855–56, vol. 31 (UNC); "Memo . . . 3 Aug. '60," Fisher Papers (UNC).

54. Cumberland Forge Ledger, 1796–97, and Daybook, 1802 (LC); Redwell Furnace Account Books, 1795–99 and 1805–15 (VHS); Ridwell Furnace Record Book (UNC); Pine Forge Account Book, 1804–08 (UNC); Account Books, 1794–1800 and 1808–12, Telfair Papers (GHS); Stump and Ricketts Ledger, 1806–23 (NYPL).

55. Paylists for 1827 and 1828, and account book, 1850–52, Leslie Papers (Duke); account books, 1794–1863, Telfair Papers (GHS); Bath Forge Wood Book, 1849–52; Bath Iron Works Negro Books, 1839–42 and 1846; Bath Forge Cash Book, 1849–51; Etna Furnace Negro Books, 1854–61 and 1856–59; Buffalo Forge Books, 1827–29, 1830–40, 1839–41, 1844–48, 1850–57; Buffalo Forge Time Book,

1830–43; and Buffalo Forge Wood Cutting and Coaling Record, 1831–41 (UV); see also memoranda of cash paid Negroes, 1854 and 1857, Weaver Papers (Duke); and "Mema of . . . cash furnished the Hands Decr. 1831," Jordan and Irvine Papers (WSHS).

56. Account Books, vols. I and II, 1854–60, Louisa Furnace (UNC).

57. Account Books, 1817, 1824, No. 3, Pettigrew Papers (NCA); vols. 19, 25, 29, 41, 43, Pettigrew Papers (UNC). The Blue Ridge Railroad accounts, Feb.–Sept., 1859, vol. 43, Hawkins Papers (UNC), indicate that some industrial slaves managed to outwit even the complicated workings of the credit system of money payments.

58. Monthly payrolls for Dec., 1860, Jan., 1861, and attached notes concerning slaveowners Bryan and Quince, London Papers (UNC); contingency bills, March 31 and June 30, 1860, Treasurers' Papers: Internal Improvements: Cape Fear and Deep River Navigation Works (NCA). Promoters of slave-based industrialization agreed with slave-employing industrialists that cash incentives improved slave discipline and increased productivity; see, for example, letter by "Hamilton," *American Farmer*, series 1, vol. 9 (Oct. 19, 1827), p. 241, which was never publicly challenged.

59. L. Baldwin to ——— Delalande, June 27, 1833, Baldwin Papers, vol. 41 (Baker); L. Baldwin to Navy Department, ca. 1830, quoted in "Slaves on a Federal Project," B.H.S. *Bulletin*, 8 (1934), 32–33. Cf. Woolley [Textile] Mill Papers (UK); Nolensville Turnpike Company Minutebook, 1855–59 (TSL); T. K. Noble to J. Morgan, Dec. 24, 1857, Hunt-Morgan Papers (UK).

60. B.H.S. *Bulletin*, 8 (1934), 32–33; Louisville *Journal*, Nov. 29, 1830, typescript, misc. papers H (Filson Club). Travelers believed that incentive payments improved discipline and productivity of slaves working in tobacco factories, fisheries, lumber and shingling operations, as well as on steamboats and railroads: Olmsted, *Seaboard Slave States*, 127–128, 153–156, and 352–355; Olmsted, *Journey Through Texas*, 19, 33; Olmsted, *Cotton Kingdom* (1953 edition), 109; Stirling, *Letters*, 242.

61. Weaver Account Books (UV and Duke); Pettigrew Account Books (UNC and NCA); Douglass, *My Bondage and My Freedom*, 253–254.

62. R. Evans, "The Economics of American Negro Slavery," in *Aspects of Labor Economics* (Princeton, 1962), 226.

63. Olmsted, *Journey Through Texas*, 19.

64. Stampp, *Peculiar Institution*, 151–153; Elkins, *Slavery*, ch. 1–3; E. D. Genovese, "The Legacy of Slavery and the Roots of Black Nationalism," *Studies on the Left*, 6 (Nov.–Dec., 1966), 9–11; E. F. Frazier, *Black Bourgeoisie* (New York, 1957). My forthcoming collection—*Slavery As It Was* (Chicago, Quadrangle Books)—will examine this question further.

65. Olmsted, *Seaboard Slave States*, 426–429.

66. D. Ross to ――― Douglass, Feb. 7, 1812, Ross Letterbook (VHS).

67. C. C. Jones to Sandy, Aug. 15, 1853, and C. C. Jones to T. J. Shepard, March 30, 1850, Jones Papers (Tulane).

68. R. Jemison Letterbooks, 1844–46, 1851–53, 1852–54 (UA); *Journals of the Alabama House and Senate*, 1845–46 session; Sellers, *Slavery in Alabama*, 131. After the Civil War, Horace—whose surname was now King—became an Alabama legislator.

69. Moore, "Simon Gray, Riverman," 472–484; J. H. Moore, ed., "A Letter From a Fugitive Slave," *JMH*, 24 (1962), 99–101.

70. For example, Frankfort *Argus*, June 3, 1829; Mobile *Register*, June 6, 1822; New Orleans *Picayune*, Dec. 8, 1840, July 7, 1841, Sept. 6, 1843, and March 2, 1839; Lexington *Reporter*, Sept. 15, 1830, Jan. 6, 1830, and March 31, 1830; Jackson *Mississippian*, Aug. 2, 1844; and Richmond *Enquirer*, Jan. 14, 1837.

71. E. Williams, "Slavery in Florida," *FHQ*, 28 (1949–50), 195–196; Ingraham, *The South West*, I, 236–237; Hunter, *Steamboats*, 459.

72. McCollam Diary, Oct. 3, 1845 (LSU); Keitt Papers (LC); Slave Time Book, Sept. 11, 1829, Graham Papers (UV).

73. D. Ross to R. Richardson, Jan. 14, 1813, Ross Letterbook (VHS).

74. W. E. Dickerson to A. Davis, April 19, 1829, Weaver Papers (Duke); D. Cogden to J. C. McRae, Nov. 6, 1852, Hugh McRae Papers (Duke).

75. R. Jemison to J. S. Clements, March 18, 1852, Jemison Letterbook (UA).

76. Testimony of William Poe, in Weld, *American Slavery as It Is*, 26; Richmond *Dispatch*, Nov. 15 and 24, 1852; C. Woodward, "A Common Carrier of the South Before and During the War," R & LHS *Bulletin*, 44 (1937), 55–56.

77. G. E. Manigault to brother, Jan. 21, 1861, Manigault Papers (Duke); B. Grist to J. Grist, Feb. 27 and April 3, 1859, Grist Papers (Duke); McCollam Diary, Sept. 16, 1845 (LSU).

78. H. Alexander to W. Hampton, Jan. 19, 1832, Hampton Papers (UNC); R. A. Moseley to W. P. Browne, Aug. 30, 1860, Browne Papers (AA).

79. Bremer, *Homes*, II, 534; Bernhard, *Travels*, II, 9; receipt, June 17, 1831, Hampton Papers (UNC); Hudson Diary, June 10 and 11, 1855 (LSU); C. W. Thruston to T. Jefferson, Nov. 18, 1834, Thruston Papers (Filson).

80. T. Maskell to S. Plaisted, Aug. 8, 1838, Plaisted Papers (LSU); J. H. Couper to F. P. Corbin, Oct. 21 and Dec. 19, 1856, Corbin Papers (NYPL).

81. Wade, *Slavery in the Cities*, ch. 4 and 7; Stampp, *Peculiar Institution*, ch. 4; Harper Diary, May 4, 1861 (UNC); Records of Pineville [South Carolina] Police Association, Oct. 2 and 8, 1823 (SCHS).

82. Wade, *Slavery in the Cities*, ch. 4 and 7; Freehling, *Prelude to Civil War*, ch. 3; Starobin, *Denmark Vesey*; Aptheker, *Nat Turner's Rebellion* and *American Negro Slave Revolts*; and Stampp, *Peculiar Institution*, ch. 3, have chronicled the several uprisings between 1790 and 1861.

83. Boston *Liberator*, Nov. 28 and Dec. 19, 1856; Nashville *Union and American*, Nov. 27, Dec. 7, 20, and 28, 1856, and Jan 3, 1857; Richmond *Dispatch*, Dec. 12, 1856 and Jan. 5, 1857; and petition cited in Phillips, *American Negro Slavery*, 485–486.

Chapter Four: Conversion, Hiring, and Integration of Work Forces

1. J. B. Smith to H. Smith, Nov. 25, 1855, J. B. Smith to George [Moore], July 26, 1853, Smith Papers and Letterbook (Duke); *Report of the Chief Engineer of the Atlantic and North Carolina Railroad . . . July 17, 1856*; Hamilton, ed., *Graham Papers*, IV, 243.

2. Hogan and Davis, eds., *William Johnson's Natchez Diary*, 156; W. Viands to I. P. Rinker, March 10, 1852, Rinker-Lantz Papers (UV); B. H. Broomhead to Bel [Smith], June 6, 15, and 24, 1857, Smith Papers (Duke); P. Ward to R. Leckie, Oct. 25 and Nov. 20, 1818, Leckie Papers (Duke); M. Jones to J. Jones, March 15, 1838, Jones Papers (Tulane).

3. Proceedings of the Board of Directors, Feb. 9 and 25, 1835, C & O Canal Papers (NA); R. Leckie to the Engineer in Chief of the C & O Canal, n.d., Leckie Papers (Duke); memorials and reports in *Senate Doc.* #277, 26 C., 1 s., March 11, 1840, pp. 183–186, 169–170, and 217; *Senate Doc.* #610, 26 C., 1 s., 1840, pp. 129–132.

4. Tift Diary, April 18 and Oct. 1, 1843 (UNC); Phillips, *Transportation*, 274.

5. Report on the Pacific Railroad, Missouri *Journal of Senate*, 18 General Assembly, 1855, appendix, p. 20; New Orleans *Picayune*, Jan. 11, 1853.

6. B. H. Latrobe to The Mayor & Council of the City of New Orleans, Sept. 17, 1819, and "Statement . . . . 17th of Sept., 1819," Latrobe Papers (Tulane); cf. Jackson *Mississippian*, May 25 and 29, 1860, on desertion of white laborers on the Mississippi Central Railroad and their replacements by slaves.

7. Letters dated Oct. 27, 1815, April 30 and June 1, 1839, Commissioner of Public Buildings of the District of Columbia, Letterbooks, vols. 7, 8, and 9 (NA, RG 42); report of July 31, 1831, Briggs-Stabler Papers (MdHS); C. Bulfinch, Report on Public Buildings, Washington, Nov., 1818, *American State Papers, Misc.*, II, 529; G. R. Baldwin to J. F. Baldwin, Feb. 5, 1837, and L. Baldwin to J. Rogers, May 11, 1832, Baldwin Papers (Baker).

8. New Orleans *Picayune*, Feb. 20, April 3 and 29, 1853; Report of the Alexandria, Loudoun and Hampshire R.R., Virginia *Board of Public Works Report*, 1854, p. 512; Barclay, *Ducktown*, 38–39, 68; Jackson *Mississippian*, April 3, 1860.

9. Hunter, *Steamboats*, 473; Lyell, *Second Visit*, II, 127, 162–163. For further evidence on the unreliability of Irish immigrants and native white Southerners, see R. Starobin, Industrial Slavery, ch. 4 and notes.

10. E. F. Niehaus, *The Irish in New Orleans* (Baton Rouge, 1965); Phillips, *American Negro Slavery*, 301–303; and Wade, *Slavery in the Cities*, 273–275, for example.

11. E. M. Lander, "Slave Labor in South Carolina Cotton Mills," *JNH*, 38 (1953), 161–173; E. M. Lander, "The South Carolina Textile Industry before 1845," SCHA *Proceedings*, 1951, 19–28; E. M. Lander, "The Development of Textiles in the South Carolina Piedmont before 1860," *CHR*, 1 (1960), 88–100; N. W. Preyer, "The Historian, the Slave, and the Ante-Bellum Textile Industry," *JNH*, 46 (1961), 67–83; Mitchell, *Cotton Mills*, 210–211; B. Mitchell, *William Gregg* (Chapel Hill, 1928), *passim;* J. G. Johnson, "Notes on Manufacturing in Ante-Bellum Georgia," *GHQ*, 16 (1932), 227.

12. Wade, *Slavery in the Cities*, 273–275; Phillips, *American Negro Slavery*, 301–303; V. A. Moody, "Slavery on Louisiana Sugar

Plantations," *LHQ*, 7 (1924), 246–247; Taylor, *Slavery in Louisiana*, 84; Sitterson, *Sugar Country*, 66; Preyer, "Textile Industry," 67–83; *Hunt's Magazine*, 40 (1859), 522; and Robert, *Tobacco Kingdom*, 206.

13. J. B. Baird to F. Carter, June 1, 1851, Carter Papers (UNC); *American Railroad Journal*, 24 (1851), 626; March 19, 1852, Notes in the Field #2, Wailes Papers (MA); McGehee Papers, vol. I, pp. 46, 74–75 (LSU); New Orleans *Picayune*, Nov. 12, 1858.

14. New Orleans *Picayune*, Dec. 11, 1856.

15. Report of Roanoke Navigation Company, and Report of James River Company, Virginia *Board of Public Works Report, 1822*, pp. 19–22; James River and Kanawha Canal Company Stockholders' Minutebook, 1836–37 (VSL); *Farmers' Register*, 4 (1837), 604–609; Report of J. C. Cabell, Virginia *Board of Public Works Report*, Jan. 31, 1839; James River and Kanawha Canal Report, Virginia *Board of Public Works Report*, 1840; *American Railroad Journal*, 21 (1848), 328; and Report of the Chief Engineer, *Annual Report of the President and Directors of the James River and Kanawha Company, Richmond, Nov. 25, 1850.*

16. Minutes of Stockholders' Meetings, 1849–1852, Cape Fear and Deep River Navigation Company Books (UNC); I. Clegg to P. Evans, March 17, 1852, Smith Papers (UNC); Treasurers' Reports, 1853, 1854, 1855, accounts, 1855–56, letters, 1855–57, and bills of slave sales, 1855–56, London Papers (UNC); account books, vols. 10, 11, 14, 15, 1852–59, Cape Fear and Deep River Navigation Company Books (UNC).

17. C. Daubeny, *Journal of a Tour* (Oxford, 1843), 140; Pontchartrain Railroad Company Minutebook, 1830–1835 (Tulane).

18. U. B. Phillips, "On the Economics of Slavery," A.H.A. *Annual Report* (1912), p. 150.

19. Charleston *Mercury*, April 1 and 3, 1856; *American Railroad Journal*, 6 (1837), 635; minutes of meeting of stockholders of Raleigh and Gaston R.R., 1860, Vass Papers (UNC); H. S. Clark to D. W. Jordan, Dec. 4, 1856, Jordan Papers (Duke).

20. *American Railroad Journal*, 1 (1832), 180; 20 (1847), 757; Phillips, *Transportation*, 150.

21. Jackson *Mississippian*, Oct. 11, 1859; *American Railroad Journal*, 9 (1839), 83; Phillips, *Transportation*, 259–261.

22. C. W. to J. Herzog, Sept. 6 and 27, 1822, July 24, 1813, Nov. 5, Dec. 3 and 31, 1814, and March 20, 1815, Wilt Letterbook

(MoHS); Richmond *Dispatch*, Nov. 30, 1853; Washington Mining Company Ledgers, 1843–48, and vol. 2, p. 258 (Duke).

23. Pendleton, "Short Account, 1796," 75–77; Lettercopybook, 1812–43, pp. 10, 73, 74, 106; F. Hall to J. Henderson, Jan. 16 and March 10, 1818; and tax receipts and hiring bills, 1860–61, Dismal Swamp Land Company Papers (Duke); F. W. Delesdernier to A. Hursey, Dec. 23, 1853, and "Copy of a bill of expenses of A. H. Hursey's Mill [ca. 1857–58]," Hursey Papers (LSU).

24. W. P. Browne to A. Saltmarsh, Sept. 24 and 27, 1859; A. Saltmarsh to W. P. Browne, Oct. 10, 1859, Browne Papers (AA).

25. J. R. Anderson to F. T. Anderson, Oct. 11, 1840, Anderson Papers (UV); Minutes of Directors and Stockholders of Tredegar Iron Company, June, 1842 (VSL).

26. Richmond *Enquirer*, June 1, 11, 12, and 15, 1847; Richmond *Whig*, May 28 and June 28, 1847.

27. Dew, *Ironmaker to the Confederacy*, ch. 2 and table I. Clearly, Anderson was determined to use whatever type of labor force—free or slave—he chose, as well as to preserve the property rights of slavery. By linking the rights of employers with the right of slave ownership, Anderson won the support of the Richmond press, which saw the Tredegar strike as a conflict between Capital and Labor, and between Slavery and Anti-Slavery. The *Whig*, for example, editorialized that in a slaveholding society workers had no right to dictate to masters what kind of labor force to employ. The *Enquirer* agreed that the Tredegar strike was "a matter of vital interest to the whole community"; if the strikers' demands were met, slave property would be rendered "utterly valueless" and employers would be at the mercy of workers.

28. Hill Papers, Brock Collection (Huntington).

29. Eaton, *Southern Civilization*, 64–65; Bancroft, *Slave-Trading*, 150; Robert, *Tobacco Kingdom*, 201.

30. Hamilton, ed., *Graham Papers*, IV, 247; hiring contracts, 1844–60 Clifton Papers (Duke); J. F. Fry to Shanks and Anderson, Dec. 13, 1850, Anderson Papers (Duke).

31. Stampp, *Peculiar Institution*, 67–72; Winston Slave Account Book (VHS).

32. Weaver Papers (Duke and UV); Jordan Papers (Duke); Jordan and Davis, and Jordan and Irvine Papers (WSHS); Robert, *Tobacco Kingdom*, 198–199.

33. Buford Papers (Duke); Morgan Papers (UK and Filson); Stampp, *Peculiar Institution*, 67–72; Sellers, *Slavery in Alabama*, 201.

34. F. Dickinson to W. Weaver, Jan. 15, 1829, Weaver Papers (Duke).

35. Hiring bonds, Jan. 2, 1847, Harper Papers (Duke); contracts for 1855, 1856, Whitford Papers (Duke); W. Harris to R. Hill, Jan. 1, 1839, Hill Papers, Brock Collection (Huntington); hiring contracts, 1844–60, Clifton Papers (Duke); hiring bond, Jan. 3, 1858, Jordan Papers (Duke); M. E. Gregory to W. Weaver, Dec. 29, 1834, J. Bibb to J. Turner, Nov. 3, 1853, and J. Coleman to W. Weaver, Feb. 19, 1856, Weaver Papers (Duke); hiring bonds, 1824–31, Jordan and Irvine Papers (WSHS); Bucklin-Beckwith contract, ca. 1850, Sublette Papers (MoHS); H. Nelson to R. Leslie, Dec. 3, 1829, Leslie Papers (Duke); and R. Allen to J. Buford, Jan. 5, 1857, Buford Papers (Duke).

36. A. Henderson to Leslie and Brydon, Aug. 17, 21, and 30, 1832, Leslie Papers (Duke); hiring bonds, Jan. 2, 1847, Harper Papers (Duke).

37. Robert, *Tobacco Kingdom*, 200; S. Drewry to J. Buford, Jan. 20 and Feb. 17, 1854, Buford Papers (Duke); R. Brooks to Jordan and Irvine, Jan. 2, 1829, and N. Mathews to J. Jordan, Jan. 18, 1831, Jordan and Irvine Papers (WSHS); Olmsted, *Seaboard Slave States*, 58.

38. Entries for Jan. 25 and 28, 1858, Gavin Diary (UNC); R. Garland to Jordan and Irvine, Jan. 3, 1830, Jordan and Irvine Papers (WSHS); C. C. Jones to T. J. Shepard, March 30, 1850, Jones Papers (Tulane).

39. H. S. Clark to D. W. Jordan, Nov. 12, 1851, and J. F. Clark to D. W. Jordan, Dec. 8, 1851, Jordan Papers (Duke).

40. Eaton, "Slave-Hiring," 663–678; Morris, "Measure of Bondage," 230–240; Wade, *Slavery in the Cities*, esp. p. 38.

41. Bancroft, *Slave-Trading*, ch. 7; Phillips, *American Negro Slavery*, ch. 20; Stampp, *Peculiar Institution*, 67–72.

42. *Ibid.*, 73, 185.

43. See appendix on slave-hiring rates in R. Starobin, Industrial Slavery, ch. 5; Gray, *Agriculture*, I, 566.

44. Stampp, *Peculiar Institution*, 72–73. Eaton and Morris seem confused about this distinction.

45. John Walker Diaries (UNC); C. White to H. Brown, Dec. 20, 1832, and other items concerning self-hired slaves Charles and

Arthur, Brown Papers (UNC); Douglass, *My Bondage and My Freedom*, 328.

46. O'Neall, *The Negro Law of South Carolina*, 26; South Carolina *Journal of the House of Representatives*, 1845 session, p. 62, and 1860 session, p. 17; Minutes of Mobile Aldermen, Jan. 10, 1856 (MCH); Mobile *Code of Ordinances* (1859), 173–174.

47. See below, chapter 6, on the campaign by white mechanics and slaveowners against the employment of slaves in certain occupations and the practice of paying slave hirelings "board money."

48. C. V. Woodward, *The Strange Career of Jim Crow* (New York, 1955, 1966), 7, 11–13; J. Williamson, *After Slavery* (Chapel Hill, 1965), ch. 10; Wade, *Slavery in the Cities*, 266–278; L. Litwack, *North of Slavery* (Chicago, 1961).

49. J. B. Smith Letterbooks and Papers (Duke); Silver Hill Mining Company Ledger, 1859–62 (UNC); Green, "Gold Mining in Virginia," 234, 263; Charleston *Courier*, July 18, 1845; *De Bow's Review*, 6 (1848), 295; Report of the Secretary of the Treasury, *House Exec. Doc. #6*, 29 C., 1 s., 1845, p. 660; M. Threlkel, "Mann's Lick,". *FCHQ*, 1 (1927), 174; Letters and affidavits, 1815–22, Taliaferro Papers (LSU); John Carter sawmill daybook, 1834–37 (UG); Lumber Daybook of Plank Road Steam Mills, 1854–55, Jemison Papers (UA); W. H. Fox to J. Fox, April 25, 1852, Fox Papers (Duke); sawmill account book, 1859–61, Affleck Papers (LSU); D. Thomas and L. Beard sawmill book, 1838–39, vol. 7, Fisher Papers (UNC).

50. P. Wager to A. Macomb, Sept. 30, 1830, describing 200 arrested miners, in J. W. Covington, "Letters from the Georgia Gold Regions," *GHQ*, 39 (1955), 407; *Harper's Monthly*, 15 (1857), 293; Gold Hill Mining Company Time Book, 1850–53 (UNC); Richmond *Whig*, Jan. 2 and June 26, 1846; Richmond *Dispatch*, Dec. 15 and 16, 1856; poet "Billy," in the Auraria, Georgia, *Western Herald*, April 9, 1833, quoted by Coulter, *Auraria*, 7.

51. Western North Carolina Railroad survey payroll, 1854, Treasurers' Papers: Internal Improvements (NCA); Raleigh and Gaston quarry time rolls, vols. 31 and 33, Hawkins Papers (UNC); reports of the Virginia Central, the Richmond and Petersburg, the Virginia and Tennessee, and the Richmond, Fredericksburg and Potomac railroads, in Virginia *Board of Public Works Reports*, 1850–61; reports of North Carolina R.R. for 1857 and 1858, in

North Carolina *Legislative Documents* for 1858, p. 17, and 1859, p. 13.

52. Reports of the James River and Kanawha Canal, Virginia *Board of Public Works Reports*, 1820, 1854, and 1861; Report of Auditor of Public Accounts, pp. 20–43, Kentucky Legislature *Reports*, Dec., 1849; Hardinsburg and Cloverport Turnpike Road Company Accounts, 1859–60 (Filson); Wailes Diary #16, Oct. 24, 1856 (Duke); New Orleans *Picayune*, Nov. 27, 1845.

53. Statements and accounts, 1858 and July 13, 1860, and time and account books, vols. 42 and 43, Hawkins Papers (UNC); statement, Aug. 11, 1855, Richardson Papers (Duke); Charleston *Mercury*, March 24, 1859; Jackson *Mississippian*, April 19, 1859.

54. Olmsted, *Seaboard Slave States*, 607, 612; New Orleans *Picayune*, Jan. 1, 1846; S. Pleasanton, Report on Savannah River Improvement, *House Doc.* #104, 21 C., 2 s., Feb. 16, 1831, p. 37; Report on Pilots' Association, Louisiana *Senate Journal*, 5 L., 1 s., March 3, 1860, pp. 91–92.

55. Robert, *Tobacco Kingdom*, tables; Hopkins, *Hemp Industry*.

56. H. A. Murray, *Lands of the Slave and the Free* (London, 1855), 168–169; Ford and Hawes Cash Book, 1844, Thruston Papers (Filson); Catterall, *Cases*, V, 290; E. Clark Ship Yard Account Books, 1838–41, 1843–56 (MA); *De Bow's Review*, 14 (1853), 622–623.

57. J. Irwin to E. Irwin, May 20, 1839, Irwin Letters (Filson); G. Pennypacker to W. Weaver, Nov. 4, 1831, W. W. Rex to D. Brady, Sept. 6, 1860, and C. K. Gorgas to D. Brady, April 2, 1860, Weaver Papers (Duke); W. W. Rex to D. Brady, Jan. 22, 1861, Weaver Papers (UV).

58. Dew, *Ironmaker to the Confederacy*, ch. 2 and table I; *Hunt's Magazine*, 28 (1853), 644–645, reported that 1045 whites and 1360 slaves worked the furnaces, while 260 whites and 410 slaves operated the forges, and 90 whites and 140 bondsmen manned the rolling mills in Tennessee's Cumberland River iron region.

59. *Hunt's Magazine*, 15 (1846), 598–599; Griffin and Standard, "North Carolina Textiles," 132–133; Jones, "Manufacturing in Richmond County, Georgia," 78–79; D. Moore to T. Moore, Nov. 5, 1817, Moore Papers (Duke).

60. Mill Ledger, 1856–70, pp. 86, 279, Wages Ledger, 1856–61, and letters dated June 2, 1861, March 13, 1862, and Nov. 19, 1863, in

Letterbook, 1859–64, Woolley Mill Papers (UK); *De Bow's Review*, 7 (1849), 372–373, 458; 25 (1858), 717; *Hunt's Magazine*, 22 (1850), 581–582; Charleston *Courier*, Nov. 23, 1836; New Orleans *Picayune*, Oct. 16, 1858; Report of the Secretary of the Treasury, *House Exec. Doc.* #6, 29 C., 1 s., 1845, p. 676, and Mitchell, *Gregg*, 100.

61. Buckingham, *Slave States*, II, 426, 411, and 112.

62. T. D. Jervey, *Robert Y. Hayne* (New York, 1909), 510–511.

63. T. B. Searight, *The Old Pike* (Uniontown, 1894), 109; Olmsted, *Seaboard Slave States*, 564; *Report of Court of Claims*, #81, 34 C., 3 s., Feb. 23, 1857; Flanders, *Plantation Slavery in Georgia*, 198.

64. W. F. Holmes, "The New Castle and Frenchtown Turnpike and Railroad Company," *DH*, 10 (1962–63), 172; Douglass, *Narrative*, 93–98. Douglass was apparently a victim of the competition for jobs between free Negro and white shipyard workers during the depression of 1837–43. When white workers struck to demand the discharge of the free Negroes, they did not object to Douglass' employment because he was a slave. According to Douglass, he was beaten because he was a black man.

65. "Memorandum of Work, Febr. 1, 1831," and "Abstract from the Rolls of Labour on the Dry Dock in the Gosport Navy Yard," 1831–1832, Baldwin Papers (Baker); "Slaves on a Federal Project," *B.H.S. Bulletin*, 8 (1934), 32–33.

66. For evidence of integration without antagonism at iron works, textile mills, internal improvement and railroad projects, and other kinds of milling and manufacturing enterprises, see Starobin, *Industrial Slavery*, ch. 4, footnote 66.

67. Richmond *Whig*, June 26, 1846; Buckingham, *Slave States*, II, 112; Auraria, Ga., *Western Herald*, April 30, 1833, quoted in Coulter, *Auraria*, 58–59.

68. According to Wyatt, "Petersburg," 12–13, the *Express* reported in 1858 that one tobacco factory employed forty white workers, whose department was kept very clean, "while all association with their 'odiferous' [black] co-laborers is entirely obviated." "A Southerner," writing to the Georgia *Citizen*, July 21, 1850, objected to the use of slave labor in cotton factories in the following terms: "*Negroes*, slaves, and White men, and *White Women*, co-operating in a cotton factory! What an association! Disgusting!"

69. Olmsted, *Seaboard Slave States*, 48; Olmsted, *Back Country*, II, 57; Olmsted, *Journey Through Texas*, 114–115; Taylor, *Slavery in*

Louisiana, 83; Morris, "Measure of Bondage," 229; Kemble *Journal*, 104, 122–126, 129.

70. Negro Time Book, Nov. 17 and 29, 1833, Graham Papers (UV), for fight between "Capt. R." and "Bryce McC."; the objection by some Moravians to employing slaves, instead of whites, in textile mills is recounted in A. L. Fries, "One Hundred Years of Textiles in Salem," *NCHR*, 27 (1950), 13.

71. Woodward, *Strange Career of Jim Crow*, 12–13.

Chapter Five: The Economics of Industrial Slavery

1. The literature on the profitability of plantation slavery is reviewed in H. D. Woodman, "The Profitability of Slavery," *JSH*, 29 (1963), 303–325, and S. L. Engerman, "The Effects of Slavery Upon the Southern Economy," *EEH*, second series, 4 (1967), 71–97.

2. H. O. Stekler, *Profitability and Size of Firm* (Berkeley, 1963), ch. 1 and 2; Conrad and Meyer, *The Economics of Slavery*, ch. 3.

3. U. B. Phillips, "The Economic Cost of Slave-holding in the Cotton Belt," *PSQ*, 20 (1905), 257–275, U. B. Phillips, *American Negro Slavery* (New York, 1918), especially chs. 18 and 19; C. W. Ramsdell, "The Natural Limits of Slavery Expansion," *MVHR*, 16 (1929), 151–171; E. D. Genovese, "The Significance of the Plantation for Southern Economic Development," *JSH*, 28 (1962), 422–437; E. D. Genovese, *The Political Economy of Slavery* (New York, 1965); D. North, *The Economic Growth of the United States, 1790–1860* (Englewood Cliffs, 1961), esp. p. 132. Cf. R. R. Russel, "The General Effects of Slavery Upon Southern Economic Progress," *JSH*, 4 (1938), 34–54, and "The Effects of Slavery Upon Non-Slaveholders in the Ante-Bellum South," *AH*, 15 (1941), 112–126, and *Economic Aspects of Southern Sectionalism*; D. Dowd, "A Comparative Analysis of Economic Development in the American West and South," *JEH*, 16 (1956), 558–574; Wade, *Slavery in the Cities*, esp. chs. 1 and 9, argues that slavery was dying in the largest southern cities and thus tends to lend weight to the old Ramsdell hypothesis.

4. See table on textile mills in appendix.

5. D. Ross to J. Staples, Sept. 16, 1813, Ross Letterbook (VHS); *De Bow's Review*, 6 (1848), 295; Charleston *Mercury*, Feb. 18,

1859; Tredegar Stockholders' Minutebook, reports for 1838–48, and Tredegar Corporate Holdings, 1866, pp. 7–9 (VSL).

6. *Report of Court of Claims*, #81, 34 C., 3 s., 1857, 62–64; L. McLane, Documents of Manufactures, *House Doc.* #308, 22 C., 1 s., 1832, 676–677; New Orleans *Picayune*, Jan. 2, 1853.

7. *Niles' Register*, 39 (1830), 271–272; Olmsted, *Seaboard Slave States*, 686–688; Report of the Secretary of the Treasury, *House Exec. Doc.* #6, 29 C., 1 s., 1845, 708–709, 748; Taylor, *Slavery in Louisiana*, 96–101; Sitterson, *Sugar Country*, 157–166, 178–184, 197, and *passim*.

8. J. E. Metts to J. R. Grist, Dec. 5, 1858, Grist Papers (Duke); letters dated 1854–60, Williams Papers (UNC); *De Bow's Review*, 7 (1849), 560–562, and 11 (1851), 303–305; Stephenson, ed., *Franklin*, 114, 177–180, 213–217; *Harper's Monthly*, 13 (1856), 451, and 14 (1857), 441; J. M. Cheney to E. Bellinger, Feb. 16, 1855, Misc. Mss. (SCHS); C. H. Ambler, ed., *Correspondence of R.M.T. Hunter*, AHA *Annual Report* (1916), 176–177.

9. Marshall, ed., *Bates Papers*, I, 111–112, 244. For lead mining, see inventory of Jan. 1, 1851, and Will of May 1, 1856, Desloge Papers (MoHS); Report on Salt Springs, and Lead and Copper Mines, *House Doc.* #128, 18 C., 1 s., 1824, 20–22, 130–133; Report of Secretary of Treasury, *House Exec. Doc.* #6, 29 C., 1 s., 1845, 660, 664–665; and *Mining Magazine*, 1 (1853), 164–166. For gold mining, see 1828 memo and undated account sheets, Fisher Papers (UNC); High Shoal Gold Mine Records (UNC); letters of 1830–33 and account book, vol. 10, 1843, Brown Papers (UNC); Expense Book of S. Burwell and J. Y. Taylor, 1832–39 (UNC); T. G. Clemson to J. C. Calhoun, Jan. 23 and 24, 1843, and T. G. Clemson to P. Calhoun, Oct. 12, 1856, Clemson Papers (Clemson); *Mining Magazine*, 11 (1858), 211 and 12 (1859–60), 365–366; *De Bow's Review*, 12 (1852), 542–543; *American Farmer*, series 1, vol. 12 (1830), 230; *Hunt's Magazine*, 31 (1854), 517.

10. See tables on railroads, canals, and turnpikes in appendix.

11. Telfair Account Books, 1794–1861, #s 90, 87, 88, 89, 152, 153, 155, and 156 (GHS); Hart Gold Mine Company Accounts, 1855–57, Latimer Plantation Book (UG); Journal of James River Steamboat Company, 1833–49 (VSL); the Palfrey Account Books, 1842–61 (LSU) reveal that Louisiana sugar plantations and mills earned substantial profits.

12. J. H. Couper Accounts, 1827–52 (UNC); the financial statements and reports for Hopeton and Hamilton plantations, 1830's to 1843, 1849, and 1853–65, and J. H. Couper to F. P. Corbin, March 28, 1859, Corbin Papers (NYPL) permit the computation of Couper's profits from rice milling beyond the year 1852; T. P. Govan, "Was Plantation Slavery Profitable?" *JSH*, 8 (1942), 513–535, demonstrates the profitability of Couper's rice milling enterprise from 1827 to 1852.

13. Account Book, vol. 4, 1833–39, 1856–61, Manigault Papers (UNC); Govan, "Was Plantation Slavery Profitable?" 513–535, demonstrates the profitable returns on Manigault's rice milling investment. For the earnings of other rice mills, see J. B. Irving's Windsor and Kensington Plantations Record Books, 1840–52, and T. Pinckney's estate appraisals and account books, 1842–63 and 1827–64 (CLS).

14. R. Evans, Jr., "The Economics of American Negro Slavery," *Aspects of Labor Economics* (Princeton, 1962), p. 217; Wall, Ebenezer Pettigrew, 308.

15. See below on the use of women, children, and superannuates in southern industries; cf. Conrad and Meyer, *The Economics of Slavery*, ch. 3.

16. Stampp, *Peculiar Institution*, ch. 9, and above chs. 2, 3, and 4. According to R. W. Fogel and S. Engerman, *The Reinterpretation of American Economic History* (New York, 1968), part 7, the manuscript census schedules reveal that about one-half of the slave population was in the labor force—a figure which is close to, if not at, the maximum possible participation rate. Since 44 per cent of the slaves were children under fourteen years old and 4 per cent were adults over sixty, virtually every able-bodied adult slave and most teen-agers were compelled to work. The slave participation-rate in the labor force was, moreover, 60 per cent greater than that of white workers.

17. See above, chapter 4, on the unreliability of white workers in the South.

18. Genovese, *Political Economy of Slavery*, 226–227; cf. below, chapter 6, on the politics of industrial slavery.

19. Genovese, *Political Economy of Slavery*, 37 note 13.

20. For evidence on this point, see Starobin, Industrial Slavery, ch. 5, note 20. The wages of white southern textile workers were somewhat lower.

21. See appendix on the cost of slave hiring in my dissertation:

Summary of Cost of Slave Hiring at Southern Industries
(in dollars)

PERIOD	DAILY	MONTHLY	ANNUALLY
1799–1833	.76	13.14	66.39
1833–52	.77	16.51	100.55
1853–61	1.44	19.68	150.00

22. Govan, "Was Plantation Slavery Profitable?" 513–535; Engerman, "The Effects of Slavery," 71–97; Stampp, *Peculiar Institution*, ch. 9; and above, ch. 3.

23. Conrad and Meyer, *The Economics of Slavery*, ch. 3; Stampp, *Peculiar Institution*, ch. 9.

24. See table on maintenance costs in appendix.

25. These prices are taken from the records of slave-employing industrial enterprises.

26. See table on maintenance costs.

27. *Ibid.*

28. *Ibid.*

29. For white wages, see Starobin, Industrial Slavery, ch. 5, note 20.

30. Boarding bills for October and Dec. 31, 1859, Treasurers' Papers: Internal Improvements: Cape Fear and Deep River Navigation Works (NCA); Jackson *Mississippian*, May 4, 1849; Graham Cotton Mill Daybook and Inventory, 1837–41 (UK); vol. 26, Hawkins Papers (UNC); account sheet, 1857–58, Jordan and Davis Papers (WSHS).

31. Norris, *Frontier Iron*, 40–41.

32. D. Myerle's testimony in *Report of Court of Claims*, #81, 34 C., 3 s., 1857; memorial of F. G. Hansford, *et al.*, Virginia *Board of Public Works Report*, *1854*, p. 403; Report of the Virginia and Tennessee Railroad, Virginia *Board of Public Works Report*, *1855*; Buckingham, *Slave States*, I, 264–265 and II, 112–113; *De Bow's Review*, 11 (1851), 319–320; Lander, "Slave Labor in South Carolina Cotton Mills," 170–171.

33. Rolls of Labor, 1831–32, and Memorandum of Work, 1831, Baldwin Papers and Selekman Notes (Baker). However, the daily rent of slave *common* laborers averaged about 72 cents, while the daily

wages of white common laborers averaged $1.01. Therefore, savings came in the cost of the more skilled hammerers, where slaves were cheaper than whites.

34. Cost of Hands for 1858, 1859, and undated, loose inserts in Jemison and Sloan Company contract account book, 1856–59, Jemison Papers (UA); Daybook and Inventory, 1837–41, Ledger and Inventory Book, 1832–45, Factory Time Book, 1847–52, Ledger, 1846–47, and Account Book, 1847–50, Graham Cotton Mill Papers (UK); Wages Ledger, 1856–61, Daybook, 1856–59, and G. Woolley to W. Peck & Sons, June 2, 1861, Lettercopybook, Woolley Papers (UK). However, the Woolley Papers reveal that common slave weavers cost almost as much to hire and to maintain as common white weavers. Again, savings came with skilled labor, where slaves were cheaper than whites.

35. Dew, *Ironmaker to the Confederacy*, 18–20, 29–32, tables, and notes for prices of Tredegar iron products; J. R. Anderson to H. Row, Jan. 3, 1848, Tredegar Letterbook (VSL).

36. J. McRae to J. Gadsden, Nov. 4, 1849, McRae Lettercopybooks (WSHS).

37. *De Bow's Review*, 19 (1855), 193–195.

38. For the cost of slave hiring and white wage rates, see my dissertation, Industrial Slavery in the Old South, appendices, and ch. 5, footnote 20. In addition, R. Mills, *Statistics of South Carolina* (Charleston, 1826), 427–428, calculated that in Charleston in 1826 black common laborers cost half as much as whites; skilled blacks averaged 82¾ cents per day, while skilled whites averaged $1.37½.

39. Dew, *Ironmaker to the Confederacy*, 32; North, *Economic Growth, passim*.

40. See works cited above in footnotes 1 and 3.

41. See *De Bow's Review*, 1846 to 1862, for such programs.

42. Roswell Manufacturing Company Stockholders' Minutes and King papers, journals, accounts, and letterbooks (GA); D. R. Williams Papers (USC); *Hunt's Magazine*, 15 (1846), 417; and 17 (1847), 323. Cf. Report of the Secretary of the Treasury, *House Exec. Doc. #6*, 29 C., 1 s. (1845), 676; Bremer, *Homes*, II, 490; *De Bow's Review*, 7 (1849), 457–458; agreement, Aug. 29, 1828, Black Papers (USC); Richmond *Dispatch*, Jan. 5, 1860; P. Woolfolk to L. Hill, Dec. 30, 1845, Hill Papers, Brock Collection (Huntington); vols. 2 and 20, J. H. Cocke Papers (UNC); Bassett, ed., *Plantation Overseer Letters*, 150–151; J. Gunnelly to M. Telfair, Jan. 11, 1835,

Telfair Papers (GHS); F. L. Fries Woollen Mill Diary, 1840–42 (NCA); Lexington *Western Review*, 2 (1820), 296–298; J. E. Colhoun Commonplace Book, p. 26 (Clemson); W. W. Davis to W. Weaver, Aug. 13, 1829, Weaver Papers (Duke); D. Ross to T. Rice, Sept. 7, 1813, Ross Letterbook (VHS).

43. Louisville *Journal*, Nov. 29, 1830, misc. papers H (Filson); Moore, *Hemp Industry*, appendix; paylists, 1827–28, Leslie Papers (Duke); Poor, *Haldeman's Picture of Louisville*, 88.

44. Northrup, *Narrative*, 211–212; *Southern Agriculturist*, 6 (1833), 518, 527, 573.

45. Liddell Papers (LSU); entry for Dec. 3, 1857, R. R. Barrow Residence Journal (UNC); "Distribution of hands in Sugar rolling, 1857," Randolph Papers (LSU).

46. Bancroft, *Census of Savannah, 1848*, 34–35; "Memoranda," vol. 4, Manigault Papers (UNC); vol. 4, p. 54, Couper Papers (UNC); *Southern Agriculturist*, 8 (1835), 169–174.

47. Webber, "Senf's Account of Santee Canal," 120; *American Railroad Journal*, 9 (1839), 80–81; Reports of Southern Railroad Company, Mississippi *Journal of House of Representatives*, regular session 1850, pp. 113, 119, 128, and called session, 1852, p. 26; Montgomery and West Point Railroad *Report*, 1850, p. 19; statement of slaves owned by Mississippi Railroad Company, Mississippi *Journal of House of Representatives*, regular sessions, 1844, p. 486, and 1841, p. 98; "Abstract of Real Estate," Aug. 9, 1839, New Orleans and Carrollton Railroad Papers (Tulane); Charleston *Mercury*, Dec. 15, 1859; *Proceedings of the Annual Meeting of Stockholders of the North Carolina Railroad*, July 14, 1853; vol. 1, Quitman Papers (MA); Hickman, *Mississippi Harvest*, 23 and tables.

48. Steiner, ed., "South Atlantic States in 1833," 348; Elmore Papers (USC and LC); —— Woods to H. Edmundson, Nov. 26, 1831, March 12 and Feb. 5, 1832, Edmundson Papers (VHS); "List of Slaves at the Oxford Iron Works . . . Taken 15 January, 1811," Bolling Papers (Duke); D. Ross to J. Duffield, Jan. 9, 1813, and Ross to ——, ca. Nov., 1812, Ross Letterbook (VHS).

49. J. E. Colhoun Commonplace Book (Clemson); De Bow, *Industrial Resources*, II, 178.

50. See, for example, Graham Cotton Mill Papers (UK); Woolley Papers (UK); and King Papers (GA).

51. Jackson *Mississippian*, March 19, 1845.

52. *De Bow's Review,* 25 (1858), 114.

53. *Southern Agriculturist,* 6 (1833), 587; *De Bow's Review,* 18 (1855), 350–351; Northrup, *Narrative,* 155–156; K. W. Skinner to C. Manigault, Feb. 8, 1852, Manigault Papers (Duke).

54. Jackson *Mississippian,* March 19, 1845; *De Bow's Review,* 11 (1851), 319–320, and 22 (1857), 394, 397; Richmond *Enquirer,* Oct. 7, 1827; *Southern Agriculturist,* 7 (1834), 582, and 4 (1831), 368; New Orleans *Picayune,* Oct. 16, 1858.

55. Fogel and Engerman, *Reinterpretation,* part 7.

56. See appendix on the cost of management in my dissertation, Industrial Slavery.

57. Moore, "Simon Gray," 472–484.

58. Account Books, 1794–1863, Telfair Papers (GHS); Northrup, *Narrative,* 89–99.

59. G. Rogers, *Memoranda of Travels* (Cincinnati, 1845), 196, 310; D. B. McLaurin to W. H. Richardson, April 19 and Jan. 27, 1855, and pass dated April 20, 1855, Richardson Papers (Duke); M. Bryan to W. W. Davis, June 30, 1846, Jordan and Davis Papers (WSHS).

60. Vols. 39, 44, 17, 30, 45, and 46, Hawkins Papers (UNC).

61. Kemble, *Journal,* 113, 116–117, 168, 176, and 187–188; C. C. Jones to Sandy, Aug. 15, 1853, and C. C. Jones to T. J. Shepard, March 30, 1850, Jones Papers (Tulane); H. T. Cook, *David R. Williams* (New York, 1916), 140; John B. Mordecai, *A Brief History of the Richmond, Fredericksburg and Potomac Railroad* (Richmond, 1941), 17; Richmond *Times-Dispatch,* Jan. 31, 1943 (VHS); Sydnor, *Slavery in Mississippi,* 7; *Farmers' Register,* 5 (1837), 315; Duke de la Rochefoucault-Liancourt, *Travels Through the United States* (London, 1799), III, 122–123.

62. Olmsted, *Seaboard Slave States,* 425–429.

63. R. Jemison, Jr., Letterbooks, 1844–54 (UA); cf. Olmsted, *Seaboard Slave States,* 553.

64. For further information and sources on slave managers in industry, see my dissertation, Industrial Slavery, ch. 3 and 5, note 64.

65. See earlier discussion on the costs of slave ownership.

66. E. M. Lander, ed., "Two Letters by William Mayrant on His Cotton Factory, 1815," *SCHM,* 54 (1953), 3–4; *American Farmer,* series 1, vol. 9 (Oct. 12, 1827), 235–314; Lander, "Development of Textiles in South Carolina Piedmont," 92; Jackson *Mississippian,*

Dec. 4, 1844; Charleston *Courier*, Feb. 19, 1845. Another industry which often used white managers was sugar milling.

67. Report upon . . . the N.C. Gold Mining Co., Sept. 5, 1832, Fisher Papers (UNC); Richmond *Enquirer*, March 23, 1839, and Jan. 9, 1840; B. Broomhead to B. Smith, Sept. 7, 1857, Smith Papers (Duke); Olmsted, *Seaboard Slave States*, 47–48; *Harper's Monthly*, 15 (1857), 297; *De Bow's Review*, 7 (1849), 546–547, and 29 (1860), 378; S. Ashmore to C. Thomas, March 26, 1860, Silver Hill Mining Company Papers (NCA).

68. Pendleton, "Short Account, 1796"; J. Baker to S. Plaisted, Nov. 23, 1839, Plaisted Papers (LSU); *Niles' Register*, 47 (1834), 55; account book, 1812–17, Telfair Papers (GHS); entry for June 6, 1857, D. C. Barrow Diaries (UG); C. L. Benson to M. Grist, Oct. 1, 1855, Grist Papers (Duke).

69. Latrobe Papers (Tulane); Baldwin Papers (Baker); C. K. Brown, *A State Movement in Railroad Development* (Chapel Hill, 1928), 12; M. S. Heath, *Constructive Liberalism* (Cambridge, 1954), 241, 261; C. Goodrich, *Government Promotion of American Canals and Railroads* (New York, 1960), 98; *De Bow's Review*, 27 (1859), 725.

70. J. M. Taylor to F. H. Elmore, June 25, 1840, and agreements of Sept. 30 and Oct. 5, 1837, Elmore Papers (LC); Richmond *Enquirer*, June 3, 1851; Jordan, Davis & Co. to W. Weaver, Nov. 24, 1830, W. Ross to W. Weaver, Nov. 27, 1831, and G. P. Taylor to W. Weaver, Oct. 7, 1831 and May 2, 1832, Weaver Papers (Duke); W. Rex to W. Weaver, Jan. 8, 1859, Weaver Papers (UV).

71. E. Steadman, *A Brief Treatise on Manufacturing in the South* (Clarksville, Tenn., 1851), 108; Columbia *South Carolinian*, Dec. 18, 1844; *De Bow's Review*, 26 (1859), 95–96.

72. *De Bow's Review*, 14 (1853), 622–623.

73. Report of the Upper Appomattox Company, Virginia *Board of Public Works Report, 1822*, p. 33.

74. Richmond *Dispatch*, Dec. 9, 1853, for example.

75. T. J. Green to the Executive Committee of the Southern Pacific R.R. Co., Oct. 14, 1856, Green Papers (UNC).

76. J. R. Anderson to H. Row, Jan. 3, 1848, Tredegar Letterbook (VSL). However, employing slave labor could not solve Tredegar's problem of competing entirely, since American labor and transportation were costly and Virginia coal and iron were of a low quality. Tredegar's "most glaring weakness" lay not in its use

of slave labor, according to Dew, *Ironmaker to the Confederacy*, p. 32, but in its "pitifully inadequate raw materials base" and in the southern transportation system.

77. See earlier discussion on the efficiency of slave labor and ch. 4 for further information on Tredegar. For sources on the use of white managers at other industrial enterprises, see my dissertation, Industrial Slavery, ch. 5, notes 66 and 77.

78. Phillips, "The Economic Cost of Slaveholding," 257–275; Phillips, *Transportation*, 388–389; F. Linden, "Repercussions of Manufacturing in the Ante-Bellum South," *NCHR*, 18 (1940), 328.

79. As a source of industrial capital, the money derived from mercantile activity—mentioned in L. Atherton, *The Southern Country Store* (Baton Rouge, 1949), ch. 6, p. 194, 204—seems less important than agricultural-based accumulation.

80. Standard and Griffin, "Textiles in North Carolina," 15–16; Coulter, "Scull Shoals," 41–43; G. A. Henry to wife, Dec. 3 and Nov. 28, 1846, Henry Papers (UNC); Spinning Book, 1806–7, Tayloe Papers (VHS); E. Carrington to A. Hamilton, Oct. 4, 1791, Cole, ed., *Correspondence of Alexander Hamilton*, 94, 145; Abdy, *Journal of a Residence*, II, 349.

81. Bill, May 9, 1829, account sheet, May 14, 1831, and J. N. Williams to J. Chesnut, May 17, 1831, Chesnut-Miller-Manning Papers (SCHS); same to same, ca. Oct., 1831, Chesnut Papers (WSHS); account sheets, 1829, 1830, June 19, 1830, and Feb. 14, 1835, Williams Papers (USC).

82. Various financial documents, Elmore Papers (LC and USC); account sheet, ca. 1840, P. M. Butler Papers (USC).

83. M. Austin, Description of the Lead Mines, 1804, *American State Papers: Public Lands*, I, 207; various letters between T. G. Clemson and J. C. Calhoun, 1842–43, Calhoun and Clemson Papers (USC and Clemson); *American Farmer*, series 4, vol. 4 (1849), 252.

84. *American Railroad Journal*, 28 (1855), 577.

85. For further information on the financing of southern transportation enterprises, see *De Bow's Review, American Railroad Journal, Western Journal and Civilian*, and the reports of boards of internal improvements and public works of the various slave states.

86. *American Railroad Journal*, 23 (1850), 9.

87. For information on the public capitalization of southern internal improvements and the ratio of public to private investment, see C. Goodrich, "The Virginia System of Mixed Enterprise," *PSQ*,

64 (1949), 366–369 and tables; C. Goodrich, *Government Promotion of American Canals and Railroads, passim;* Taylor, *Transportation Revolution, passim;* Heath, *Constructive Liberalism,* 287–289; Smith, *Economic Readjustment of an Old Cotton State,* 179–183; J. W. Million, *State Aid to Railways in Missouri* (Chicago, 1896), 232–236; D. Jennings, "The Pacific Railroad Company," *Missouri Historical Society Collections,* 6 (1931), 309; T. W. Allen, "The Turnpike System in Kentucky," *FCHQ,* 28 (1954), 248–258 note; C. B. Boyd, Jr., "Local Aid to Railroads in Central Kentucky," *KHSR,* 62 (1964), 9–16; S. J. Folmsbee, *Sectionalism and Internal Improvements in Tennessee* (Knoxville, 1939), 28, 122, 135, 265; S. G. Reed, *A History of Texas Railroads* (Houston, 1941), *passim;* M. E. Reed, "Government Investment and Economic Growth: Louisiana's Ante-Bellum Railroads," *JSH,* 28 (1962), 184, 189; and railroad reports in *De Bow's Review,* 26 (1859), 458–460, and 28 (1860), 473–477; *American Railroad Journal,* 28 (1855), 771; and the *Western Journal and Civilian,* 14 (1855), 292. Taylor, *Transportation Revolution,* 92, estimates that in 1860 about 55 per cent of the investment in railroads in the eleven Confederate states came from state and local authorities. This accounts for neither private investment in internal improvements other than railroads, nor investment generally in such states as Maryland, Kentucky, and Missouri.

88. For federal funding of southern enterprises, see Goodrich, *Government Promotion,* 156–162; Taylor, *Transportation Revolution,* 49–50, 95–96, 67–68; Reed, "Government Investment . . . Louisiana's Railroads," 184, 189.

89. For foreign funding of southern enterprises, see Kemble, *Journal,* 104–122; Hidy, *House of Baring,* 281, 330, 336; Ratchford, *American State Debts,* ch. 5; McGrane, *Foreign Bondholders and State Debts,* p. 89, and ch. 9–13; *Niles' Register,* 29 (1825), 178; 40 (1831), 270; and 42 (1832), 91; Governor's Message, Milledgeville *Federal Union,* Nov. 6, 1849, and Dec. 2, 1845; Barclay, *Ducktown, passim;* correspondence for 1845–48, and 1855–61, Gorrell Papers (UNC); Green, "Gold Mining, Virginia," 357–365; Green, "Gold Mining, Georgia," 224–225; *American Journal of Science,* 57 (1849), 295–299.

90. Taylor, *Transportation Revolution,* 97–102, and *passim.*

91. Financial documents and letters, Elmore Papers (LC and USC), and P. M. Butler Papers (USC).

92. W. P. Browne to G. Baker, Jan. 30 and 31, 1857, Browne Papers (AA).

93. Reports of Upper Appomattox Company, Virginia *Board of Public Works Reports, 1816*, p. ii, and *1835*, p. 42; Reports of Roanoke Navigation Company, Virginia *Board of Public Works Reports, 1823*, p. 69, *1838*, pp. 98, 100, *1839*, p. 125, and *1854*, pp. 487–488.

94. Report of Slate River Company, Virginia *Board of Public Works Report, Jan. 24, 1828*, p. 23; *American Railroad Journal*, 5 (1836), 817; J. Andreassen, "Internal Improvements in Louisiana," *LHQ*, 30 (1947), 46–47.

95. A. C. Caruthers to W. B. Campbell, Jan. 28, 1838, Campbell Papers (Duke), for the entire scheme.

96. Smith, *Economic Readjustment of an Old Cotton State*, 115–134; G. R. Woolfolk, "Planter Capitalism and Slavery: the Labor Thesis," *JNH*, 41 (1956), 103–116.

97. Genovese, *Political Economy of Slavery*, 20, 24–25, 34, 37 note 13, 159–172, 185, 276–277; North, *Economic Growth*, 126, 130, 132, 166, 170, 172–176, 205–206.

98. Genovese, *Political Economy of Slavery*, *passim*; North, *Economic Growth*, *passim*. For further discussion of southern income distribution, see Engerman, "Effects of Slavery," 71–97; F. L. Owsley, *Plain Folk of the Old South*, *passim*; F. Linden, "Economic Democracy in the Slave South," *JNH*, 31 (1946), 140–189.

99. However uneven income distribution was *within* the South, recent comparisons of regional and national wealth for 1840 and 1860 suggest that southern income levels and rates of growth compared favorably with those of the free states. See Engerman, "Effects of Slavery," 71–97, especially note 35, and R. Easterlin, "Regional Income Trends, 1840–1950," in S. Harris, ed., *American Economic History* (New York, 1961), 525–547. If one revises upward the maintenance cost of slaves (as Genovese, *Political Economy of Slavery*, 275–280, has done, and as I have also done above), then the size of the southern market and the demand for manufactured goods also increases.

100. Dew, *Ironmaker to the Confederacy*, 32; North, *Economic Growth*, 122–126; Genovese, *Political Economy of Slavery*, 159–165; W. Miller, "A Note on the Importance of the Interstate Slave Trade of the Ante-Bellum South," *JPE*, 73 (1965), 181–187.

101. Taylor, *Transportation Revolution*, chs. 1 and 10; Griffin, "Origins of Southern Cotton Manufacture, 1807–1816," 5–12;

Griffin, "South Carolina Homespun Company," 402–414; and Starobin, Industrial Slavery, ch. 1 and tables.

102. Taylor, *Transportation Revolution*, chs. 1 and 10; Eaton, *Southern Civilization*, chs. 9 and 10; Stampp, *Peculiar Institution*, 398–399.

103. Genovese, *Political Economy of Slavery*, 165–166.

104. Stampp, *Peculiar Institution*, 397. Though limited markets restricted southern industrialization, the extent of this phenomenon should not be exaggerated. Plantation self-sufficiency, slow urbanization, and other market factors did not restrict consumption entirely. Recent studies have also shown that plantation and slave consumption were higher than once thought, and that some southern businessmen found substantial markets outside of the slave states. See Genovese, *Political Economy of Slavery*, 25, 159–162, 170, 185, and 276–277; and North, *Economic Growth*, 130.

Chapter Six: The Politics of Industrial Slavery

1. Previous discussions of the debate over and the campaign for industrial slavery have suffered from several shortcomings. Opinion on the use of slave labor in industries has generally been confused with actual employment. The "boosterism" which permeated many magazines, such as *De Bow's Review*, has not been adequately accounted for. The debate was not confined simply to the question of textile manufacturing, but embraced the industrialization process as a whole. The controversy began in the 1790's and continued in the 1820's, long before the most intensive period of debate in the 1840's and 1850's. See, for example, P. G. Davidson, "Industrialism in the Ante-Bellum South," *SAQ*, 27 (1938), 405–425; J. G. Van Deusen, *The Economic Bases of Disunion in South Carolina* (New York, 1928); C. S. Boucher, "The Ante-Bellum Attitude of South Carolina towards Manufacturing and Agriculture," *Washington University Studies*, III (St. Louis, 1916); F. Linden, "Repercussions of Manufacturing in the Ante-Bellum South," *NCHR*, 18 (1940), 313–331; N. W. Preyer, "The Historian, The Slave, and The Ante-Bellum Textile Industry," *JNH*, 46 (April, 1961), 67–83; H. Collins, "The Southern Industrial Gospel before 1860," *JSH*, 12 (1946), 386–402. Cf. E. D. Genovese, *The Political Economy of Slavery* (New York, 1965), chs. 8, 9.

2. Goodrich, *Government Promotion*, 87; J. Cooke, ed., *The Reports of Alexander Hamilton* (New York, 1964), 115–205; R. W. Griffin, "The Origins of Southern Cotton Manufacture, 1807–1816," *CHR*, 1 (1961), 5–12; McColley, *Slavery and Jeffersonian Virginia*, 20.

3. U. B. Phillips, *Life and Labor in the Old South* (New York, 1929), 177; cf. Bruchey, ed., *Cotton and the Growth of the American Economy*, tables.

4. *Ibid.*; Taylor, *Transportation Revolution*, esp. ch. 5 and 8.

5. Baltimore *American Farmer*, series 1, vol. 9 (Sept. 28, 1827), 219, 244; cf. Lexington *Western Review*, 2 (June, 1820), 296–298; Richmond *Enquirer*, Oct. 9, 1827.

6. Unless otherwise indicated the next several paragraphs are based on articles and letters in the Baltimore *American Farmer*, series 1, volume 9, October, 1827, through April, 1828, and volume 10, December, 1828. Cf. *Southern Agriculturist*, 1 (1828), 358.

7. *American Farmer*, series 1, vol. 9 (Oct. 5, 1827), 225–226; *Southern Agriculturist*, 1 (1828), 548; Cook, *Williams*, 143–144.

8. Clark, *Manufactures*, 620, appendix XI; J. Madison to H. Clay, April 2, 1833, Colton, ed., *Correspondence of Henry Clay*, 359. Cf. "Hamilton," in *American Farmer*, series 1, vol. 9 (Oct. 19, 1827), 241, and the *Farmers*' original editorial query for further information on the tariff issue.

9. North Carolina Legislative Papers, 1828 (NCA); *American Farmer*, series 1, vol. 9 (Jan. 18, 1828), 346–348, and (Jan. 25, 1828), 353–354.

10. Alabama *Journal of the House of Representatives*, session 1828–29, pp. 7–8.

11. *American Farmer*, series 1, vol. 9 (March 14, 1828), 410, and vol. 10 (April 4, 1828), 19–20.

12. Phillips, *Transportation*, 114; Georgia *Journal of the House of Representatives*, regular session, 1825, p. 21; H. Fulton, *Reports on the Internal Improvement of the State of Georgia, Nov. 22, 1827*; Governors' Messages, Milledgeville *Federal Union*, Oct. 23, 1830, Dec. 25, 1833 and Nov. 5, 1834.

13. Alabama *Journal of House of Representatives*, session 1828–29, pp. 10, 12–13, 15.

14. North Carolina *Journal of the House of Commons*, session of 1829–30, p. 146, cf. p. 14.

15. Louisiana *Journal of the Senate*, 11 L., 2 s., Feb. 19, 1834, pp. 55–56; Report of the Committee on Internal Improvements, *ibid.*,

12 L., 1 s., March 6, 1835, pp. 42–43; Louisiana *Journal of House of Representatives*, 5 L., 2 s., 1861, p. 61.

16. Mississippi *Journal of the House of Representatives*, regular session, 1830, p. 144, and 1836, p. 320; *Proceedings of the Railroad Meeting . . . at Natchez . . . 10th October 1834.*

17. Mississippi *Journal of the House of Representatives*, regular session, 1838, pp. 99–101, and 1839, pp. 297–298.

18. Mississippi *Journal of the House of Representatives*, regular session, 1846, pp. 69–74, and 1850, pp. 113–125; *De Bow's Review*, 9 (1850), 349.

19. Phillips, *Life and Labor*, 177; cf. Bruchey, *Cotton*, tables.

20. *Ibid.*; Phillips, *Life and Labor*, 177.

21. Van Deusen, *The Economic Bases of Disunion in South Carolina*, 270–271, 279–281, and Linden, "Repercussions of Manufacturing," 325–326, discuss how some southern textile and iron manufacturers, represented by Gregg and Hammond, began to favor protective tariffs to foster southern industrial self-sufficiency. For the continuing campaign for slave-built transportation enterprises, see Starobin, Industrial Slavery, ch. 6, note 21.

22. J. H. Hammond, "Anniversary Oration . . . 1841," 3–23; cf. Mississippi *Journal of the House of Representatives*, regular session, 1844, p. 51.

23. Charleston *Courier*, Nov. 22 and Dec. 10, 1844; T. P. Martin, ed., "The Advent of William Gregg and the Graniteville Company," *JSH*, 11 (1945), 398–401; cf. *American Farmer*, series 4, vol. 1 (June, 1846), 369.

24. *De Bow's Review*, 8 (1850), 24–29.

25. *Ibid.*, 8 (1850), 518. Support for Gregg's position came from the Jackson *Mississippian*, Jan. 19, 1849; from Lewis Thompson, Dec., 1858, Thompson Papers (UNC); and from J. M. Wesson to J. F. H. Claiborne, Aug. 11, 1858, Claiborne Papers (UNC).

26. G. Fitzhugh, *Sociology for the South* (Richmond, 1854), 144–148.

27. C. G. Memminger to J. H. Hammond, April 28, 1849, Hammond Papers (LC).

28. *De Bow's Review*, 10 (1851), 57; *The Plough, the Loom, and the Anvil*, 4 (1851), 112. Supporters of Memminger's position are listed in my dissertation, Industrial Slavery, ch. 6, note 28.

29. J. J. Briggs to D. Daniel, July 9, 1839, Paton Papers (NCA).

30. H. W. Benham to J. G. Totten, May 1, 1839, *House Doc.* #201, 26 C., 1 s., p. 24. Cf. Irwin Letters, 1836–40 (Filson); Samuel

Walker's Elia Plantation Journal, ca. 1856–57, pp. 28–29 (Tulane); Pendleton *Farmer and Planter*, 6 (1855), 35; and Charleston *Courier*, May 22, 1832.

31. See above, Chs. 4 and 5.

32. Olmsted, *Back Country*, I, 199–200 and notes.

33. Milledgeville *Federal Union*, July 15, 1851; New York *Daily Tribune*, July 7 and 18, 1851; W. Gregg to J. H. Hammond, Dec. 1, 1848, Hammond Papers (LC); petitions, 1794, 1818, ca. 1840, Legislative Papers: Slavery Petitions (SCA); Nashville *Republican Banner*, June 12, 1858; Taylor, *Slavery in Arkansas*, 111.

34. *Niles' Register*, 44 (1833), 375; Milledgeville *Federal Union*, Jan. 6, 1846; Lyell, *Second Visit*, II, 81; W. E. B. DuBois, *The Negro American Artisan* (Atlanta, 1912), 31–32.

35. Richmond *Dispatch*, Oct. 25, 27, and 28, 1852, March 23, 1853, Dec. 24, 1857, and Jan. 18, 19, and 28, 1858; Richmond *Southern Planter*, 13 (1853), 23.

36. South Carolina *Journal of House of Representatives*, session of 1857, pp. 164, 273, session of 1858, pp. 9, 45, 60, 69, 151, 265, and sessions of 1859, 1860; petitions, Nov. 16, 1858, 1859, and n.d., Legislative Papers: Slavery Petitions (SCA); Charleston *Mercury*, March 12, 1859; *De Bow's Review*, 26 (1859), 600; message of Governor W. H. Gist, South Carolina *Journal of House of Representatives*, regular session, Nov., 1860, p. 18. For the objections raised against certain industrial uses of slave labor in Maryland, Virginia, Tennessee, Mississippi, and Louisiana, see Starobin, Industrial Slavery, ch. 6, note 36.

37. Phillips, ed., *Plantation and Frontier Documents*, II, 367–368; Milledgeville *Federal Union*, July 6, 1858 and July 5, 1859; Augusta *Southern Cultivator*, 18 (1860), 54, 204–205, 288–289, and 19 (1861), 152.

38. Heath, *Constructive Liberalism*, 353; Flanders, *Slavery in Georgia*, 205–207; Linden, "Repercussions of Manufacturing," 313–325; Genovese, *Political Economy of Slavery*, ch. 8 and 9; Russel, *Economic Aspects of Southern Sectionalism*, 53–55, 219.

39. Jackson *Mississippian*, Jan. 7, 1859.

40. Genovese, *Political Economy of Slavery*, ch. 10.

41. E. H. Berwanger, *The Frontier Against Slavery* (Urbana, 1968), 7, 10; McColley, *Slavery and Jeffersonian Virginia*, ch. 8.

42. R. Love to A. Jackson, Nov. 17, 1831, in Bassett, ed., *Jackson Correspondence*, IV, 376; Milledgeville *Federal Union*, Jan. 1,

1831; J. W. A. Sanford to G. R. Gilmer, Sept. 26, 1831, Sanford Letterbook (GA); J. E. Hays, ed., Cherokee Indian Letters, Talks and Treaties, 1786–1838, 3 vols., Project #4341, W.P.A. typescript, 1939, pp. 219–271 (GA); T. C. Bryan, ed., "Letters Concerning Georgia Gold Mines," *GHQ*, 44 (1960), 341.

43. Berwanger, *Frontier Against Slavery*, ch. 3; D. Beasley, "Slavery in California," *JNH*, 3 (1918), 40–44; the Jackson *Mississippian*, April 1, 1850, contained an advertisement entitled "California, The Southern Slave Colony," inviting Southerners to send their names, number of slaves, time of departure, etc., to "Southern Slave Colony," Jackson, Mississippi. This project, which may have been related to James Gadsden's described below, contemplated a settlement of 5,000 whites and 10,000 slaves.

44. *Congressional Globe*, 31 C., 1 s., p. 202; Genovese, *Political Economy of Slavery*, 256–260 and notes. The Charleston *Courier*, April 30, 1845, expressed similar feelings at an earlier date.

45. J. Gadsden to T. J. Green, Dec. 7, 1851, Leidesdorff Papers (Huntington).

46. H. Mann, *Slavery* [1850], 324–330.

47. Mississippi *Journal of the House of Representatives*, called session, Nov. 18, 1850, p. 10; Genovese, *Political Economy of Slavery*, 256–260; *Congressional Globe*, 31 C., 1 s., p. 731.

48. Richmond *Dispatch*, May 12, 1852.

49. M. W. Cluskey, ed., *Speeches, Messages and Other Writings of the Hon. Albert G. Brown* (Philadelphia, 1859), 588–599; *De Bow's Review*, 13 (1852), 54; Charleston *Mercury*, Feb. 28, 1860.

50. M. J. Cheney to E. Bellinger, Feb. 16, 1854, Misc. Mss. (SCHS).

51. Genovese, *Political Economy of Slavery*, 263.

52. *De Bow's Review*, 13 (1852), 54; J. Gadsden to T. J. Green, Dec. 7, 1851, Leidesdorff Papers (Huntington).

53. *De Bow's Review*, 20 (1856), 640–641; T. J. Green to the Executive Committee of the Southern Pacific Railroad, Oct. 14, 1856, Green Papers (UNC).

54. H. Wish, "The Revival of the African Slave Trade in the United States, 1856–1860," *MVHR*, 27 (1941), 569–588; R. Takaki, "The Movement to Revive the African Slave Trade in South Carolina," *SCHM*, January, 1966, 38–54.

55. South Carolina *Journal of the House of Representatives*, regular session, 1856, pp. 35–37.

56. Richmond *Whig*, March 16 and June 8, 1857.

57. *De Bow's Review*, 24 (1858), 421–422; cf. Jackson *Mississippian*, June 17, 1859.

58. Charleston *Standard*, quoted in Olmsted, *Back Country*, II, 137–138; Savannah *Daily News*, Feb. 15, 1859.

59. Jackson *Mississippian*, May 24, 1859; E. B. Bryan, *Minority Report on the Slave Trade* (Columbia, 1856), 4; C. W. Miller, *Address on Re-opening the Slave Trade* (Columbia, 1857), 4, 8.

60. L. W. Spratt, *Report of the Slave Trade Committee, Southern Commercial Convention, Montgomery, Alabama, May, 1858*.

61. Jackson *Mississippian*, April 26, May 13, May 20, and June 14, 1859; *De Bow's Review*, 27 (1859), 364; Charleston *Mercury*, May 17 and 18, 1859. Cf. Jackson *Mississippian*, Oct. 4, 1859, Feb. 3, 4, and 7, 1860; and J. G. M. Ramsey to L. W. Spratt, April 13 and 20, 1858, Ramsey Papers (UNC).

62. Charleston *Mercury*, 1859–61; *Southern Literary Messenger*, 32 (1861), 409–420.

63. T. P. Martin, "Conflicting Cotton Interests at Home and Abroad," *JSH*, 7 (1941), 180–194; Van Deusen, *Economic Bases of Disunion in South Carolina*, 306; and De Bow, *Industrial Resources*, I, 233–237, stress the fear by northern manufacturers of southern industrial competition.

64. Jackson *Mississippian*, May 4, 1849, Dec. 6, 1850; cf. Charleston *Courier*, Jan. 28, 1845.

65. Report of the Committee to Investigate the Southern Railroad Company, Mississippi *Journal of the House of Representatives*, regular session, 1850, pp. 632–633; *De Bow's Review*, 11 (1851), 316–319. Cf. message of Governor John S. Roane, Arkansas *Journal of House of Representatives*, 1850–51, pp. 40–41.

66. *De Bow's Review*, 12 (1852), 182–185.

67. New Orleans *Picayune*, Nov. 12, 1858; Jackson *Mississippian*, Sept. 2, 1859; cf. Richmond *Dispatch*, Feb. 11, 1859; "The South, in the Union or Out of It," Jackson *Mississippian*, Oct. 29, 1860; cf. P. L. Rainwater, "Economic Benefits of Secession: Opinions in Mississippi in the 1850's," *JSH*, 1 (1935), 471–474; Vicksburg *Whig*, Jan. 18, 1860.

68. Though I do not completely agree with Eugene Genovese's interpretation (*Political Economy of Slavery*, ch. 8) of the politics of slaveowning planters and industrialists, I have drawn on some of his evidence for this paragraph.

69. R. A. Wooster, *The Secession Conventions of the South* (Princeton, 1962), 16; Dew, *Ironmaker to the Confederacy*, ch. 3 and 4; Bonner, *History of Georgia Agriculture*, 91–92; B. King to W. E. Baker, Dec. 13, 1860, King Papers (GA).

70. Genovese, *Political Economy of Slavery*, ch. 8; Wooster, *Secession Conventions, passim.*

71. Genovese, *Political Economy of Slavery*, ch. 8; materials on Confederate congressmen kindly furnished by Professor Richard E. Beringer of California State College, Hayward, Calif.

72. South Carolina *Journal of the House of Representatives*, called session, Nov., 1861, p. 36; cf. Message of Governor John Letcher, Virginia *Journal of the Senate*, regular session, 1861–62, p. 19.

73. Genovese, *Political Economy of Slavery*, 206–207, suggests that some Southerners considered "a Prussian road to industrial capitalism, paved with authoritarianism [and] benevolent despotism." For an excellent discussion of industrial "revolution from above"—something which southern secessionists contemplated—in Germany and Japan in the late nineteenth century, see B. Moore, Jr., *Social Origins of Dictatorship and Democracy* (Boston, 1966), chs. 5, 7, 8, and 9.

Appendix

Table 1. Earnings of Slave-

COMPANY	LOCATION	PERIOD
a. Woodville	Woodville, Miss.	1850–61
b. Tuscaloosa	Scottsville and Tuscaloosa, Ala.	1841–58
c. Barrett and Marks	Tallapoosa County, Ala.	1845
d. Mississippi	Bankston, Miss.	1849
		1850–60
e. Martin and Weakly	Florence, Ala.	1850–60
		1855
f. Bell	Huntsville, Ala.	1850–60
g. Saluda	Columbia, S.C.	1840–50
		1849
h. Vaucluse	Aiken, S.C.	1849
		1855
i. DeKalb	Camden, S.C.	1838–48
		1849–60
j. Various factories	Augusta, Ga.	1850–60
k. Arcadia	Pensacola, Fla.	1845–60
l. Roswell	Roswell, Ga.	1842
		1843
		1844
		1845
		1846
		1847
		1848
		1849
		1850–53
		1854
		1855
		1856
		1857
		1858
		1859
		1860
		1861

DIVIDEND ON COMMON STOCK	NET PROFIT AS A PERCENTAGE OF NET WORTH	AVERAGE (%)
10–15		12.5
10–15		12.5
	15	15
"Large dividends"		
	37	37
	10–14	12+
	50	
	"Eminently successful . . . has been for many years [1850's] been paying large profits."	
"Doing a flourishing business . . . pays large dividends."		
5		5
	15.6	15.6
	"Is making money."	
10+		
15		About 13
20–30		25
"The most successful of the cotton factories operating in . . . Florida."		
20		
18		
22		
20		
20		
14		
12		
12		
Dividends not discussed at stockholders' meetings.		
10		
17.5		
10		
10		
10		
15.5		
19		15.2
13		
	GRAND AVERAGE:	16

Sources for Table 1:

a. Vol. I, part 1, p. 46, McGehee Papers (LSU).

b. New Orleans *Picayune,* Oct. 16, 1858; R. Griffin, "Cotton Manufacture in Alabama," *AHQ,* 18 (1956), 294.

c. Report of the Secretary of the Treasury, *House Exec. Doc.* #6, 29 C., 1 s., 1845, p. 649.

d. J. H. Moore, "Mississippi's Antebellum Textile Industry," *JMH,* 26 (1954), 86–90; *Niles' Register,* 75 (1849), 344.

e. Charleston *Mercury,* Feb. 26, 1858.

f. *Hunt's Magazine,* 38 (1858), 509.

g. New Orleans *Picayune,* Oct. 23, 1845; Vicksburg *Whig,* Nov. 12, 1849.

h. *De Bow's Review,* 7 (1849), 457–458, and 18 (1855), 787–788.

i. *Ibid.,* 7 (1849), 372–373, and 18 (1855), 787–788.

j. *Ibid.*

k. R. Griffin, "The Cotton Mill Campaign in Florida," *FHQ,* 40 (1962), 269.

l. Roswell Manufacturing Company's stockholders' minutes, 1842–1861 (GA); Charleston *Mercury,* Feb. 26, 1858.

Table 2. Earnings of Slave-employing Canals and Turnpikes, 1805–1861

COMPANY AND LOCATION	PERIOD	DIVIDEND (%)	PROFIT RATE (%)	AVERAGE (%)
a. Louisville and Portland Canal, Kentucky	1831–42	8–10		14.7
	1843–55	20		
b. New Orleans Navigation Company, Louisiana	1805–27	6		7.2
	1828	10		
	1829	20		
	1830	19		
	1835	5		
c. Dismal Swamp Canal, Virginia	1850's	6		6
d. James River Canal, Virginia	1808–20	12–16		14
e. James River and Kanawha Company, Virginia	1835–60		"Never profitable to the stockholders"	0
f. Roanoke Navigation Company, Virginia	1836	1.5		1.5
g. Barataria and Lafourche Canal, Louisiana	1832	30		
	1833–52		Heavily in debt	
	1853–60		Little debt	
h. Lynchburg and Salem Turnpike, Virginia	1834	4		4

Sources:

a. G. M. Bibb, Report on the Louisville and Portland Canal, *House Doc.* #66, 28 C., 2 s. (1845), pp. 7–9, 39; Paul B. Trescott, "The Louisville and Portland Canal Company, 1825–1874," *MVHR*, 44 (1958), 695, 698, 686, reports that "once completed, the canal made large profits."

b. Louisiana *Journal of the Senate*, 1827, p. 17; 1829, p. 55; 1830, pp. 47–48; 1831, pp. 38–39, 56; 1836, p. 41.

c. Frederick L. Olmsted, *A Journey through the Seaboard Slave States* (New York, 1861), 151 note.

d, e. Wayland F. Dunaway, *History of the James River and Kanawha Canal Company* (New York, 1922), 34–36, 45, 182–183.

f. Virginia *Board of Public Works Report*, 1836, p. 48.

g. Louisiana *Journal of the House of Representatives*, 1848 session, pp. 148–150; Louisiana *Journal of the Senate*, 1853, p. 28.

h. Virginia *Board of Public Works Report*, 1835, pp. 59–60.

Table 3. Earnings of Slave-

Bold figures indicate dividends on common stock; other figures

COMPANY	1835	'36	'37	'38	'39	'40	'41	'42	'43	'44	'45	'46	'47
Montgomery & West Point										3	3		
Mobile & Ohio													
Georgia			6½	7	8	8	4.1	10	7.1	6.5	5.5	7.8	4½
Central of Georgia						3.4		2.7	4½	6	6	6	5.7
Macon & Western													
Southwestern													
Western & Atlantic													
Lexington & Frankfort													
Louisville & Frankfort													
Pacific													
Charlotte & South Carolina													
Raleigh & Gaston													
Wilmington & Weldon													
Wilmington & Manchester												6	
Greensville & Roanoke					3.1	3.2	5.7	3.4	2.7	2.3	3.0	3.7	4.2
South Carolina	6	6	6	6	2	4.3	3	5	5.3	5	5⅔	5⅓	5.8
Memphis & Charleston													
Nashville & Chattanooga													
Louisa				4½	6	4½	0	0	6	6	6	6	6
Petersburg	10	10		7½	6½	3	7	0	0	3	3½	7	7
Petersburg & Roanoke						(7 to 10 per cent)						7	7
Richmond, Fredericksburg & Potomac				7				7		6	6		7
Virginia Central													
Richmond & Petersburg												3.6	4.1

Sources:

The American Railroad Journal; De Bow's Review; Hunt's Merchants' Magazine; The Journal of the Franklin Institute; The Farmer's Register; New Orleans Picayune; Virginia Board of Public Works Reports; Southern Quarterly Review; Mississippi Central Railroad Report, May 1, 1860; Ulrich B. Phillips, A History of Transportation in the Eastern Cotton Belt to 1860 (New York, 1908); B. H. Meyer and Caroline E. MacGill, History of Transportation in the United States before 1860 (Washington, 1917); H. D. Dozier, A History of the Atlantic Coast Line Railroad (Boston, 1920); Cecil K. Brown, A State Movement in Railroad Development (Chapel Hill, 1928); Samuel M. Derrick, A Centennial History of the South Carolina Railroad represent net earnings expressed as a percentage of net worth.

'48	'49	'50	'51	'52	'53	'54	'55	'56	'57	'58	'59	'60	'61	'62	AVERAGES	
	8½	9½					8			10	10					7.4
						1.2	2.7	5.4	6.9	10.5	8.0	16.2				7.3
6	6½	7	7	7	7½		3½	7½	8	6	7½	8–15			6.3	6.2
8	7–12½	8	8	8	8	14	21.0	19.8	15.4	21	22.6	20.3			10.9	11.1
12.3	17.5	15.2	9.9	12.3	12.1	12.0	14.2	10.4	9.0	11.4	14.5	18.6				13.0
			8	8	8		9	8	8	8	8	13			9.2	
					7.0	10.4	13.2	15.0	14.3	12.4	13.9	12.8	16.8			12.9
			9.9	11.4	12.3	13.3	8.0									10.9
			6	6			6				6				6	
				5	5		5	5	5	5	5	5				5
			5	5	6					13					5.5	9
				6	10½						9					8.5
		6		6						7	8				6.8	
					15					14	8.5					10.9
		7.3			9.2											4.3
2½	4	6	7	7	8	8½	9	10	8	8	8½	7			6.6	3.9
										10	12½	12				11.5
					3.5	5.7				5.6	13.7					7.1
4	4														4.4	
7	7	7	7	7	7	7	0	3	6	6	7½	10	9	12½	6.2	
															7	8.5
		7			7	12						7			6.8	8.3
			7		10	4½	6				7				10	6.1
3.7	2.8	3.9	3.9	4.5	4.2	6.2	6.6	6.0	6.2	7.0	6.5	6.7				5.1
												GRAND AVERAGE:			7.1	8.3

(Columbia, 1930); A. G. Smith, *Economic Readjustment in an Old Cotton State: South Carolina, 1820–1860* (Columbia, 1958); Robert Black, *Railroads of the Confederacy* (Chapel Hill, 1962); John B. Mordecai, *A Brief History of the Richmond, Fredericksburg and Potomac Railroad* (Richmond, 1941); Dorothy Jennings, "The Pacific Railroad Company," Missouri Historical Society *Collections*, 6 (1931), 288–314; Charles W. Turner, "The Louisa Railroad, 1836–1850," *NCHR*, 24 (1947), 34–57; Charles G. Woodward, "A Common Carrier of the South Before and During the War," R&L HS *Bulletin*, 44 (1937), 48–63.

Scattered information is available for a score or more other southern railroads.

Table 4. Annual Maintenance Cost per Industrial Slave, 1820's–1861 (in dollars)

LOCATION	YEAR	FOOD OR BOARD	CLOTHING	FOOD PLUS CLOTHING
1. Maramec Iron Works, Missouri	1820's–30's	36.50	29.20	
2. Calhoun's woolen mill, South Carolina	1830	23	5	
3. River snag boats	1829–39			120
4. Various sugar plantations, Louisiana	1830			50
5. Pine Forge, Virginia	1831–33	72		
6. Savannah River Improvement Project, Georgia	1835	54.75		
7. Robert Leslie's tobacco factory, Petersburg, Va.	1835	30		
8. William Clark's hemp factory, Kentucky	1838	72		
9. LaGrange and Memphis R.R., Tennessee	1839	96		
10. Nesbitt Iron Manufacturing Company, S.C.	ca. 1839	73		
11. Cherokee Iron Works, South Carolina	1839–40	10	3	
12. Sugar plantations, Louisiana	1845	10 (pork)	15	30+
13. Graham cotton mill, Kentucky	1847–50	35 low 40 typical 50 high	7.50	
14. Louisa R.R., Virginia	1851	75		33.25–34.25
15. Turpentine distillery, Alabama	1848			30
16. South Carolina R.R., South Carolina	1849		16	
17. A cotton mill, Mississippi	1847	73		
18. Public improvement projects, Virginia	1849	25		
19. Rocks Mill, Virginia	1838–50	120.45		

	Date			
20. Vicksburg and Jackson R.R., Mississippi	1848–50	28 low 31–45 average 33.50 high	25	
21. Chesterfield R.R., Virginia	1851	52		
22. Virginia Central R.R., Virginia	1852	43	14+	
23. James River and Kanawha Canal, Virginia	1854	42		
	1858	42–48		
24. Gold Hill Mine, North Carolina	1855	46.40	24.50	
25. Nolensville Turnpike Company, Tennessee	1854	29	11.65	
	1855	21	14.30	
	1856	15	6.87	
	1858	20.67	10.83	
	1859			
26. Hardinsburg and Cloverport Turnpike Co., Kentucky	1859–60	125	20	
27. Charleston and Savannah R.R., South Carolina	1855			
28. Cape Fear and Deep River Navigation Co., N.C.	1859	109		
29. Blue Ridge R.R., South Carolina	1860	60		
30. Silver Hill Mine, North Carolina	1860	60		60
31. Richmond, Fredericksburg and Potomac R.R., Va.	1860			
32. J. H. Couper's rice plantation, Georgia	1859	23		22–25
33. Woodville mines, Virginia	ca. 1850's	110	15	
34. Evans's estimate		24		
35. Olmsted's estimate of a sugar plantation	1850's	91.25	15	
36. W. Dearmont, builder, Georgia	1850–61			
AVERAGES:	1820's–61	51.57	14.50	44.94

Sources for Table 4:

1. Flyleaf notation, woodchopping book, vol. 10, James Collection (UMo).
2. J. E. Colhoun Commonplace Book, 1836–37 (Clemson).
3. H. Shreve, Report on Public Works, *House Doc.* #93, 26 C., 1 s., 1840, pp. 6, 9, 11–12.
4. *Niles' Register,* 39 (1830), 271.
5. Account book, vol. 8, 1831–33, Shenandoah County, Virginia, Collection (UNC).
6. Reports, 1835, Mackay-Stiles Papers, series B (UNC).
7. Bill, Dec. 31, 1835, Leslie Papers (Duke).
8. Accounts, ca. 1838 (Filson).
9. Report, July 17, 1839, *American Railroad Journal,* 9 (1839), 80–81.
10. Undated memo, ca. 1839, Elmore Papers (LC).
11. Statement, 1839–40, Elmore Papers (USC); cf. J. A. Black report, 1840, Elmore Papers (USC).
12. Report of the Secretary of the Treasury, *House Exec. Doc.* #6, 29 C., 1 s., 1845, pp. 708–709, 748.
13. Account Books, 1847–50, 1851, Graham Papers (UK).
14. Report, Nov. 20, 1848, Virginia *Board of Public Works Report, 1848,* p. 431.
15. *De Bow's Review,* 7 (1849), 560–562.
16. Report, 1847, *American Railroad Journal,* 21 (1848), 293–298.
17. Jackson *Mississippian,* May 4, 1849.
18. *Patent Office Report,* 1849, II, 141.
19. Account book of estate management, pp. 82–84, Muse Papers (Duke).
20. *De Bow's Review,* 9 (1850), 456.
21. Cited in R. Evans, Jr., "Some Aspects of the Domestic Slave Trade, 1830–60," *Southern Economic Journal,* 27 (1961), 336 table.
22. Account, March, 1852, box 201, Brock Collection (Huntington).
23. Report, Oct. 30, 1858, Virginia *Board of Public Works Report, 1858,* p. 277; report of 1854, in *ibid., 1854,* p. 394.
24. Account book, vol. 3, 1854–61 (UNC).
25. Nolensville Turnpike Company Minutebook, 1829–65 (TSL).
26. Hardinsburg and Cloverport Turnpike Accounts, 1859, 1860 (Filson).
27. See footnote 21 above.
28. Bills, Oct., Dec. 31, 1859, Cape Fear & Deep River Works, Treasurers' Papers (NCA).
29. Statement of costs, July 13, 1860, Hawkins Papers (UNC).
30. Ledger, p. 219 (UNC).
31. C. W. Turner, "The Richmond, Fredericksburg and Potomac," *CWH,* 7 (1961), 259.
32. J. H. Couper to F. P. Corbin, March 28, 1859, Corbin Papers (NYPL).
33. F. Green, "Gold Mining in Antebellum Virginia," *VMH,* 45 (1937), 361–362.
34. See footnote 21 above.
35. F. L. Olmsted, *A Journey in the Seaboard Slave States* (New York, 1861), 686–688.
36. Account book, ca. 1850–61, Dearmont Papers (Duke).

Bibliographical Essay

This book is based on a wide variety of printed and manuscript sources, the most important of which are the business records of southern industrial enterprises and the personal papers of slaveowning businessmen. Some secondary books and articles mentioned in the Notes provided thoughtful guidelines, but it was the primary materials which proved most crucial to the research. However, since a full bibliography of all of the documents used in this study appears in my dissertation, Industrial Slavery in the Old South, 1790–1861 (Ph.D., University of California, Berkeley, 1968)—available from University Microfilms, Ann Arbor, Michigan—only the most important primary sources are summarized below.

Printed Sources

The most useful printed sources included slave narratives, travelers' accounts, federal, state, and local records, company reports, journals, newspapers, and miscellaneous books and pamphlets. Practically all of the slave narratives listed in Charles H. Nichols' *Many Thousand Gone* (Leiden, E. J. Brill, 1963) were read, and as it happens, a large proportion of fugitive slaves were either artisans or industrially employed bondsmen. Their narratives and letters, therefore, provide valuable personal testimony about living and working conditions at southern industries and about the motivations and reasons for the escape of slaves. Among the most interesting of these narratives were: Charles Ball, *Fifty Years in Chains: or, The Life of an American Slave*, New York, H. Dayton, 1860; Leonard Black, *The Life and Sufferings of Leonard Black, A Fugitive From Slavery*, New Bedford, Mass., Benjamin Lindsey, 1847; Henry Box Brown, *Narrative of Henry Box Brown*, Boston, Brown and Stearns, 1849; William Wells Brown, *Nar-*

rative of William W. Brown, A Fugitive Slave, Boston, Anti-Slavery
Office, 1847; Henry Clay Bruce, *The New Man. Twenty-nine Years
a Slave. Twenty-nine Years a Free Man*, York, Pa., P. Anstadt and
Sons, 1895; Frederick Douglass, *Narrative of . . . an American Slave*,
Boston, Anti-Slavery Office, 1845; and *My Bondage and My Freedom*,
New York, Miller, Orton and Mulligan, 1855; Benjamin Drew, ed.,
*North-Side View of Slavery, The Refugees, or Narratives of Fugitive
Slaves in Canada*, Boston, J. P. Jewett and Co., 1856; Francis Fedric,
Slave Life in Virginia and Kentucky, London, Wertheim, Macintosh
and Hunt, 1863; Moses Grandy, *Narrative of the Life of Moses
Grandy*, Boston, O. Johnson, 1844; William Hayden, *Narrative*, Cin-
cinnati, Published by the Author, 1846; Rayford W. Logan, ed.,
*Memoirs of a Monticello Slave . . . Isaac, One of Thomas Jefferson's
Slaves*, Charlottesville, University of Virginia Press, 1951; John H.
Moore, ed., "A Letter from a Fugitive Slave," *Journal of Mississippi
History*, 24 (1962), 99–101; Solomon Northrup, *Twelve Years a Slave*,
Auburn, N.Y., Derby and Miller, 1853; James W. C. Pennington, *The
Fugitive Blacksmith*, 3rd ed., London, Charles Gilpin, 1850; Kate
Pickard, ed., *The Kidnapped and the Ransomed; Being the Personal
Recollections of Peter Still and His Wife "Vina," After Forty Years
of Slavery*, Syracuse, William T. Hamilton, 1856; Peter Randolph,
Sketches of Slave Life, 2nd ed., Boston, Published for the Author,
1855; and Carter Woodson, ed., *The Mind of the Negro as Reflected
in Letters Written During the Crisis, 1800–1860*, Washington, The
Association, 1926.

Numerous travelers visited the slave states between the Revolution
and the Civil War, and in many cases they recorded vivid descriptions of industrial work sites and urban scenes. Most travelers made
a grand tour skirting the periphery of the region, but some managed
to find their way through the interior. Practically all of the accounts
listed in Thomas D. Clark's *Travels in the Old South*, 3 vols., Norman,
University of Oklahoma Press, 1956–59, were read, and more than a
hundred of them contained interesting descriptions. However, the
most valuable ones for this study were: Frederika Bremer, *Homes of
the New World*, 2 vols., New York, Harper and Bros., 1853; James S.
Buckingham, *The Slave States of America*, 2 vols., London, Fisher and
Co., 1842; Frances Anne Kemble, *Journal of a Residence on a Georgia
Plantation in 1838–1839*, New York, Knopf, 1961; Charles Lyell, *A
Second Visit to the United States*, 2 vols., New York, Harper and
Bros., 1849; Frederick Law Olmsted's several works—*A Journey in the*

Back Country, 2 vols., New York, G. P. Putnam's Sons, 1907; *A Journey Through Texas*, New York, Dix, Edwards and Co., 1857; *A Journey in the Seaboard Slave States*, New York, Mason Brothers, 1861; and *The Cotton Kingdom*, 2 vols., New York, Mason Brothers, 1861; James Stirling, *Letters from the Slave States*, London, John W. Parker and Son, 1857; B. C. Steiner, ed., "The South Atlantic States in 1833, as seen by a New Englander [Henry Barnard]," *Maryland Historical Magazine*, 13 (1918), 267–386; [A New England Traveler], "Original Correspondence," Lexington, Kentucky, October 16, 1830, reprinted in the Louisville *Journal*, November 29, 1830, typescript, misc. papers H (Filson Club); William Cullen Bryant, "A Tour in the Old South [1843]," in Parke Godwin, ed., *Prose Writings of William Cullen Bryant*, 2 vols., New York, Russell and Russell, 1964; J. D. Legare, "An Account of an Agricultural Excursion made into the South of Georgia in the Winter of 1832," *Southern Agriculturist*, 6 (1833), 518–529, 576–577; and the excellent travelogues featured in *Harper's Monthly Magazine* for 1853, 1856, 1857, 1859, 1865, 1873, and 1879.

Of the large number of magazines and journals published in the antebellum period, the following were especially useful for information on the economics and politics of industrial slavery: *De Bow's Review*, 1846–66; *American Farmer*, 1819–60; *Southern Cultivator*, 1843–61; *American Railroad Journal*, 1832–61; *Farmers' Register*, 1833–43; *Harper's Monthly Magazine*, 1850–66; *Hunt's Merchants' Magazine*, 1839–62; *Journal of the Franklin Institute*, 1825–65; *Mining Magazine*, 1853–60; *Niles' Weekly Register*, 1811–49; *American Cotton Planter*, 1853–61; *American Journal of Science*, 1818–62; *Southern Agriculturist*, 1828–46; *Soil of the South*, 1851–56; *Western Journal and Civilian*, 1848–56; and the *Southern Planter*, 1840–61.

Many newspapers from the 1820's to the 1860's were read; but those yielding the most valuable material—especially on the hazards of industrial work, the frequency of slave escapes, other resistance activity, and the politics of industrial slavery—were the Charleston *Courier*, Charleston *Mercury*, Jackson *Mississippian*, Milledgeville (Ga.) *Federal Union*, Mobile *Register*, Nashville *Republican Banner*, Nashville *Union and American*, New Orleans *Picayune*, Richmond *Dispatch*, Richmond *Whig*, Richmond *Enquirer*, and the Boston *Liberator*. All of these newspapers reprinted items from other journals beyond their immediate area. Dwight L. Dumond's *Southern Editorials on Secession*, New York, The Century Co., 1931, is a worthy compilation.

The records of federal, state, and local governments contain a wealth of information on southern society which has not been fully utilized by historians. The *American State Papers* series, *House Executive Documents, House Reports,* and *Senate Documents* from the 7th (1802) through the 37th (1862) Congresses, as well as the *Annual Reports of the Commissioner of Patents,* 1844–57, include relevant sources on southern manufacturing; lead, salt, and gold mining; the construction of levees, roads, waterways, bridges, and public buildings; the operation of armories and navy yards; the employment of slaves by the army, navy, and customs service; and the problem of accidents and explosions on steamboats. The debates in the *Congressional Globe* for the 1840's and 1850's detail the politics of southern expansionism. The journals of both the upper and lower houses of the legislatures of Alabama, Arkansas, Florida, Georgia, Kentucky, Louisiana, Maryland, Mississippi, Missouri, North Carolina, South Carolina, Tennessee, and Virginia contain fascinating documents on the use of industrial slaves on the state level from the War of 1812 to the Civil War. The appendixes to these journals, especially, include the annual messages of governors, which provide insight into local political controversies of the period.

The reports of various state agencies, such as boards of public works, in turn embrace information pertaining to state projects of internal improvements as well as to various private river, road, turnpike, canal, bridge, ferry, and railroad companies. In addition, the printed censuses, lists of taxpayers, codes, ordinances, mayors' reports, and business directories were consulted for such cities as Charleston, Mobile, New Orleans, Savannah, Louisville, and St. Louis. J. K. Menn's The Large Slaveholders of the Deep South, 1860 (Ph.D., University of Texas, 1964) lists the occupations and slaveholdings of those Southerners with over fifty blacks. *Lloyd's Steamboat Directory and Disasters on Western Waters,* Cincinnati, J. T. Lloyd, 1856, provides graphic information on the hazards of steamboating. The annual reports of various railroad, mining, canal, and gas companies, dozens of which appeared in pamphlet form, supplement the official records.

Many pamphlets, books, and documentary collections were especially helpful at certain points in the study. Among scores of others consulted, the following were useful: James H. Hammond, "Anniversary Oration," Nov. 25, 1841, *Proceedings of the State Agricultural Society of South Carolina,* Columbia, A. S. Johnston, 1841; C. W. Miller, *Address on Re-opening the Slave Trade,* Columbia, Carolina

Times, 1857; Robert Mills, *Statistics of South Carolina*, Charleston, Hurlbut and Lloyd, 1826; Thomas Spalding, *Observations on the Method of Planting and Cultivating the Sugar-Cane in Georgia and South Carolina*, Charleston, Agricultural Society of South Carolina, May 17, 1816; E. Steadman, *A Brief Treatise on Manufacturing in the South*, Clarksville, Tenn., n.p., 1851; Helen T. Catterall, ed., *Judicial Cases Concerning American Slavery and the Negro*, 5 vols., Washington, D.C., Carnegie Institution, 1926–37; U. B. Phillips, ed., *Plantation and Frontier Documents: 1649–1863*, 2 vols., Cleveland, A. H. Clark Co., 1909; J. D. B. De Bow, ed., *The Industrial Resources of the Southern and Western States*, 3 vols., New Orleans, *De Bow's Review*, 1852–53; "Slaves on a Federal Project [the Gosport Navy Yard in the 1830's]," Business Historical Society *Bulletin*, 8 (1934), 32–33; Edward B. Bryan, *Minority Report of the Committee on Federal Relations, Respecting Certain Resolutions Relating to the Importation of Slaves*, Columbia, S.C., n.p., 1856. Moreover, the following editions of the papers of southern businessmen yielded significant evidence: Eugene C. Barker, ed., *The Austin Papers*, 4 vols., Austin, University of Texas Press, 1926; T. Conn Bryan, ed., "Letters Concerning Georgia Gold Mines, 1830–1834," *Georgia Historical Quarterly*, 44 (1960), 338–346; James W. Covington, ed., "Letters from the Georgia Gold Regions," *Georgia Historical Quarterly*, 39 (1955), 401–409; J. G. DeR. Hamilton, ed., *The Papers of William A. Graham*, 4 vols., North Carolina State Department of Archives and History, 1957–61; Herbert A. Kellar, ed., *Solon Robinson, Pioneer and Agriculturist*, 2 vols., Indianapolis, Indiana Historical Bureau, 1936; E. A. Davis, ed., *Plantation Life in the Florida Parishes of Louisiana, 1836–1846, As Reflected in the Diary of Bennet H. Barrow*, New York, Columbia University Press, 1943; Thomas M. Marshall, ed., *The Life and Papers of Frederick Bates*, 2 vols., St. Louis, Missouri Historical Society, 1926; and Wendell H. Stephenson, ed., *Isaac Franklin, Slave Trader and Planter of the Old South*, Baton Rouge, Louisiana State University Press, 1938.

Manuscript Sources

Even more vital to this study than printed primary materials were the surviving manuscript collections of southern industrial enterprises and the papers of slaveowning businessmen themselves. These manuscripts comprise a wide variety of documentary evidence without which the day-to-day operations of slave-employing industries cannot be fully comprehended. The letters, letter copybooks, diaries, receipts, contracts, and notebooks of many different kinds of businesses in all of the slave states were consulted. In addition, the account books, daybooks, ledgers, payrolls, timebooks, contracts, and stockholders' minutebooks were used. City records, town tax rolls, federal census schedules, and state legislative papers and petitions were also very helpful. Almost half of these sources can be read at the University of North Carolina at Chapel Hill and at Duke University nearby; but many important collections had to be tracked down at nearly forty other libraries, historical societies, and government archives. Though they do not represent all of the manuscripts researched, those handwritten materials which were crucial to this study are listed below alphabetically according to their location in various state depositories:

ALABAMA

Alabama Department of Archives and History, Montgomery
  William Phineas Browne Papers
Huntsville Public Library, Huntsville
  Patton, Donegan and Company Records
Mobile City Hall, Mobile
  Committee Reports of Aldermen, City of Mobile, 1833–34 (typescripts)
  Minutes of the Common Council, City of Mobile, 1844–49, 1851–59 (typescripts)
  Minutes of Aldermen of the City of Mobile, 1824–32, 1839–47, 1850–61 (typescripts)
  Mobile Tax Books, 1851, 1860
University of Alabama Library, Tuscaloosa
  Robert Jemison, Jr., Papers, Account Books, and Letterbooks
  Shelby Iron Works Collection
  Gavin Yuille Papers

CALIFORNIA

Huntington Library, San Marino
  Robert and Lewis Hill Papers
  Leidesdorff Papers
  Midlothian Mining Company Documents
  Richmond Mining Company Papers
  Virginia Railroads Papers

GEORGIA

Emory University, Atlanta
    Allatoona Iron Works Ledger
    Eureka Copper Mining Company Lettercopybooks
    Slavery Papers
Georgia Department of Archives and History, Atlanta
    W. R. Bivins Journal (film)
    Cherokee Indian Letters, Talks, and Treaties, 1786–1838, ed. by
        Mrs. J. E. Hays, 3 volumes, W.P.A. project #4341 type-
        scripts, 1939
    Roswell Manufacturing Company and Barrington King Papers,
        Account Books, Minutebook, and Lettercopybooks (film)
    John W. A. Sanford Letters (film)
    Savannah Tax Rolls, 1860 (film)
    Western and Atlantic Railroad Account Books
Georgia Historical Society, Savannah
    Charles and Louis Manigault Records (typescripts)
    Fraser-Couper Papers
    Telfair Family Papers and Account Books
University of Georgia Library, Athens
    David C. Barrow Papers and Diaries
    John Carter Daybooks and Accounts
    M. Dennis Ledger
    Latimer Plantation Book, containing Hart Gold Mine Company
        Accounts

KENTUCKY

The Filson Club, Louisville
    Clark Papers and Accounts
    George W. Erwin Papers
    John Irwin Letters
    Hardinsburg and Cloverport Turnpike Road Company Papers
    John Wesley Hunt Papers
    J. H. and C. C. Morgan and Company Papers
    James Rudd Account Book
    Thruston Family Account Books and Papers
University of Kentucky Library, Lexington
    Squire Gaines Account Book
    Robert Graham Cotton Mill Books
    Hunt-Morgan Papers

George Woolley Cotton and Woolen Mill Account Books and
Letterbooks

LOUISIANA
Louisiana State University, Baton Rouge
Thomas Affleck Papers and Account Book
W. A. Britton Account Book of Nautilus Mutual Life Insurance
Company of New York
Clinton and Port Hudson Railroad Company Account Books and
Papers
East Feliciana Parish Archives Collection
Asa Hursey Papers (film)
Liddell Family Account Books and Papers
Joseph Mather Plantation Journal
Ellen E. McCollam Diary (typescript)
James S. McGehee Papers (typescript)
Samuel McCutchon Journals and Papers
William J. Minor Journals and Papers
Palfrey Family Papers, Account Books, Ledgers, and Diaries
Samuel Plaisted Letters
Pré Aux Cleres Plantation Journals
John H. Randolph Accounts and Papers
Steamer *Savage* Accounts
Lewis Stirling Diaries, and Papers
James G. Taliaferro Papers
Calvin Taylor Ledgers, Diaries, and Papers
New Orleans Public Library
Commissioner of Public Roads and Streets, Record of Work in
1st Municipality, 1839–43
Journals of the Deliberations of the Council of the 1st Municipal-
ity, 1836–45
Police Department, List of Prisoners not on chaingang, and ne-
groes on chaingang, 1825–51
Police Department, Lists of Negroes Employed on Public Works,
1823
Police Jury, Petitions for Emancipation of Slaves, 1827–34, 1843–
46
Tulane University Library, New Orleans
C. C. Jones Books, Diaries, and Papers
Kuntz Collection

B. H. Latrobe Papers
Memoranda of Artesian Well . . . New Orleans, 1854–55
John McDonogh Collection
New Orleans and Carrollton Railroad Company Papers
Pontchartrain Railroad Company Minutebook
Slave List, 1854–55
Trouard Account Book of Lumber Yard
Samuel R. Walker Journal (typescript)

MARYLAND
Maryland Historical Society, Baltimore
    Briggs-Stabler Papers
    Shipyard Account Books in Matthew Marine Collection
    Northampton Furnace Account and Time Books in Ridgely
        Collection
    J. J. Williamson Account Books

MASSACHUSETTS
Baker and Houghton Libraries, Harvard University, Cambridge
    Loammi Baldwin Papers
    Benjamin Selekman Notes
    Palfrey Family Letterbooks and Papers

MISSISSIPPI
Mississippi Department of Archives and History, Jackson
    Ebenezer Clark Ship Yard Log Books
    Steamboat *Vesuvius* Account Book, 1821–23
    John A. Quitman Account Book, 1841–53
    Benjamin L. C. Wailes Notebooks, Diaries, Surveys, and Papers

MISSOURI
Western Historical Collection, University of Missouri, Columbia
    Lucy Worthington James Collection, containing Maramec Iron
        Works Records
    Washington County, Missouri, Lead Mining Collection
Missouri Historical Society, St. Louis
    Desloge Family Collection
    Ste. Genevieve Town Archives Account Books, List of Hands
        called to work, 1836, and Bills of Sale
    Slavery Papers

Sublette Papers

J. B. Vallé and Mathew Ziegler Ledgers, Journals, and Estate Book

Christian Wilt-Joseph Herzog Letterbook

Columbia University Library, New York City

Robert H. Montgomery Accountancy Manuscripts

Dr. Allard B. Flagg Account Book and Papers, and Slavery Manuscripts, in Plimton Collection

Police Reports, 3rd Municipal Police District of the City of New Orleans, Louisiana, 1833, in Slavery Collection

New York Public Library, New York City

Francis P. Corbin Papers

Houmas Plantation Account Book

Steamboats *Mount Vernon* and *Monticello* Account Book

J. Stump and D. Ricketts Ledger

Duke University Library, Durham

Francis T. Anderson Papers

William Blanding Journal

William Bolling Papers

John Buford Papers

William B. Campbell Papers

John L. Clifton Papers and Ledger

Francis P. Corbin Papers

Dismal Swamp Land Company Account Book, Letterbooks, and Papers

Samuel Smith Downey Papers

John Dunn Steamboat Payroll Book

John Fox Letter, 1852

John Berkeley Grimball Papers

James R. and Richard Grist Records

Henry St. George Harris Papers

Steamers *Heroine, et al.* Receipt Book

M. Jones Account Book

Daniel W. Jordan Account Books and Papers

W. Robert Leckie Journals and Papers

Robert Leslie Account Books and Papers

Louis Manigault Journals and Papers
McRae Family Papers, Letterbooks, and Account Books
Thomas Moore Letters
James B. Richardson Papers
Joseph Belknap Smith Diaries, Account Books, Letterpressbook, and Papers
William T. Sutherlin Account Books and Papers
James Thomas, Jr., Papers
Benjamin L. C. Wailes Diaries and Letters
Washington Mining Company Ledgers
William Weaver Ledger and Papers
John Whitford Papers
North Carolina Department of Archives and History, Raleigh
Joseph and Alexander Brevard Books and Papers
Charles Fisher's Report on the Establishment of Cotton and Woollen Manufactures, in Legislative Papers, 1828
Francis Levin Fries Diary (typescript)
Benajah Nicholls Papers
North Carolina Railroad Company Account Books and Papers
David Paton Papers
Ebenezer Pettigrew Books and Papers
Rose Bay and Swan Quarter Turnpike Company Minutes and Accounts
Silver Hill Mining Company Papers
Treasurers' Papers: Internal Improvements: Letters, Papers, and Journals
John D. Whitford Books, Minutes, Reports, and Papers
Southern Historical Collection, University of North Carolina Library, Chapel Hill
Arnold-Screven Papers and Account Books
R. R. Barrow Residence Plantation Journal (typescript)
Battle Family Papers
Bayside Plantation Journal
Bertie County, North Carolina, Miscellaneous Records
Walter Brashear Papers
Brevard-McDowell Papers
Hamilton Brown Papers and Account Books
Burton-Young Contract, 1853
William H. Burwell Account Books
Cape Fear and Deep River Navigation Company Books

Farish Carter Papers and Account Books
J. F. H. Claiborne Letter, 1858
John H. Cocke Records (film)
James Hamilton Couper Notes and Accounts
James Hamilton Couper Letters, 1833–37 (film)
William L. Criglar Papers
Charles Fisher Account Books
Gales-Seaton Papers (typescripts)
David Gavin Diary (typescript)
Gold Hill Mining Company Records
Ralph Gorrell Papers
Thomas Jefferson Green Papers
John Berkeley Grimball Diary (typescripts)
Wade Hampton Papers
James C. Harper Diary (typescripts)
Hawkins Family Papers and Account Books
The Hayes Collection (film)
Ernest Haywood Collection
Gustavus A. Henry Papers
John Hogg Account Books
William Alexander Hoke Account Book of High Shoal Gold
    Mine
Holt Diary (typescript)
Franklin A. Hudson Diaries (typescripts)
Joseph A. Linn Papers
William L. London Collection
Louisa Furnace Account Books
Mackay-Stiles Papers and Account Books
Charles and Louis Manigault Records
McBee Family Papers and Account Books
John Nevitt Plantation Journal (typescript)
Pettigrew Papers and Account Books
George W. Polk Papers
Polk-Yeatman Papers
J. G. M. Ramsey Letters, 1858
Ridwell Furnace, Virginia, Record Book
Account Books of Pine Forge, Shenandoah County, Virginia
Silver Hill Mining Company Ledger
Peter Evans Smith Papers and Accounts
James R. Sparkman Papers and Account Books

William E. Sparkman Journal
Thomas Sparrow Papers
Stonebraker-McCartney Family Papers (film)
Elizabeth Furman Talley Papers
Lewis Thompson Papers and Journals
Nelson Tift Diary (film)
William D. Valentine Diaries
William W. Vass Papers
John Walker Diaries (film)
Richard H. H. Walton Account Books
Henry Clay Warmoth Journals
Maunsel White Papers and Letterbook
Sarah Hicks Williams Papers
Robert W. Withers Papers (film)

SOUTH CAROLINA
Charleston Library Society, Charleston
    Dr. John B. Irving Journal
    Thomas Pinckney Estate Books
Clemson University, Clemson
    John C. Calhoun Papers
    Thomas G. Clemson Papers
    John Ewing Colhoun Commonplacebook (typescript)
South Carolina Historical Society, Charleston
    R. F. W. Allston Diary and Papers
    John Ball Plantation Clothing and Blanket Books
    John Ball, Jr., Back River Plantation Book
    Chesnut-Miller-Manning Papers
    Coffin Point Records
    Manigault Family Account Books, Letterbook, and Papers
    Pineville Police Association Records
    Charles Senf's Report on Santee Canal, Nov. 11, 1800
    St. Stephen's Parish, Board of Commissioners of High Roads
        Minute Book, 1789–99
    St. John's Parish, Minute Books of Commissioners of High Roads,
        1760–1836, 1825–53
    Francis W. Weston's Laurel Hill Rice Mill Account Book
South Caroliniana Library, University of South Carolina, Columbia
    Ball Papers
    John S. Black Account Books and Papers

Pierce Mason Butler Papers

Franklin Harper Elmore Papers and Accounts

J. D. Frost Account Book

John C. Calhoun Papers

Chesnut-Williams-Manning Papers

James Gadsden Papers

James H. Hammond Account Books and Papers

Lancaster County, Board of County Commissioners Minutebook, 1849–68

David R. Williams Papers

South Carolina Archives, Columbia

F. H. Elmore document on Nesbitt Manufacturing Company, Legislative Papers: Public Improvements, Manufacturing, Petitions, Iron Manufacturing, 1836–39

Legislative Papers: Public Improvements: Manufacturing, Roads, Railroads, Cities, and Ports, 1780's–1865

Legislative Papers: Slavery Papers, 1790–1865

TENNESSEE

Tennessee State Library, Nashville

Gallatin Turnpike Company Minutebook, 1830–65

Knox County Road Commissioners Minutebook, 1808–19

Lebanon and Nashville Turnpike Company Account Book and Minutebook

Nashville and Charlotte Turnpike Company Minutebook, 1831–60

Nolensville Turnpike Company Minutebook, 1829–65

VIRGINIA

Virginia Historical Society, Richmond

Daniel Anderson Accounts

Henry A. Edmundson Papers and Daybook

Redwell Furnace Account Books

David Ross Letterbook

Tayloe Family Records

Bickerton Lyle Winston Account Book

Virginia State Library, Richmond

City of Richmond Personal Property Tax Book, 1861

James River and Kanawha Canal Stockholders' Minutes

James River Steamboat Company Journal of Steamboat *Thomas Jefferson*

Legislative Petitions

Tredegar Iron Works Records

Virginia Manufactory of Arms Letterbook and Papers

Armory Iron Company Papers in Board of Public Works Records, 1845–48

Alderman Library, University of Virginia, Charlottesville

Anderson Family Papers

William W. Davis Papers

Graham Daybooks, Timebooks, and Ledgers

Heth Papers

Richmond Police Guard Daybook, 1834–43

Rinker-Lantz Account and Time Books and Papers

Weaver-Brady Records

WASHINGTON, D.C.

Library of Congress

American Colonization Society Records

Hill Carter Plantation Journals

Cumberland Forge Account Books

Franklin Harper Elmore Papers

James H. Hammond Papers

Daniel W. Lord Journal of a Trip

Miscellaneous Slave Papers

James Monette Plantation Diary (typescript)

Zachary and Richard Taylor Papers

National Archives

Commissioner of Public Buildings of the District of Columbia Letterbooks (RG 42, film)

Naval Records Collection of the Office of Naval Records: Logbook and Payrolls (RG 45)

Potomac Canal Company and Chesapeake and Ohio Canal Company Records (RG 79)

Records of the Bureau of Yards and Docks and Records of Naval Shore Establishments: Payrolls and Journals (RG 71)

Records of the Office of the Chief of Engineers: Account Books, Checkrolls, and Reports (RG 77)

Records of the Office of the Chief of Ordnance: Record Books
and Reports (RG 156)
Records of the Office of the Quartermaster General: consolidated
correspondence file: slaves (RG 92)
Manuscript Census Returns, 1790–1860 (RG 29)

WISCONSIN
State Historical Society of Wisconsin, Madison
Chesnut Papers
Jordan and Irvine Papers and Account Books
Jordan and Davis Papers
John McRae Lettercopybooks

Index

Abolitionists, 192, 205, 232

Accidents, 44–45

Adams, John Quincy, 192, 203

African slave trade, movement to reopen, 222–25, 228

American Farmer, 193–98

Anderson, Joseph Reid, 125–28, 177–78, 229; *see also* Tredegar Iron Works

Architects, use of slaves as, 30

Army Department, employment of slaves, 33

Arson, 81

Austin, Moses, 24, 93, 181

Backwardness of South, 7–8, 11, 13, 163–64, 186–89, 232

Bakery, slaves employed in, 19

Ball, Charles, 38

Barrow, R. R., 64

Bates, Frederick, 49, 150

Bell, John, 15, 89, 114, 230; *see also* Cumberland River Iron Works

Benjamin, Judah P., 19

Black Heath Coal Company, 23, 48

Blacksmiths, use of slaves as, 15

Board money payments, 211–13

Brick manufacturing, employment of slaves, 19

Bridge building, employment of slaves, 30

Brown, Albert G., 216, 219

Brown, Andrew, 108–9, 172

Brown, John, 225

Brown, William Wells, 30

Bryant, William Cullen, 92

Buckingham, James Silk, 140–41, 144

Butler, Pierce Mason, 180, 183

Calhoun, John C., 24, 150, 181, 229

California, 205, 216–20

Canals, employment of slaves, 28–29

Cape Fear and Deep River Navigation Works, 29, 100–101, 102, 122, 158

Capital invested in industries, 11, 147, 156–57, 178–82

Caribbean, 205, 214, 220

Caruthers, A. C., 185

Caruthers, R. L., 229

Cherokees, 215

Chesnut, James, 180

Cities, 7–9, 186

Civil War, 146, 190, 231–32

Class relationships, 6, 208–10, 231–32

Clay, Henry, 18, 69, 81, 197

Clothing, 35, 54–57, 93, 132, 157

Coal mining, use of slaves, 22–23

Codes, 7

Competition, advantages of slave labor in, 147, 163–78

Compromise of 1850, 226, 227

Conditions, comparison of slave and free labor, 35–37

Confederacy, 228–30

Conspiracies, 88–90

Construction of national Capitol, 32

Conventions, commercial, 211, 225

Conversion: from free to slave labor, 120–28; from slave to free labor, 116–19

Costs: comparison of slave and free labor, 158–62, 195–96; food, clothing, housing, and supervision, 157; of foreign managers, 173; maintenance, 157; of slave hirelings, 155, 162, 274; slave managers, 172–73; on South Carolina R.R., 160–61; supervision, 168–91; at Tredegar Iron Works, 160; white labor, 158, 162; women and children, 166

Cotton ginning, use of slaves, 22

Cotton pressing, use of slaves, 22

Cotton prices, 191, 203, 205

Cotton seed oil extraction, use of slaves, 22

Cotton textile manufacturing, employment of slaves, 12–14

Couper, James H., 113, 152

Cuba, 220–21

Cumberland River Iron Works, 15, 52, 140; see also John Bell

Davis, Jefferson, 216, 221

De Bow, J. D. B., 3, 190

De Bow's Review, 150, 167, 207, 227, 228

Discipline, 91–115

Diseases, 31, 62–68, 118, 132

Dismal Swamp Land Company, 63, 124, 150

Douglass, Frederick, 29, 98, 136, 143, 144, 270

Draymen, slaves employed as, 30

Dredgeboats, slaves used on, 32

Efficiency of slave labor, comparison with free labor, 14, 147, 153–63

Elmore, Franklin Harper, 180

Expansionism, 204–6, 214–21

Explosions, 43–47

Federal government, employment of slaves, 32–33

Ferries, use of slaves on, 29

Fights, 86

Firemen, employment of slaves as, 31

Fires, 42–43, 81

Fisher, Charles, 197–98

Fisheries, employment of slaves, 26–27

Fitzhugh, George, 209

Flexibility of slave capital, 182–86

Flooding, 47

Food, 35, 50–54, 93, 157

Fortifications, use of slaves to build, 32

Franklin, Isaac, 26

Free blacks, 4, 88, 89, 114, 138, 192, 212, 270

Free labor, 4, 116–28, 137–45, 154–55; *see also* White labor and Immigrant labor

Fugitive slaves, 29, 30, 38, 81–83, 84–85, 112, 114

Gabriel Rebellion, 88, 89

Gadsden, James, 217, 221

Gallego Mills, 21–22

Garbagemen, use of slaves as, 31

Gas works, employment of slaves, 31

Genovese, Eugene D., 99, 188, 214, 287

Goldmining, use of slaves, 23–24, 216–20

Gosport (Norfolk) Navy Yard, 32, 67, 103, 118, 143, 159–60, 174

Grandy, Moses, 29

Gray, Simon, 108–9, 169, 172

Green, Thomas Jefferson, 177, 217, 221

Gregg, William, 119, 155, 206–7, 209, 229

Gristmilling, use of slaves, 21–22

Hamilton, Alexander, 179, 191

Hammond, James Henry, 90, 206, 207–8, 209

Hampton, Wade, 117, 180

Harper, William, 210

Haxall Company, 21–22, 149

Hazards, 42–50, 131–33

Health, 62–68

Hemp manufacturing, use of slaves, 17–18

Hiring, 12, 48, 57, 95, 102, 111, 128–37, 186

Hiring out own time, 135–37; *see also* Self-hire

Holidays, 41, 57, 95–98

Horace (King), 30, 107–8, 171–72, 173

Hospitals, 69–71

Hours of work, 37–41

Housing, 35, 57–62, 93–94

Hunt-Morgan family, 18

Immigrant labor, 117–19, 122, 137–45; comparison with slaves and poor whites, 154–55

Imprisonment, 113

Incentives, 95–104

Insurance, 71–74, 254–55

Insurrections, 88–90

Integration, 137–45, 158–62

Internal improvements, use of slaves at, 28–30

Iron manufacturing, use of slaves, 14–15

Iron mining, use of slaves, 22–23

Jackson, Andrew, 215

Jacksonian Democrats, 203

James River and Kanawha Canal, 29, 31, 60, 116, 122, 139

Jefferson, Thomas, 191
Jemison, Robert, Jr., 30, 107–8, 160, 172, 173, 229
Jones, C. C., 106–7
Jones, Thomas P., 195–96
Jordan, Daniel W., 26, 130

Keelboats, use of slaves on, 30
King, Barrington, 229

Leadmining, use of slaves, 24
Leslie, Robert, 17, 101
Levees, 31, 32
Louisiana Revolt of 1811, 88
Lumbering, use of slaves, 25–26

McDonogh, John, 19
Madison, James, 197
Managers: slave, 91, 105–9, 169–73; white, 168–69, 173–78
Manigault family, 152
Mann, Horace, 218
Maramec Iron Works, 15, 159
Maybank, Sandy, 106–7, 171, 172–73
Mechanics, use of slaves as, 18
Medicines, 68–69
Memminger, C. G., 209–10, 213
Midlothian Mining Company, 46, 47, 124, 138, 144
Mining, 214–19, 223–24
Missouri debates, 192
Money payments, 98–104

Nashville Convention of 1850, 218, 229
Nathan, 170, 173
Nationalism, 205, 226–30, 232
Naval yards, employment of slaves, 32
Navy Department, employment of slaves, 33
Nesbitt Manufacturing Company, 15, 166, 174, 180, 182–83
New Orleans Gas Company, 93, 94
New Orleans Water Works, 118, 174
North Carolina Conspiracy of 1860, 89
Northrup, Solomon, 167, 170
Nott, Josiah C., 73
Nullification, 197, 226
Number of industrial slaves, 11–12, 236–37

Olmsted, Frederick Law, 62, 80–81, 105, 171, 173
Overseers, see Managers
Oxford Iron Works, 14–15, 55, 166

Paper manufacturing, use of slaves, 19
Passes, 91
Passive protests, 77–80
Patrols, 114
Pettigrew, Ebenezer, 101, 102, 104, 153

Pickens, F. W., 230

Plank roads, use of slaves on, 29

Plantation slaves, comparison with industrial slaves, 9–10, 35–36, 50–51, 83–84

Planter class, 5, 179–83, 208–9, 231–32

Politics of industrialists, 228–32

Poor whites, 4–5, 13, 120–21, 206, 207–9, 214; comparison with slaves and immigrants, 154–55

Pratt, Daniel, 19, 155

Printing of newspapers, with slave labor, 19

Processing of crops, use of slaves, 19–22

Productivity of slaves, 154–55

Profitability: of canals, 151; extractive industries, 149–50; industrial slavery, 5, 146–53, 290–95; iron works, 149; lumbering, 150; mining, 150; railroads, 151; rice milling, 152; sawmilling, 152; slave hiring, 152–53; steamboats, 152; of textile mills, 148–49

Proslavery ideology, 6, 116, 128, 137, 144–45, 189, 192

Prosser, Gabriel, 88, 89

Public: employment of slaves, 30–33, 109–203; funding of industry, 182; works, use of slaves on, 31

Punishment, 7, 109–15

Quarrying, use of slaves, 32

Quitman, John A., 29, 166, 218

Racial relationships, 6, 137–45, 270

Railroads, use of slaves, 28, 221–23

Rebellions, 88–90

Religion, 7, 91–93

Repression, 88, 91–115

Republican Party, 90, 114, 217, 225, 232

Resistance, 75–91

Rhett, Robert Barnwell, 225

Rice milling, use of slaves, 20–21

River improvement, use of slaves for, 28–29

Road work, use of slaves for, 31, 32

Roanoke Navigation Company, 29, 122, 184

Routinizing of work, 91–92

Ruffin, Edmund, 62, 171

Runaways, 81–85, 112, 114, 133, 256–57; see also Fugitive slaves

Salt mining, use of slaves, 24–25

Saluda Cotton Factory, 13–14

Sawmilling, use of slaves in, 20, 25–26

Secession, 206, 225–30

Self-hire, 135–37, 211–12

Segregation, 137, 141–43

Shipyards, employment of slaves, 29–30

Shoes: manufacturing, use of slaves, 19; see Clothing

Singing, 18, 27, 30, 92

South Carolina Railroad, 28, 123, 217

South Carolina Union Factory, 179–80

Southern Pacific Railroad, 118, 177, 221

Spalding, Thomas, 98

Spratt, L. W., 225

State slaveownership, 31, 199–203; see Public

Steamboats: disasters, 43–44; use of slaves on, 30

Stirling, James, 75, 91

Stone quarrying, use of slaves, 32

Strikes, 118–19, 122, 125–28, 142, 266, 270; see also Tredegar Iron Works

Sugar milling, use of slaves, 19–20

Swamp refugees, 84–85, 112, 114

Tanneries, use of slaves, 19

Tariff, 192, 193, 196–97, 203, 205

Taylor, James H., 207

Taylor, Zachary, 26, 40

Telfair, Alexander, 101, 152, 170

Tennessee-Kentucky Conspiracy of 1856, 89–90, 114

Textile manufacturing, use of slaves, 12–14

Theft, 78–80

Thomas, James, Jr., 17

Tilden, Samuel J., 24, 150

Tobacco manufacturing, use of slaves, 15–17

Towns, 8; see also Cities

Tracking with dogs, 112–13

Trade between South and West, 192

Transcontinental railroad, 221–22

Transportation, use of slaves, 28–30, 199–203

Treasury Department, employment of slaves, 33

Tredegar Iron Works, 15, 59, 94, 100, 125–28, 140, 142–43, 149, 177–78, 229, 266, 278

Turner, Nat, 88, 89

Turnpikes, use of slaves on, 29

Turpentine extraction and distilling, use of slaves, 26

Upper Appomattox Company, 176–77, 184

Urban slaves, 9–10; comparison with rural slaves, 11–12, 50–51, 54–55, 57–58, 83–84

Vesey, Denmark, 88, 89, 192, 208

Washington, George, 77, 191

Water works, use of slaves, 31

Weaver, William, 52–53, 55–57, 79, 101, 103–4, 129, 130, 174–75

Whipping, 109–10

White labor: artisan movement, 211–14; unreliability, 194–95; wages, 100, 155, 158

White panics, 88–90, 115

Williams, David R., 179–80, 196–97

Women and children, employment in industries, 11, 153, 164–68, 193–94

Woodville Manufacturing Company, 13, 120

Yancey, William Lowndes, 229

Yeomanry, 4–5, 206–9, 214